# THE CASH COWBOY COMBO!

PAXTON S. FINNEGAN

# CONTENTS

# A Special Gift

As a token of my appreciation, I'd like to offer you a free online copy of *The Law-Abiding Pirate*, my guide to further secure your money against the ravages of inflation through the fledgling world of cryptocurrency, and the ancient art of treasure hunting for gold, silver, and other precious metals! Visit the link below or scan the qr code to my website and let us know to which email address you would like your gift to be sent. Enjoy!

## www.paxtonsfinnegan.com

(PS: Yes, that might be a pen name. Either that or my parents wanted everyone to think that I was named after a Confederate General from the Civil War.)

# YOU CAN'T HAVE MY MONEY!

### A 6-STEP GUIDE TO GROW TAX-FREE WEALTH AND RETIREMENT INCOME BY SMART INVESTING IN AFTER-TAX ACCOUNTS, ACTIVE-MANAGED FUNDS, AND CASH-VALUE LIFE INSURANCE

**Paxton S. Finnegan**

When you grow up on a ranch, getting trampled by cows on a semi-regular basis, you tend to develop a passive attitude toward the rest of the goings-on of your everyday life. Sure, times may be tough at the moment. But I'm not getting trampled by a cow, so it's not so bad. That's just how life is.

However, I quickly learned that this is a bad attitude to adapt when it comes to finances. While focusing on the various ways in which "It could be worse" in any given scenario will help us to appreciate the blessings in our lives, it does run the risk of developing an apathetic outlook on future planning. For the longest time, I thought I'd save enough for a comfortable retirement just by doing things "the way we've always done it": Get a job. Work hard. Buy a house. Save when you can. Have a nest egg for retirement.

And suddenly I was in my mid-30s, trying to think if I'd ever once had $10,000 sitting in a basic bank account. A few quick calculations on a napkin told me that I needed new ways of both growing my income and planning for my retirement.

The problem is that, although we all want to make the best decisions we can for ourselves, there's a lot of important things to know that just don't get covered in the classroom. We end up learning our financial skills from our peers, and our families. We can learn a lot of wise sayings about saving from family but it takes more than just budgeting some monthly cash into a savings account to feel secure when your hair starts turning grey. Especially when times get tough, and the budget we've carefully built starts getting ornery.

It's the nature of the beast for money matters to get tricky, but it's also in the nature of the community to share our skills so we can all learn from one another. This book is here to help you take steps towards setting up a solid life for yourself before you reach the end of your career, as well as making plans for the security of your family.

Education doesn't matter. I'll be a blue-collar grunt till the day I die, God willing. Income level, while something we all strive to improve, doesn't matter as much as we think it does. Even with a small monthly amount budgeted towards smart investments, we can build a confident future.

We can be in middle-management, hitting it hard from nine to five. We can be that teenager working our first job, flipping hamburgers. Or we could be a grey-haired Granny wondering if our lifetime of work will tide us over to our final resting place. It doesn't matter where on the spectrum we fall. There are all kinds of seminars and books teaching people a new way to get rich, or the perfect stocks and innovations to invest in, and I do not question the validity of any of them: Many people following them have achieved great success, while others have failed. That's just not what I'm interested in. I'm interested in a road-map that can be followed by anyone, regardless of our income level, to maximize the potential growth and savings of whatever money we have. I've worked with a lot of impoverished people in my lifetime, some self-afflicted, and others failed by a lack of basic financial methodology in school. I want to help them get on a better course, even while working a minimum-wage or part-time job. And, even if we have been blessed with the highest levels of education and a great income, this book can help us solidify those earnings into a rock-solid retirement.

Because we've all seen entire industries collapse overnight, and the richest among us lose everything. We need more than income. We need an underpinning financial plan to anchor us through tumultuous times, keeping us on a course toward success.

If done right, our job becomes the least important part of the process.

We'll learn about when our bank is our best friend, and when we're better off remembering that they're a business first. We'll learn how to best utilize our existing debts, and how even debt can play a huge role in enabling us to maximize our long-term investments. We'll learn about exciting new strategies for growing investments through things as basic as our mortgages and life insurance coverage. And, above all, we'll learn how to keep our lifelong earnings from being gouged by the omnipresent tax-man at the end of the day.

I can't speak for the entire world's economic system. Every national government will have an entirely different financial and banking system and different levels of economic opportunity for the ground-level working folks. Even in the United States, a lot of investment opportunities will vary greatly from state to state. However, what I did notice over several years of research was the strong parallels in financial opportunities and economic strategies across North America. These have enabled some free trade opportunities which the rest of the world would normally find difficult, seen first in NAFTA and later in the USMCA. International transactions have never been easier, business people frequently work on both sides of borders, and even basic banking needs and investment products have borrowed freely from one another. This more strongly aligns daily strategies which the average person can use, regardless of what country they live in. For that reason, I've tried to incorporate investment variations that will be useful to over 300 million American readers, as well as to their almost 40 million northern neighbors in Canada. While the names and specific details of some products may vary by region, I will try to group similar tools for ease of understanding, or discuss ways to implement methods not fully available in our area yet.

Even if every specific option is not available to our state or province, the trend has been that something else very similar may be available if we do a little digging, or the strategies which have been most successful in one nation can be readily adapted for use in another. Find the one that appeals most strongly to you, regardless of its country of origin, and see how easily it can be implemented into your daily financial strategy. Strengthening the financial foundations of everyday citizens in allied nations leads both countries to stronger trade agreements, more widely available investment products, and a truly enviable international relationship.

Fair warning: You'll hear me sing the praises of Capitalistic freedom and Judeo-Christian values in this book, and make jokes about the Commies and blue-haired people. Just in case my approval of international banking parallels was leading any of you to believe that I have globalist sympathies. Nope. Throughout history, the world has functioned most efficiently and thrived most financially when nations embraced and balanced personal freedoms, financial opportunity, and military strength. Freely borrowing, analyzing, and adapting international ideas is a major key to the prosperity of any sovereign state, but keep a watch set on the gates.

Seriously, the title of this book is *You Can't Have My Money!* Did you think you were going to find that Socialism blueprint hyped by your blue-haired Gender Studies professor in here?

# 1

# WE DON'T ALL DIE FROM BLACK LUNG AT AGE 45 ANYMORE: HOW VACCINES, ADVANCES IN TECHNOLOGY, HIGHER STANDARDS OF LIVING, AND A BUNCH OF LONELY SOLDIERS COMING HOME FROM STOMPING ON NAZIS CHANGED THE WESTERN WORLD FOREVER.

Gather round, folks, and let's take a look back to the last century. The Greatest Generation set us up on a path to prosperity that no one else in history can boast of, but it's important to note a few things they overlooked, quite understandably at the time. Once we know these things, it becomes easy for us to correct their missteps to make the most of the unprecedented opportunities they afforded to us.

## A New Life

September 1945: World War II had just ended, and the ramifications of this would be huge for low-wage, blue-collar workers throughout the North American continent.

Because the inefficacy of cavalry and bayonet charges had been made brutally clear in the corpse-filled no man's land between Gallipoli trenches in World War I, factories were now churning out tanks, planes, amphibious landing craft, and industrial vehicles. These incredible advances in land, air, and sea vehicles required concurrent advances in factory automation to assemble them. When peacetime finally arrived, a whole new industrial stage had been set, and nobody was ready to set-strike them after the curtain dropped and just go back to the horse and buggy. For the first time in history, auto-mated factory-production jobs were the norm, and workers for them were in high demand, not just for the military, but for the average citizen.

Backing our growing production base would be the advent of nuclear power: Another World War II innovation of conflict-resolution that nobody was ready to put into the dust-bin of history after General Douglas MacArthur had his infamous "No BS" sit-down—and equally infamous "god-shatter-ing" photo taken—with Emperor Hirohito of Japan. The greatest and most terrible innovation in the history of mankind was first adapted to civilian electrical generation in 1958. It was an era of unprecedented optimism, and people spoke of the inevitability of flying cars without sarcasm.

Soldiers who'd been putting off starting a family for years were now ready for their stateside hero's welcome, which, as it turned out, involved a lot more than just brass bands and parades. The population boomed, and birth rates rose at an incredible rate across the world. In the United States alone, 76 million babies were born during this period, with a total of 90 million born across North America in the 18 years between 1946 and 1964.

In the 20th century alone, the world population went from 1.7 billion to over 6 billion people. This number is made all the more shocking when we stop to consider the hundreds of millions who died within that same century as a result of two world wars and the genocidal rise of Communist regimes across the world in the aftermath.

More people being born, along with the peace and advances we already made, meant more people were reaching adulthood.

Because medical advances in vaccines, antibiotics, surgery, sterile medical storage, and hygiene made it easier to live longer, we got a far larger quantity of mature minds sharing great ideas. This led to still greater leaps forward in technology, lifestyle, and even workplace safety standards.

In the wake of the horrors of war was a renewed love for life, and that didn't just apply to the family setting. Hard hats, gloves, and steel-toed boots may seem like nothing special until you see the old black-and-white photos of construction crews building the Empire State Building without them. Men who had survived storming the beaches of Normandy were not exactly looking forward to coming home only to die in some cost-cutting mining operation, and they made dang sure that every employer in the USA knew it. Unions were rapidly formed to ensure fair treatment and pay for all workers, plus improved safety standards. After a few more years, the black-lunged coal miner carrying a pickax and a caged canary was suddenly operating an automated boring machine in a ventilated shaft with radon detectors and an emergency beacon on his belt.

More hands working together meant more hands to lay the wires and cables for infrastructure, funneling electricity and telephone reception into every home. Shortly thereafter, somebody invented this thing called the Internet.

As a result, the exchange of ideas would continue to compound itself.

Through all these advances, even the most impoverished nations saw an incredible rise in their overall wealth and life expectancy in less than a century of development. The amazing advances in health, technology, and professional practice fed back into itself, making it possible for larger amounts of people to live and succeed together, and then in turn support, and perhaps even become, the minds who'd think up the next wave of advances.

With fewer and fewer people needed to handle the now-automated necessities of survival like farming, construction, resource gathering, and energy production, even more have been freed to specialize in new areas of art, technology, and research. Gone are the days when a peasant farmer could produce enough grain to feed himself and three family members. One farmer with a tractor and combine harvester can now produce food for hundreds of people. All of this has led to even further development in increasingly esoteric fields of knowledge, full of serendipity to keep us propelling forward.

I have literally never used the word serendipity before, outside of referencing a pink sea dragon from a children's book. That just goes to show how deeply awed the past century has left me.

### The Unexpected Mule in It All

But, of course, sometimes a stubborn mule manages to sneak among your selectively-bred champion Thoroughbreds. Despite the surge of innovation, one aspect of our day-to-day lives refused to budge, especially among those of us who aren't exactly ranked amongst the financial elite: We didn't know how to plan for retirement.

Ask a pioneer in the 1850s what his retirement plan was, and you'd probably get a blank stare and a demand to get your DeLorean off his silver claim. He planned to cut timbers, plant crops, milk cows, pan gold, and shoot game until he died of black lung at age 45. The dreams of "striking it rich" and "living like kings" were frequently spoken of, but rarely attained. Very often, there was no distinction between working years and sunset years: We worked right into the sunset and hoped that we didn't accidentally snuggle up under a smallpox blanket in the process. And we didn't mind, because work was just as much a part of a happy life as a family was.

It's also important to note that even the rare few who did find fortunes in previous centuries often didn't know how to manage their treasures, further evidence that we can learn new things all the time and still never learn from the past. The famous Canadian gold miner, William "Billy" Barker, first struck it rich in 1862, sifting an incredible 1/3 oz of gold per pan, and eventually pulling up gold nuggets by the bucketful from a 60-foot shaft. The resulting gold rush led to the creation of one of the most famous northern boomtowns, Barkerville, British Columbia, where gold-panning is still a popular tourist attraction today.

Billy Barker died penniless in 1894, and I doubt he was very happy about it.

Now, that's not to say that people nowadays aren't happy, or that we don't have a variety of tools and options for dealing with the retirement mule. For example, we have our typical High-Interest Savings Accounts (HISA) offered by most banks, generally offering annual returns of 1% to 1.5%. For those who want to feel secure in their sunset years, we also have our Individual Retirement Accounts (IRA), or its Canadian counterpart, the Registered Retirement Savings Plan (RRSP).

People looking to squeeze more productivity out of this mule have also been getting into the stock market or looking at mutual funds. Others think they'll be fine with only a workplace pension, and others do nothing more than drop all their spare change into a 4-gallon water jug on the kitchen counter for 50 years.

Even the white-collared professional can be stuck with surprisingly old-fashioned ideas, amongst other blind spots. Mistakes that happened in 1929 repeated in 2007 in the form of great market crashes, showing that, on some levels, things haven't changed much. Because of our long lives, we now have more time than ever to see ourselves make the same mistakes all over again. We need to find ways to avert that calamity, using the tools available to us. Unfortunately, we more often than not have to unearth these tools on our own. That's where this book can help us.

### *I Know I Won't Work as Well When I'm an Old Buzzard*

When I was a 4-year-old kid, I would say, *"Waaah! Why are the cookies always on the top shelf?!"* Then, around the time I turned 40, I started saying, *"Gaaah! My back! Why is everything always on the bottom shelf?!"* Just because we're living longer doesn't mean we're necessarily able to work longer. We now have a prevalence of both junk food and sedentary jobs, ranging anywhere from office workers slumped over their computers to long-haul truck drivers. This means that a lot of our current aging population has nowhere near the vim and vigor of Grandpa Finnegan who died by chopping a mighty Redwood down on himself at age 93.

Despite rising life expectancy, most people still dislike the idea of working once we get into our sixties or seventies. Even before we reach that point, our relatively comfortable lives mean more and more people are aiming to retire at fifty or even forty, as higher quality of life makes it easier for us to push ourselves harder while we're young to enjoy a well-earned retirement early on.

However, regardless of how hard we work, or whether we retire at 40 or 70, we're going to need careful planning. Odds are, we're more than able to live into our 90s. The last thing we want is for our savings to dry up mid-retirement because we under-estimated our longevity by a few decades.

### Become the Nine

When I started to research and discuss with a few true financial wizards with whom I was blessed to be associated, I came across a simple phrase: 91 and 9. We're going to want to remember that one.

It means that 91% of people start their retirement fearful for their financial security. In a room of 1,000 people, 910 of them risk entering retirement unfulfilled, and with limited means to generate sufficient wealth using the time they have left. In the wake of the COVID-19 pandemic, some experts estimate that this number will rise as high as 97%. Other recent studies have shown that the number one fear of senior citizens is outliving their retirement funds, superseding even fears for their physical and mental health.

At the time of this writing, this problem of only 91% of people feeling comfortable about their retirement is consistent across North America, which is yet another reason that I felt it was important to cover strategies that could be utilized in both the USA and Canada: With numbers that bad, we need to look to the strategies being used on the other side of our border, for either direct copying or at least inspiration.

What we'll soon discover is that, despite some differences in terminology and financial products, the basic strategies work similarly well in both countries, and many could even be implemented in such diverse places as Australia, Mexico, the UK, or any other number of nations with a reasonable degree of economic freedom. The strategies parallel each other in many ways, so, no matter which country we live in, we can still find something that will get our money working harder for us.

This is one way to stumble across unexpected treasures. Sometimes, the economic norms practiced by our community, region, or even country simply don't work out as well as we'd hope. In these cases, it's the wise person who's able to look to their neighbor for help. Not in handouts, but in knowledge. With the shared knowledge of nations, it isn't just our next-door neighbor who we can feed for a lifetime by teaching him how to fish.

Even if it means pointing our financial telescope across state or provincial lines, or even if it means pointing that same scope across a sovereign state border, it's a good idea to seek inspiration from others. Especially when they're the ones succeeding.

However, we first need to take a look at some people who didn't succeed. Because there's a very good chance that we're doing the same thing they did.

# 2

THE YOUNG, EAGER, AND
WOEFULLY UNPREPARED LIFE
INSURANCE AGENT: 3 TALES OF
HOW STICKING TO THE "HOW IT'S
ALWAYS BEEN DONE" MENTALITY
CAN LEAD TO FINANCIAL DISASTER.

**Storytime!**

E arlier, I mentioned just a couple of the ways that modern people prepare for their futures: HISAs, 401(k)s, and IRAs, or RRSPs for those in Canada. Then there are mutual funds, separate accounts, segregated funds, cash-value insurance products, Roth IRAs, and Tax-Free Savings Accounts.

Let's keep all of those in the back of our minds, as we'll be looking at each of them in-depth later on. Until then, let's look at...

## Dan's Story

Dan is a police officer in his early 40s who lives in Denver, Colorado, with his wife and their four children. Given the high-risk nature of his job and the fact that he did not decide to serve his community until he was already in his early 30s, he decided to provide additional security for his family by purchasing a life insurance policy to be paid out to his family in the event of his untimely death.

Dan placed a call to a local agency and was offered a home visit to discuss his options. Two days later, he opened his front door to greet a young, well-dressed, and extremely eager life agent. After hearing the enthusiastic pitch, Dan wasn't fully certain of the details, but he was given every reassurance by his agent that the policy would be a perfect fit. Dan met all the qualifications, and the pre-authorized monthly payments were very reasonable. He signed for the policy. Dan now had a life insurance policy he was able to dutifully pay month after month, year after year. Or so he thought.

What neither he nor his agent realized was that no policy could sustain itself on the type of plan he had been offered. All policies need a certain amount paid to be viable. It's like a form of community donation:

If the fund doesn't get enough paid in initially, then it won't have enough to help a person when they fall on hard times.

Almost ten years later, Dan was horrified to realize that his life insurance policy had been underfunded from the very beginning to the point where its cash value was only two years away from completely killing itself off. It is important to note that he had not been given notice from the insurance company regarding this underfunding. He had begun investigating on his own after a few years since something about his payment plan just didn't sound right to him.

When Dan realized how underfunded his policy was, he faced a stark choice: Pay up the staggering balance owing now to restore the full fund value, and henceforth pay increased premiums, or let the policy drop. He left messages with the agency, requesting a follow-up meeting to discuss other solutions. To this day, the agency has never returned his calls.

Dan had no choice but to cancel his policy with no hope of recovering any of the tens of thousands of dollars he had been paying for nearly a decade.

Having lost the feeling of security for his family's future, he had to start the long process of seeking out another, more credible company, with more knowledgeable agents to help guide him to a sustainable choice. He has since found relative success, but his earlier financial loss still hurts him. He treated a relatively new form of insurance the way his father or grandfather may have approached the life insurance policies of their generation, and he got burned for it.

Even as he's recovering, his plans for financial security have been set back by years.

Insurance policies aren't necessarily just "fire and forget" or "shoot and scoot." We can't always just set up a monthly payment to cover our premiums and be done with it. As interest rates and policy charges of a life insurance policy change, so must the amount that must be paid to keep the policy active.

For example, a common trait of some Universal Life Insurance policies is that, as a cost for its relative flexibility compared to other life insurance plans, we need to pay more as we age. Others will have an investment portion that accrues interest on our payments to keep the fund value high. But Dan had never been told that. He was told that as long as he paid what the agent said he should, then everything would be fine.

### Stacy's Story

Stacy is a single mom from Chicago, Illinois, whose 14-year-old daughter Alana has a physical and learning disability. Whereas Dan often worried about what his family would do once he was gone, Stacy was more concerned with her daughter's future as a growing teen and future adult.

Going off the advice she had been raised with, Stacy decided to build up some cash through a mutual fund. Throughout her adult life, she had been told how hands-off and convenient they are, and how great they can be for building long-term wealth.

In simple terms, a mutual fund is when multiple investors pool part of their resources together and then give control over that pool to a team of finance managers and advisors. The management team smartly invests the fund to generate profit for all of the individual investors.

That's the theory at least, but we all know there can be a big difference between theory and actual practice.

Stacy was continually frustrated by what turned out to be a very passive management team with a grossly hands-off approach to investing,—the managers apparently believing that the "hands-off" description applied equally to all parties involved—and because she was only one small cog in the mutual fund, she found it very difficult to keep her participation in it aligned to her wants and needs. When it came to investment choice, there was not a lot of flexibility to be found in passive mutual funds.

All of that hassle, and she didn't even have the peace of mind in knowing that it was at least working. As it turned out, different parts of the fund would often suffer, and as a result, she would suffer. Her stress would mount as she became increasingly aware of how her investments would fall short of the returns she needed to help her daughter live the life she wanted.

Sadly, her management team wasn't just passive when it came to money, but also when it came to client support.

Anyone who's dealt with passive management in customer service knows that, when their system starts getting screwy like this, there's no one on hand to help you. At least, no one who works there.

But at least you'll still get that customer satisfaction survey in your email within 15 minutes of slamming down the phone.

Taking matters into her own hands, Stacy tried to make up for the consistent losses of the fund by investing in other funds that are lower risk. Sadly, lower risk historically means lower returns, and this was the end result of her investments. She earned back a fraction of what she had planned and budgeted for.

While she managed to make ends meet, the way that single mothers always seem to do, giving her daughter that chance of a better life meant Stacy had to replan her entire retirement: The strategy change she was forced to make for the family to survive ultimately crippled their long-term finances. Stacy was left with no choice but to start structuring the rest of her life on a far more modest budget.

But what of the managers? What of the people who were supposed to be looking after the money she entrusted them with? A sad fact of life is that, whether a fund gains or loses money, the managers still get paid so long as the fund exists. They were never operating with her best interests in mind and had no real motivation to do so. In their minds, so what if one investor pulls out? They lost zero sleep, while Stacy was losing all of it.

### Roy and Annie

Meanwhile, in Canada...

Roy and Annie are an elderly couple living in farm country outside of Edmonton, Alberta, who find themselves going through a disappointing retirement. People often say old habits die hard, and their old habit was spending decades listening to financial advice from their local bank.

A lot of the advice was good enough to build trust, trust which would become habitual credulity towards their bank tellers, but it turned out that Roy and Annie may have trusted too much. Either that or the bank assumed too much about this couple's knowledge of tax laws.

Regardless of whether trust or apathy was to blame, their bank failed to warn them about a key detail present in one of the services they were offering. For decades, the bank tellers were saying, over and over again, "Now is the best time to contribute to one of our offered RRSPs!" (Again for the sake of parallels, it is important to note that this same scenario regularly plays out in the case of elderly Americans who contributed a lifetime of payments to the RRSP's US counterpart, the traditional IRA.)

It seemed like a great decision at the time.

"RRSP income is exempt from tax while it remains in the plan," the bank teller assured them. "You can even deduct contributions from your annual income tax."

On the surface, this seemed like a great way for Roy and Annie to save their money for old age in a place that wouldn't be whittled away by taxes. Since all RRSPs are registered with the Canadian government, and since the government is usually interested in encouraging its citizens to save and plan for the long term, the plan seemed solid.

RRSP funds, like IRAs, are indeed tax-exempt while in the plan, but no one at the bank said anything to Roy and Annie about how that money would be taxed once withdrawn from the plan. Maybe these days we'll see a warning about this on official websites, but it's hardly written in bright red letters.

Imagine being in this couple's shoes. Roy and Annie made a home together, raised a family, and worked hard their whole lives. Whatever they earned, they spent carefully, budgeted well, and even invested wisely, seeing great gains for their future in compounding growth.

They did everything according to the accepted plan. By the time they were getting old and grey, they had squirreled away a respectable amount of money to ensure their wellbeing for the rest of their lives. Then retirement came, and they made their first withdrawal from their RRSP.

Only now, if Roy and Annie want $60, they need to take out $100.

The government never touched their RRSP while it was sitting tucked away and useless, but, as soon as that fund matured to the point of mandated withdrawals, Canada started helping itself to huge swathes of the money Roy and Annie were banking on for their everyday needs.

Ultimately, nearly 40% of what they withdrew had to go towards various back-end taxes. Fine print that not a single bank teller warned them about when encouraging them to sign up for an RRSP. Why? Because that particular RRSP was an investment product specific to their bank, so naturally it is the first thing their bank offered, as we'll discuss further in the next chapter.

Imagine saving up a specific amount for when we're no longer able to be effective in the workplace, only to be told at the last minute that we're only going to get slightly more than half of that back. We're well past our prime, and there's nothing we can do about it.

The older we get, the harder it becomes to bounce back. That's because we have far less recovery time before we need to worry about retiring and building up old-age security. And, in Canada, that's not just a generic phrase: Old Age Security, or OAS, is an additional payment made by the Canadian government to seniors citizens. However, portions of it can also be clawed back by the government based upon how much the individual has contributed to and withdrawn from their RRSP: The mandatory withdrawals are considered taxable income, and the amount of OAS a person is entitled to will be scaled according to their level of income.

The RRSPs that kept getting pitched to Roy and Annie by their small-town banker—who they knew better as "Sharon from church"—became their primary investment tool. They'd made the wrong choice of where to contribute the bulk of their investment money from day one because other options had never been discussed. Some had not even been invented yet, such as the Tax-Free Savings Account, or TFSA, which quietly arrived without Roy and Annie's knowledge in 2009. Not only were they never fully apprised of the limitations specific to their current investment tool, but they were never told the benefits of something new.

**The Takeaway**

We've just examined three key examples of what are considered to be staples for preparing our future and the futures of our family: Life insurance, mutual funds, and retirement accounts.

Just like Dan, Stacy, Roy, and Annie, we have likely been told that investing in any of those choices is just the rational and responsible thing to do. We've been told that it's not just rational and responsible, but also the *safe* thing to do. This is what I have seen friends, colleagues, and even mentors tell each other for decades. And bankers, of course.

However, we see here that none of those options are inherently safe, and, even if they are that generally means a lower return on our investments or a lower overall fund value. It's easy to hit a snag, even when we think we're being responsible. To meet a modern

THE CASH COWBOY COMBO! | 43

life's demands, it's not enough to just go with what people say we should do just because it looks like the most sensible choice. (I'll withhold my rant about the entirety of the Federal Reserve system for another book.)

It's important to look at each person's choice critically. Let's walk through how they could've done better for themselves, and what we can do differently if we ever find ourselves in their shoes.

The truth is, with the smallest of changes in strategy and approach, all of their stories could've been completely turned around. Many of their lives have started turning around for the better once they internalized the hard lessons they learned, and many others who were willing to listen to them found their own lives going much better for it. My own life included, as I could now look for alternatives to the choices they had made.

One story on its own won't always have all the answers, but once we collect more together, we begin realizing some remarkable things. Much of the advice below feeds into the strategies I'll be describing later on, but I'll also be covering some smaller common-sense stuff: Things we really ought to know, but don't usually get warned about when told to invest or insure ourselves in "the most responsible way."

### Dan's Alternate Ending

The first thing Dan could've done was a little more research on his insurance company. Generally, the longer-lived and better-established a company is, the more certain we can be that it'll payout and remain strong throughout our lives, ready to lend us the aid we've been contributing to. Even if it costs a little more, we'll have the security of knowing that we're investing in a policy where the company knows what it's doing, and isn't just going to drop the ball when we need it.

However, beyond the hypothetical, Dan was dealing with a long-term, reputable agency, and not some scammer. So the next thing he could've done is take a little time to double-check everything the agent said, particularly regarding the actual operation and coverage of his specific policy. It's entirely possible that the young, eager life agent was simply inexperienced, and did not yet know how to build rapport and trust with his clients by explaining the policy in thorough, yet simplified, detail. A more thorough explanation of what was needed and what would be provided could have saved Dan a lot of grief.

No matter how sincere the agent is, there's a good chance that they don't know everything about what they're selling, especially when it comes to complex financial matters. As far as both Dan and the agent knew, they had worked out a deal where Dan was getting what he needed, with the agent probably knowing little more about Dan than his health status and annual income.

No one can fully know our circumstances, nor do most strangers care to. Not until a representative demonstrates a sincere desire to sit down and get to know us should we consider them as an option. This usually means finding an agent who plans on collecting information and conducting a full break-down of our economic situation to come up with a detailed life plan. In short, they can't do that in one evening sitting around our kitchen table. If they show that they are willing to take a few extra days to come up with a customized solution for us, then that is the company we should probably be dealing with, as opposed to some young guy in a suit who constantly hears Alec Baldwin in his ear, muttering, "Always be closing."

It isn't always easy to think of the questions we need to ask in this situation, but it does demonstrate how important it is to get advice and speak to financially savvy people we can trust before we make big, life-changing decisions.

### Stacy's Alternate Ending

It's easy to see how Stacy may have been bamboozled. She was often told that passive investment is historically the safer, more responsible long-term option. She had then heard that mutual funds are the ideal passive method to build extra income through initial investments, and countless people that she knew had been investing in them for years. When she heard this, she felt that they would only be passive in the sense that she wouldn't have to directly handle them. After all, that's what she was entrusting the mutual fund's professional finance team with in the first place.

Sadly, it turns out that 'passive' is kind of a loaded word in the world of mutual funds. "Passive is good" is the conventional wisdom, but passive mutual funds aren't the only way. Since she was already willing to pay a team to handle things for her, Stacy could've instead benefited from finding an active-managed fund instead. These are much more flexible in the sense that their professional managers actively monitor the accounts. They are willing and able to seize opportunities as they come by, or divert funds to a safer place when the market changes for the worse.

Active management means placing our money in the hands of people who will make bigger investments where repayment is most likely, and smaller investments where repayment is less likely while following the standard mutual fund method of dividing our investment into several different funds, generally in an 80/20 split based on our risk tolerance. The difference is in protective measures. For example, in a traditional mutual fund, if our 80% share suffers, we lose part of our investment, while our 20% share remains stable. However, an active manager has the entrusted ability to switch the market shares when things are not looking well: If our 80% share appears to be at risk of losing value, it can be switched with our 20% share, so the drop in our investment is minimized. The managers know to be that sensitive, even when choosing different bond options within a single company, and they're hands-on enough to be making those decisions constantly.

It's the exact opposite of the passive, "do it as we've always done it" way. If Stacy had combined this more active strategy with something like an active-managed mutual fund or segregated fund, she wouldn't just be smiling by now, she'd be laughing.

### Roy and Annie's Alternate Ending

The knee-jerk response is to say that Roy and Annie should've ignored their bank teller's suggestions. Instead of putting almost all their eggs in one highly taxable basket, they could've diversified, and sought out other ways to contribute to their future, such as in (when it became available) a Tax-Free Savings Account—the Canadian equivalent of a Roth IRA.

Other strategies such as income-splitting could've also been used, but a good TFSA, perhaps operating within an actively managed investment fund, would have been the best way to minimize the clawback they experienced on their cash and OAS when they were finally withdrawing funds in retirement. Like the Roth IRA, there are no annual income tax deductions attached to contributions into the TFSA. However, once the full tax for that year is paid, the funds grow tax-free for the remainder of their investment period, so long as the annual contribution limit is not exceeded: The current limit as of this writing is $6,000 annually, so a simple contribution of $500 a month can safely grow our investment for as long as we like.

And, at the end of the day... when you take out $100, you get $100.

We will be taking a closer look at several different investment tools in the following chapters, which at first can seem a little complicated when we are dealing with different countries. Even in the US, some tools will differ slightly or at least have names that vary from state to state. However, it is noteworthy that many of the products were inspired by each other, although subsequently developed with slight variations in different nations or states. We will always be sure to emphasize which parallel product or strategy can be used, regardless of our region.

# 3

THAT'S HOW THEY GET YOU: THE
RED, FLASHING, EARDRUM-
BURSTING WARNING BELLS WHEN
YOUR BANK TRIES TO SELL YOU A
MORTGAGE, MORTGAGE LIFE
INSURANCE, AND HIGH-LIMIT
CREDIT CARDS.

Although it can feel convenient to take advantage of every product our bank offers us, there's usually a better option out there. Figuring out what to do with that fact will be the first step in this book.

**Step 1: Learn to Look Beyond Your Bank.**

I have no problem with banks. For my part, I've been a steadfast customer to local banks, often for decades at a time, and they have come through for me in many difficult times. I have nothing but gratitude for the promotions they offered that ultimately saved me untold sums over the years.

All that being understood, it's still just a bank, and a bank is a business. They provide a service to us in exchange for a modest fee. It's not an exclusive relationship. Roy and Annie treated their bank too much like one,—after all, it was "Sharon from church"— and this is what stopped them from diversifying enough to truly be secure.

A bank won't feel insulted if we shop around before making our investments, but too many people only have one thought when it comes to managing their money: "Go to the bank!"

Most of us still put more confidence into something that's a little more brick-and-mortar than online investing or a faceless institution or product from out of state. People then justify not using anything else with feelings of community loyalty, which is just a home-town guilt trip. Openness to new financial options does not make one a "playa," or whatever it is that the kids are saying these days.

Banks are great at making money, but, let's be honest, most of them aren't so good at making *us* money. If they were equally good at both, they would've warned Roy and Annie about the back-end taxes during the RRSP pitch. Bankers thrive from bringing business to their specific institution. (Do you really believe that the maximization of a bank teller's Christmas bonus is contingent on how many IRAs they *didn't* sell that year?)

Keep banks on their toes. Keep them honest. Shop around, and let them know up-front that we are doing so. Sometimes that's all the motivation they need to find the best option for us.

### What Can We Expect From Our Bank?

Although this might change soon, our bank should be offering what is considered to be a full range of accounts, including both traditional IRAs and Roth IRAs, the Roth generally being more interesting for readers of this book who are interested in minimizing our taxation in retirement. However, it's equally likely that all the accounts they offer are nothing more than savings accounts, which can be helpful but aren't the best quality choice for long-term investment. Normally, it's not a banker who'll help us find our ideal investment account, but a broker instead. We'll look more closely at brokers later on.

Besides general investment and retirement accounts, bankers will leap at every chance to offer three services: mortgages, mortgage life insurance, and high-limit credit cards. I accepted all three without question when I was younger and buying my first house.

All three services have a better alternative. Switching to these saved me a great deal of money that would otherwise have gone to needless expenses with diminishing returns. Without those savings, I wouldn't have felt comfortable enough to explore the wealth creation strategies we'll cover in later chapters. That is why it is our first step: It opens to door to better things.

### Getting a Better Mortgage, Brokers, and More

We aren't replacing the service of a mortgage, but rather where we get it from. When we're looking to get money for our first home, our first instinct is a mortgage offered by our bank. After all, mortgages are one of the longest-running, slowest-burning, but most reasonable-looking loans we can have.

Mortgages take a house we would never have been able to afford on our own, and give us the power to start living in it for a reasonable monthly rate. When I went to my bank for my first mortgage, I signed everything they put in front of me, while understanding pretty much none of it.

A couple of years down the road, my financial situation got difficult, and my bank couldn't help in a meaningful way, so, for the first time, I thought about speaking to an independent advisor.

It turned out that the mortgage I'd taken out, while pretty normal, was adding to my problems. I was put in touch with a mortgage broker, which was like having my eyes opened to a whole new world. While a bank will typically only offer its own mortgage plans, a broker can show us a plethora of available options, and help us get in touch with whoever is offering the best choices.

All I had to do was ask my broker to switch my mortgage from the bank's to a new one I wanted. Although the principal amount of money I had to pay didn't change, the way that payment was divided, and the far lower interest rate, meant that I ended up saving thousands of dollars in the long run. Even when my new monthly mortgage payments conveniently offered to roll up and combine my property taxes,—which had previously been socking it to me to the tune of about $2,000 a year—I still ended up paying less per month than I had been previously. This led to a snowball effect as all the money I saved through that switch could now be invested, and the effect of that is strongly felt in my life today.

Always find a broker who comes very well-recommended. Ask what fees we need to pay them and, for the love of all-holy green-and-viscous *cow cud*, take our time in deciding what rates are best for us. Don't just take the first option we find. The greatest benefit of a broker is that they can find almost every mortgage option available. Let's use that.

Brokers are also great for helping us to invest. Aside from mortgages, they are comfortable browsing through all sorts of investment markets, particularly the stock market. While a lot of brokers are content just to perform the orders we give them, most modern brokers are more than happy to perform double-duty as financial advisors in their own right.

Between brokers and regular advisors, it becomes easy to form well-rounded opinions on what to do with our money, so long as they're fully licensed. For instance, a US broker must be licensed with both FINRA and the SEC. Always do the homework.

Brokers not only help us invest but also diversify. Diversification is a great way to reduce the risks of strategies such as Stacy's mutual funds, or Roy and

Annie's retirement account. For instance, having a smaller stake in two mutual funds in unrelated industries would've given Stacy more stable security than her large stake in a single fund. Double stakes would have also made it easier for her to abandon ship and reinvest in a better one when the time came.

### What About Mortgage Life Insurance?

**To be clear:** A mortgage is a good thing, and life insurance is a good thing. Mortgage life insurance, on the other hand...

"That's a whole 'nuther animal," as Dad used to say.

It is a reassuring feeling to get insured, and equally satisfying to be called a "policyholder" by our bank. That's one of those labels that make us feel that we've officially "made it" as an adult. Thus, when our bank offers to include mortgage life insurance in the monthly payments of our first home, it just feels like an extra layer of security for a nominal fee.

What's the difference between mortgage life insurance and standard life insurance? From a bank's perspective, the primary difference is that it's either illegal for them to sell life insurance, or else heavily regulated and restricted. Mortgage life insurance was developed as a legal workaround that has the added benefit of being an easy upsell for the bank.

Unlike a standard policy, mortgage life insurance doesn't offer a tax-free cash payout to a beneficiary when we die. Instead, it fully pays off the mortgage balance still owing on our home.

While it might seem responsible, and even charitable, to know that whoever we are leaving our house to won't have to pay a dime for it in the event of our death, there are three major problems with this if we do a little homework.

**Problem 1:** Our beneficiary gets a free house, but that's it.

They could just as easily get a lump sum of tax-free cash—equivalent to the balance owing on the home, along with a considerable amount extra—from any decent life insurance policy, whether whole life or term. Mortgages are some of the easiest and slowest-burning debts to manage, especially with a good broker. Opting for mortgage insurance over a standard policy is like being a nurse who treats the guy with a papercut before she pays any attention to the purple-faced guy who's complaining of a stabbing chest pain that keeps radiating into his left arm.

Life insurance policies allow us to decide where the death benefit will be paid. For example, many policyholders leave directions for their mortgage to be paid off first, then pay any other large debts, and finally, pay the remainder to a beneficiary. Death brings expenses, particularly if the decedent was the household's primary source of income. Funerals alone can cost thousands of dollars... a truly disgusting fact when you stop and think about it.

But millions of people still elect for mortgage life insurance. Is there a silver lining?

**Fun fact:** Nope!

**Problem 2:** Mortgage life insurance pays out less money the longer we pay into it.

Normally, the providing bank will arrange for the insurance premium to be conveniently rolled up into our regular mortgage payment, so we're still only making one monthly payment. However, we're paying extra for diminishing returns: The longer we make payments, the smaller the balance left owing on our mortgage. And the less the bank has to pay out if we happen to kick it.

It's pretty obvious why banks love this, but the whole idea of insurance is that we should see growing rewards for long-term contributions, not penalization. Standard policies promise a larger payout in exchange for long-term payment of our premiums. Mortgage life insurance is a complete reversal of that.

**Problem 3:** Mortgage life insurance pays out the balance owing on mortgages in just 12% of all claims.

TWELVE. FREAKING. PERCENT. 88% of the time, the issuing bank is content to just take our money, promise to pay a consistently lowering amount, and then refuse to even do that.

Numbers are nothing without human faces relating to them. 100 people died. 100 families lost a loved one. 12 families got a paid-off home. 88 families were told, "No."

Now multiply those people exponentially until we have national statistics.

Mortgage life insurance is high-risk and low-benefit. It just isn't worth it. There are far better types of insurance out there, such as ACTUAL life insurance, health insurance, disability insurance, critical illness insurance, and estate planning. These can all be invaluable when we need them, help us tackle urgent overwhelming circumstances, and are open to rewarding us for being a long-term contributor... sometimes even before we die, as in the case of cash-value insurance. We'll discuss insurance options further in Chapter 8.

### *Meanwhile, in the Land of Credit...*

Credit cards are the third bank-given service that should trigger alarm bells whenever they're offered. Like mortgages, credit cards can be helpful and have even become necessary for such modern conveniences as airline and hotel reservations, online shopping, and even security deposits. Also like mortgages, it's vital we don't just accept the first set of terms offered.

There is wisdom in having no more than one card at a time. Banks and credit card companies love to go wild with offers, and, if we are too quick to accept, we'll easily end up with three or more cards, all of them crying out to be used.

It is stressful having to keep track of multiple sources of debt, and that stress can lead to a lot of wasted time and energy as we get bogged down in uncertainty. If we're in this situation, the best thing we can do is consolidate our credit balances.

What this means is taking out a loan on a lower interest rate than most of our cards and other debts, yet also large enough to pay off all of them. Yes, we still owe just as much money after taking the consolidation loan as we did before, but now we only owe it to one institution, and we are paying one low-interest rate. We have a variety of loan options: A consolidation loan, a repayment plan arranged by a debt consolidation company, a line of credit, or a lower-interest credit card.

I cannot recommend consolidation strategies enough, as many credit cards out there charge over 20% interest. This is what I call "high," but what the typical bank in the US might call "average." Paying 2o% or more in interest can get ridiculous when we consider the things we use credit cards for: Food, clothes, entertainment, and other consumables that don't generate long-term value.

Paying with credit instead of cash means making life much more expensive without meaningfully raising its quality. Consolidation is the first step towards breaking a bad credit habit.

**Tips on Consolidation**

Unfortunately, some lending institutions really enjoy getting our regular high-interest payments and will not authorize a consolidation loan to be negotiated. If we're unable to consolidate our credit but have a steady income, there's another way to get our credit under control, called the Debt Avalanche. In this method, we make the required minimum payments to our credit debt and other loans, but then use any extra money we have to make overpayments on the one debt with the highest interest rate. We keep doing this until that debt is fully paid off, and then we move on to overpaying the debt with the second-highest interest. And then the next. If we can maintain paying the same amount we began the Avalanche with, our subsequent debts will be paid off much faster as each subsequent debt gets more money paid to it per month until it is eliminated.

For a simple example, let's say that we have three credit cards with large balances owing: One with 25% interest, one with 15% interest, and one with 8% interest. All of them have minimum payments of $100 a month, so we pay a total of $300 a month. We can budget out an additional $50 a month for an overpayment,—for a new total of $350 a month—so we now can pay $150 a month toward the 25% interest card. If the 25% card also carries the largest balance, then this method is doubly beneficial. Then we simply continue to pay $350 a month until the Avalanche is complete.

When the 25% card is fully paid off, our best option is to cancel it. If we still have balances owing on the other two cards,—which we may or may not, as the payment priority is based on the cards' interest rates and not the total balance owing—we then immediately move on to paying the same monthly amount of $350, but now focusing an overpayment of $250 onto our 15% card. Once that card is paid off, we cancel it and move on to our final debt—the 8% card —towards which we are now paying the full $350 a month, $250 more than its required minimum payment.

We can see how this is a fantastic method for keeping our interest rates from spiraling out of control, which is the single greatest danger of credit cards: Spiraling interest on a credit card is the evil twin of compounding interest on an investment.

By the time we are done, we will have paid off all of our credit card debt at an expedited rate, canceled any superfluous cards, and be left with only a single low-interest card. If managed carefully, this can save years of payments and thousands of dollars in interest.

Another method to consider is the Debt Snowball, which follows the same process as the Debt Avalanche, except that we focus the initial overpayment on the debt with the smallest balance owing. When that debt is paid, we continue paying the same amount every month, but the increased overpayment is now dedicated to the next-smallest debt. By the time we have only our largest debt remaining, we will likely be overpaying it by hundreds of dollars a month, which can also eliminate all debt in an expedited time frame.

The Debt Snowball and Debt Avalanche can work for a wide variety of debts, but, as a general rule, the Debt Avalanche is preferable when we have a wider range of interest rates, which is why it is recommended for credit card debt. If our interest rates are comparable across all debts, then the Debt Snowball is less of a risk and is also generally easier to keep track of, as our debt primacy is simply arranged in ascending order.

In either case, the key is to decide on a total monthly payment which we can easily manage over a prolonged period of time—the combined minimum payments of all cards or debts, plus a small initial overpayment—and then keep paying that same amount every month until all debt is gone.

**What Should We Do Next?**

Once our debt is consolidated, simplify immediately. Keep one credit card with a low-interest rate and preferably a low spending limit. If we want to make a large purchase, we can simply continue the Avalanche or Snowball even after all our debt has been eliminated: To carry on with the previous example, we would then have a fully paid-off credit card and we would be putting an additional $350 of free cash into it every month that can be spent without penalty of interest or debt, while still racking up any reward points our card offers. If we are saving up for specific short-term purchases, rather than long-term investments, this is a very easy way to do it.

Remember, we can often overpay credit cards or lines of credit indefinitely, so a low spending limit is not necessarily prohibitive to our purchases, and far less likely to turn into a monster: It is far safer to have a credit card with a $1,500 spending limit and $5,000 overpaid onto it than it is to just have a card with a $6,500 spending limit. Both cards can buy that $6,500 fishing boat, but one will leave us with only $1,500 in debt while the other will leave us with $6,500 in debt.

Having more cards on hand just adds the temptation of outright maxing them before we rein ourselves in. Lower spending capacity and lower interest mean that we'll be less likely to push ourselves beyond our means, and less likely to curse our decisions later on. Having only one card means we'll also be more likely to stop sooner before our debt situation feels too insurmountable and we need another consolidation.

For me, the most effective method is to keep my remaining credit card frozen. And that's literal, not a cute way of saying call the bank to put a hold on spending: Literally put your credit card in an airtight container, put that in a bucket of water, and put it in your freezer. If we need it, we have to thaw it.

90% of the time, by the time the card is thawed out, we realize that we didn't need the item anyway. That may sound crazy, but it's not. Almost *everything* we buy with credit cards is an impulse item.

## Bottom Line

While our bank certainly can have the best products for our needs, it doesn't help to rush in. That's how we end up with steep mortgage rates, unhelpful insurance schemes, and too many dang credit cards.

The important thing to say is, "Thanks. I'll think about it."

This gives us time to do our research, talk to an advisor, and use modern technology like the Internet to get a wider perspective on what the world has to offer. Rushing in while ignoring the alarm bells is how they get you.

# 4

## SMASH THE HIERARCHY: REVERSING OUR THINKING ON THE FIRST PLACES WE SHOULD BE CONTRIBUTING OUR MONEY TO.

There's the traditional way of investment focus and debt repayment, but we'll soon see that there's quite a difference between the traditional way and what actually works.

**Step 2: Embrace the Concept of Using Other People's Money.**

I hope you have both a strong stomach and a strong love of beef steak because I'm going to tell you in grim detail a war story from my youth: The Battle of Ear-Tag D17.

D17 was a mild-mannered Black Angus/Hereford-crossed "Black Baldy" cow—black body, white face, with a much-in-demand marbling quality—who inexplicably became a homicidal lunatic 18 seconds after giving birth to her first bull calf. A lot of cows get overprotective of their babies, but this psychopath was one for the annuls of cowboy history. Black Baldies are a notably passive breed, perhaps because they do not fully comprehend how delicious they are. Cutting against either the grain or knowledge base of the breed, D17 must have known exactly how delectable her newborn veal was destined to be because she put me through a wooden-planked wind fence the first time I approached her floundering neonate to check his airway for amniotic fluid. Not only was it EXCRU-CIATINGLY PAINFUL, but it was also maternally negligent: Baby cows drown in their own amniotic fluid all the time!

During her magical first two weeks of motherhood, D17 managed to trample almost every member of my family. At one point, I considered giving her an actual name as opposed to just her ear-tag designation,—and had even narrowed my choices down to either a notably berserk Viking warrior from my distant ancestry or the *Enola Gay*—but it was my older brother who eventually said, "We don't speak the name of the devil."

Blue-haired animal lovers with no comprehension of just how epic a tomahawk steak can be may shriek like harpies when I tell them this next part, but I quickly ditched my traditional cattle cane in favor of a 2x4 every time I was required to venture into the maternity pasture. Cattle canes are constructed from a sturdy plastic polymer that can be used to guide or prod inattentive calves on cattle drives and can also give a stinging *Whack!* to their defiant mamas when necessary. However, when dealing with bovine juggernauts, a 2x4 has a little more stopping power.

The Battle of Ear-Tag D17 took place on what would normally be a 10-minute cattle drive, moving about 30 pairs of new calves and their mothers from the maternity pen to the south pasture. The adorable naivety of cattle canes had become a thing of the distant past, and every member of my family was now packing 2x4s. D17 saw us coming through the gate and met us at full stride.

For the next 30 minutes, the battle raged in a whirling dervish of literal blood, sweat, and tears, topped with an occasional spray of manure. (Not sure if you're aware, but cows will "fury poop" when sufficiently agitated) Heroes arose, cowards fled, ballads were inspired, and we had barely progressed 20 feet closer to the south gate.

My 2x4 had gone MIA in the chaos—or perhaps D17 had eaten it in an attempt to absorb her enemy's life force— and my nemesis could immediately smell my weakness. Abandoning her trampling of Dad for a moment,—which I'm sure he appreciated—she locked onto me like a laser-guided missile and charged.

The skull of a charging cow is basically an 800 lb anvil coming at you at 20mph, and I was too far away from the fence to clamber to safety. All I had time to do was snatch up a nearby boulder—which I probably could not have budged from the ground in a less adrenaline-fuelled circumstance—and lob it straight up in the air like a mortar round.

To the great surprise of both of us, the boulder dropped straight down onto the crown of D17's head with resonating *"BONK!"* Her charge was stopped on a dime, which seemed to fly in defiance of most laws of physics. For a long moment, two bug-eyed foes stared at one another in stunned silence as the rock dropped to the ground like the hammer of Thor. Then D17's front legs buckled underneath her, and she pitched forward with her jaw in the dirt and butt in the air like a terrified peasant prostrating before the emperor.

"*BAAAAAAAAAWWWLL!!!*" she announced, which I later learned was the bovine term for unconditional surrender, but which I initially mistook for a death knell.

"Holy crap, I killed her!" I blurted.

Then D17 rose to her feet, shook her head a couple of times, led her oblivious offspring to the south gate leading to greener pastures... and never bothered anyone again for the remainder of her many years on the ranch.

I don't know if you'd call it cognitive recalibration, mild brain damage, or just a Windows update. Whatever the designation, it was a brutally transformative moment that changed everyone's life for the better, including hers, and led to a happier future.

I bring this up because, looking back on my love-hate relationship with so many aspects of finance, I think it's sometimes necessary to have something similar happen to us to reevaluate our financial planning. Getting a similar butt-kicking on a psychological level can do our wallets a world of good.

*The Rock*

The three stories we covered earlier are all good examples of cow-bonking rocks, and they all send a clear message: How we're doing things now—and even historically—isn't necessarily how we should be doing things going forward.

At the time of this writing, most people are throwing the first fruits of their paycheck into paying down mortgages and other debts. Fair enough. We all want to be debt-free.

Conventional wisdom states that a mortgage is the most important debt to pay off first because it's the biggest and therefore most scary. The second priority is any secondary debts. Then we'll pay into a child's college fund, life insurance, and, a long way down the road, maybe we'll consider contributions to an IRA or RRSP. In the interests of parallel strategies within this book, we will often refer to those two investment tools collectively as IRA/RRSPs due to their strong similarities.

After-tax funds such as Roth IRAs and TFSAs—which we will likewise refer to collectively as Roth/TFSAs in circumstances where they have closely aligned uses in both the US and Canada—are viewed as the lowest priority of all, and many times they are never even considered. When hard times arise, they are often the first monthly expense to be canceled.

The bonk on the head we got from the three stories in Chapter 2 should tell us that a complete reversal of these priorities has become necessary. We live in the Land of Opportunity, and we need to make the most of that.

A strategy that has been gaining a lot of momentum in recent years puts the investment primacy on Roth/TFSAs, followed by insurance products. Both of these, when handled well, are great ways to grow our investments for later in life. Using this model, only after our Roth/TFSAs are maxed out should our conventional IRA/RRSPs be tended to.

Our mortgage, because it has a low interest rate and relatively well-spaced installments, simply does not need to be a priority, no matter how big and scary it may appear.

Of course, we must still make the payments needed to eventually clear what we owe on our house, but strategies such as mortgage prepayment and over-payments can be avoided altogether while still enabling us to save and invest respectably. We do not necessarily benefit from clearing our mortgage early, and we might even lose out on huge investment growth. As in all cases, our circumstances will differ, and some people have been very happy paying off their mortgage early. However, bear with me for a moment, and let's see if another option makes sense to you.

First, we need to get comfortable with spending other people's money.

### Other People's Money

Other People's Money, or OPM. My first experience with this phrase occurred when I was a kid. A local businessman from Texas liked to claim that OPM was his secret to success, and he may have been telling the truth. I'll probably never know for certain, because he was shortly thereafter accused of defrauding his business partners and employees, and fled the country. I'm not sure if he eventually ended up in a mansion or a gutter, but, either way, the OPM acronym left a bad taste in my mouth.

Even outside of that experience, the term sounds slightly sinister and self-serving when taken out of context. But the fact is that virtually everyone utilizes OPM, and we use it almost every day of our lives. Any form of loan, mortgage, or credit technically fits that designation.

People like to offer their money all the time... but only so long as it's on credit. Credit and home mortgages are the most common forms of OPM. Usually, credit agreements are set up to chiefly benefit the lender, but, if we know what we're doing, we can use the money they give us to not only procure important amenities, such as a house to stay in but also divert money into places that will generate far more value for us in the long run. Now, investing in leverage like this can be quite risky, so we don't want to rush anything or get emotional while doing it. (Be under no illusion: HGTV programs lie to all of us about the "indescribable joy" of homeownership.) Let's break things down together.

Firstly, when I talk about leverage, I'm not talking about borrowing money to invest straight into something else. What I'm saying is that when we take out a mortgage or if we happen to already have some other large slow-burning debt, paying it all off right away isn't our only option.

A lot of people think paying every spare dollar they have into removing debts right away is the best idea or even the only responsible action for their family. At the time, it often seems like a great idea. This is because people often believe that the only alternative is reckless spending, along with mounting interest and a never-ending rack-up of debt.

So, fearing this one extreme, we are tempted to swing to the other, to the point where we wind up paying off our home an entire decade ahead of schedule, and our credit card debt even earlier than that.

This is a tempting prospect for sure. A whole decade of no interest building up against us? An early return to being debt-free? That sounds fantastic.

However, there are notable alternatives to this strategy, or rather to this blind refusal to maximize the potential of our OPM. Even if we are this aggressive at paying off our house, we're still going to take about 15 years at best to do so. And during that time, because every spare dollar is going into clearing our house debt in under two decades, we're also having around 15 years of absolutely zero growth in our savings.

We'll be 15 years closer to retirement age without anything meaningful in the bank to show for it. We'll have the relief of not being in the red, or being in debt, but not necessarily for long. I think we can do better than that.

Try this: When we're in mortgage debt, instead of aggressively paying it all back as quickly as possible, simply make the minimum payments required. That's the first thing we do.

Next, take the non-linear approach. People like to work in a sequential, "one after the other" sort of way with their money. This is why Debt Snowball and Debt Avalanche strategies are so popular, and, to be clear, I am not diminishing the value of those strategies, particularly for people struggling with excessive debt. They work by tackling one thing at a time in a logical order. In fact, the method I'm going to describe next is a variation inspired directly by those strategies: Maximizing the potential of OPM while making only minimum payments.

When we're comfortable with OPM, we can put our extra money into growth accounts while simultaneously keeping our debt under control.

So, we'll be working with our money in a staggered way, putting some of it on one side to meet our requirements with debt, while putting the rest on the other side to start growing and generating long-term returns. There's no reason why we can't do these two things at the same time. Being debt-free is not a prerequisite for making meaningful investments and generating meaningful growth. If it was, we'd see far fewer entrepreneurs setting themselves up for quick success, as many of them have to take on debt to get the equipment necessary for their business. Even the most successful titans of industry often carry a lot of debt, which puzzled me when I was younger: Why would billionaires still have debt? Was their wealth actually a sham or scam?

No. They just know how to make a ton of money while paying their debts in the most efficient way possible.

So, like the billionaires, we need to retrain our brains to be comfortable with staggering money in this way. No one says we have to take big risks. Most of us aren't setting up an international real estate empire: We're just doing a little simple math. In this chapter, I'll be giving mathematical examples of great OPM management in action, so we can see how it works.

### *Some Rules About OPM*

OPM is a great way to smash the "hierarchy of primacy" which we have all been lulled into thinking is just the way things are. Let's say we have a 25-year mortgage on our home, and we know that, with a little budgeting, belt-tightening, and overpayment, we could reduce that amortization period by 10 years.

Make the minimum payments instead.

And let's be clear about that. That means making only 1 full mortgage payment every month. Don't even switch to the biweekly payment system which gives us 13 full payments per year, and shaves off one year in every twelve from our amortization period. Yes, it would mean paying off our house in the full 25 years instead of the 15 that can be so tempting. However, the investment interest we can generate in our favor over those same 25 years through contributing to growth accounts will more than makeup for having to pay interest on our house for an extra decade.

Using OPM means we cannot clear all our debts as quickly, so it's important to know when to use it.

**Rules:**

1. We only use OPM, staggering our money between debt and growth contributions, when our debts are low-interest. A mortgage is a great example of low-interest debt. Some credit cards, and even car payments or payment plans on home furnishings, may also have a low enough APR to work as a source of OPM.

2. Always think twice before using OPM if it means delaying high-interest debt, such as that from a high-interest credit card. If the growth account we're contributing to has a lower rate of return than the debt we have to pay off, we're going to have a hard time, or even risk seeing our high-interest debt spiral rapidly beyond what we've budgeted for. The better solution is to Avalanche or Snowball our debt until we only have low-interest debts remaining, and switch back to staggering OPM from there.

3. In some cases, both strategies can overlap and save precious time if we have sufficient funds and can budget them both carefully: We can initiate an OPM strategy for our

investments and low-interest debt while simultaneously enacting an Avalanche or Snowball strategy for our higher-interest debts. If we can do this successfully, we may be in an even better position once our highest-interest debts are eliminated, i.e., we will be accustomed to budgeting overpayments, so we can then divert those previous payments toward our OPM strategy. However, if we do not have sufficient income to overlap strategies without stretching our money too thin, just do them sequentially: Eliminate high-interest debt first, then use OPM for what's left.

Now, here are some reasons why using OPM can be so good when dealing with mortgage debt in particular:

Firstly, we don't get anything tangible out of paying off our home. It becomes easier to sell once it's fully paid off, but even so, it's not easy to quickly convert where we live into cash when we fall on hard times and need to support ourselves with drastic actions. In other words, our home is likely our most valuable asset but also has the lowest liquidity.

So, aggressively paying off our mortgage, even when all other debts are out the way, can leave us quite brittle to outside tragedies. Our home will also almost certainly lose value over time due to the way real estate works, meaning our home just isn't a great appreciating investment, even if we regularly maintain and renovate it. It's great at keeping us warm and safe, but we already get both those perks even while we're paying it all off. Even the increased value from maintenance and renovations are only really worth the time and expense if we can be reasonably confident that they are adding at least 1.5x our investment, or even double, to our home value: For every $1,000 we spend on fixing up the place, we should be able to add at least $1,500 to our asking price., and $2,000 is better. As a home ages, this is not always possible. No matter how many improvements we've made to an ancestral property, some buyers will always show a preference for a new home.

We need to value a home for what it is: A place we can proudly call our own, and even pass on to our kids. In a financial downturn, it might become a burden if we haven't planned sufficiently in other areas. Using OPM to invest can leave us with a handy source of cash for when the going gets tough, and prepare us to enjoy our castle throughout a prosperous retirement.

Next, because paying off a mortgage even at max speed takes so long, it's important to also consider inflation. A dollar today is worth less than a dollar yesterday. The dollar of tomorrow will be worth even less. This isn't just me being a doomer, or boomer, or whatever it is the kids are saying these days. This is just how it is for economies worldwide. Inflation happens, and, when it does, individual banknotes buy less: Less electricity, less water, less bread, you name it. The pace of inflation will often even outpace the interest rate of our bank's High-Interest Savings Account, as we will discuss further in Chapter 5.

Because the minimum rates of a mortgage don't change, and can even be reduced with help from a broker, this means we're effectively paying less each month. If we have to pay a minimum of $900 per month for 25 years, then that's what we'll still pay to the end, even when inflation means that $900 is only effectively worth $600 by the end. In this way, infla-tion can work in a long-term mortgage's favor, espe-cially when we consider that most long-term employees will also see pay increases over the years:

Their wages go up as the value of their mortgage payment comes down.

Likewise, the interest we think we're saving by paying off the mortgage early is likely going to matter a lot less than we think, again because of inflation. Even if inflation only occurs at a rate of 2% each year,—again more than most High-Interest Savings Accounts can offer as compensation—over 15 years on an aggressive mortgage payoff, that's still enough to make, say, a $70,000 saving on interest worth tens of thousands of dollars less.

On the flip side, growth accounts and investment accounts are great ways of effectively preserving and even increasing the value of our money despite inflation. The sooner we put money in such a place, the sooner we're protecting its value from the ravages of time which, as we'll see below, will be far more impactful in the long run.

### *Math Time: Being Aggressive*

Before I show the math behind using OPM properly, let's look at the scenario of an ambitious power couple who thought three caramel macchiatos at Starbucks were a better investment than this book.

We're going to use a very simple example where things like inflation or interest variation don't exist. Because we aren't factoring for inflation, our results from this example will be better in practice than they look here. However, it's important to note that while our example will use a fixed mortgage for simplicity, not all mortgages have unchanging interest rates, i.e., many fixed-rate mortgages will be subject to change after 5 years. For that reason, we always take our time, read the fine print, and ask lots of questions for understanding before we sign off on such a big loan, and never forget the option of using the services of a mortgage broker to find the best rates, even years from now.

Now, imagine that we're first-time homebuyers looking at acquiring a $250,000 mortgage loan. According to the offered contract, we'll be charged a consistent 4% interest, with minimum monthly payments totaling $1,188.80. This means we'll be paying off $14,265.60 a year, and our debt will be fully paid off in, um... 30 years. Any first-time homeowner will surely cringe when they think about paying $1,188.80 each month for 30 years, and this is what leads to the natural, but sub-optimal, urge to aggressively pay off our mortgages at an expedited rate.

Let's assume that we, the power couple, are young and married. We're respected professionals, and we don't want to be paying off our new house for 30 years. So we commit to paying the whole dang thing off in 20.

To pay off our house 10 years earlier, we'd need to put another $321.82 towards it each month. Added onto the minimum monthly rate, that's $1,510.62 we'll be paying each month, just for our home loan. For the moment, we assume that going higher than that wouldn't be comfortable for us, which is reasonable.

That extra $321.82 will amount to an extra $3,861.84 spent each year. Maybe this seems a little steep, but we know we can meet that faster pace, and fully owning our house a decade earlier is tempting, so we do it.

Partway through, we decide to go hard or go home. Why pay only once a month, when we can instead pay once a fortnight? We re-space our payment schedule, decide to skip Starbucks for a while, and we are now eking out $19,638.06 towards our mortgage each year, an impressive annual increase of $5,372.46. This is the point where we've gone full-on aggressive, and have little or nothing to spare for savings at the moment. But we're good at sticking to plans once we've made them, so we can do it. And it means we can now pay off our home in 18 years instead of 20.

We do it. It's 18 years later, we fully own our home, and we're feeling pretty happy. Also, our family has expanded, and we now have a 12-year old daughter, Li'l Sue. We decide that our disciplined overpayments have prepared us to now build our savings. Being familiar with the concept of both the Debt Snowball and Debt Avalanche, we agree that the same amount we used to spend on mortgage payments can now just get dropped into a growth account instead. We've got our groove on, we've kept up with all other living expenses, and it feels like a breeze to begin investing at a rate of $1,636.50 a month. That's an impressive amount for any family to put away for retirement.

Imagine we are Canadian,—stay with me, America, this applies equally as we'll see—and therefore have our choice of HISAs, TFSAs, and RRSPs. HISAs don't have the interest rate that we'd hope for, so that one's out, which leaves us with a choice between TFSAs and RRSPs, and the "TF" portion of TFSA is immediately intriguing. However, much like the

Roth IRA, a TFSA only allows us to invest $6,000 in it per year without any serious penalties... namely full-rate taxation on the entire contribution amount. So, to our dismay, we find our ability to save being bottlenecked.

Now, we could split our investments, putting $6,000 into a TFSA and the remaining $13,638.06 into an RRSP, although that feels a little more complicated than necessary. However, we then realize that an RRSP allows up to 18% of our pre-tax income to be contributed to it. Let's say we've been earning a combined gross income of $120,000 a year. In that case, our contribution limit is $21,600. Awesome! Our entire investment budget is less than that, $19,638.06. So we can quite comfortably sink everything we used to put into mortgage payments into an RRSP instead, without fear of penalty as we're still under the contribution threshold. Forget that silly TFSA and its measly $6,000 contribution cap...

We find a good RRSP fund with a consistent 8% rate of return, and faithfully make contributions to it for the next 12 years. So, 30 years after we first took that mortgage loan, we end up with full homeownership and a cool $372,672.81 tucked away. Well, almost... It's closer to $223,603.69 after the 40% in back-end taxes are paid. Kind of makes us wish we could have utilized that TFSA instead.

This same situation for a couple in the good old US of A would be even more tricky as both IRAs and Roth IRAs have a contribution cap of $6,000 a year, which increases to $7,000 a year for those over the age of 50, which in our example was 3 years ago. We can own multiple IRAs, but their combined contribution totals cannot exceed $6,000 or $7,000 a year. By this time, we realize that our best option is to skip the income tax breaks of the traditional IRA in favor of the tax-free withdrawals of the Roth IRA, so our annual investments of $19,638.06 would be divided as follows: $6,000 in a Roth IRA with impressive 8% returns, and, thinking that the rest is just gravy, we decide to simply dump the balance of $13,638.06 into a High-Interest Savings Account earning an impressive—for a bank—2% a year.

After 9 years, we begin putting $7,000 a year into our Roth IRA, and only $12,638.06 into our HISA. At the end of our 12 years of investments,—and after the interest earned in our HISA is hit every year at the marginal tax rate on our tax return—we will have a paid-off home and tax-deducted cash amounting to about $297,097.57. And we just turned 53, and Li'l Sue just started her second year of college.

Now, when we factor in other things such as promotions, pay raises, and pension funds, this doesn't look like a bad outcome, and, to be fair, it is far more of an accomplishment than many families will ever achieve.

But I can do you one better.

### *Math Time: Using OPM*

I'm about to hit you in the head with a rock.

Let's rewind our clock by 30 years. We're now 23 years old again, we actually skipped the three trips to Starbucks and bought this book instead, and we're looking over our mortgage for this same house. Paying it all off in 18 years would mean spending $19,638.06 per year on the mortgage. But paying it across the full 30-year amortization period means spending only $14,265.60 a year.

However, we are still willing to work hard for our future. We could still afford to pay the $19,638.06 into the mortgage, but instead of doing that, we're just going to make the minimum payments, leaving us with an additional $5,372.46 each year to invest where we wish. That's low enough to fit snugly into a Roth IRA or TFSA without any penalties since both allow us to make annual contributions of $6,000. Our advisor finds us a Roth/TFSA with a fantastic average return rate of 8%, just like in our last scenario, so we place our additional $5,372.46 into it each year... for the next 30 years. While we can only put so much into one of these accounts each year, there's no limit to how much the accounts can hold in total.

This money will remain tax-exempt, even when we withdraw it, so we can be confident that it won't be ripped from us as we make withdrawals in retirement.

That's $5,372.46 a year, broken down into small payments of $447.70(2) per month. In 30 years, it will grow into a tax-free pool of $608,605.44.

We're now 53 again. But, in America, we have more than double the amount of money we would have had after-tax if we went with the aggressive repayment method and over 3.75x more than if we had just tucked away that extra $5,372.46 into a sock drawer every year. In Canada, although we come out with the same $608,605.44 in both countries, we'd have earned almost 3x more than we would have with the aggressive 18-year plan.

**One last "BONK!" for the road...**

And this is the big one.

Rental properties are often viewed as the absolute worst form of OPM, as we don't have a home to call our own, no matter how long we keep shoveling in payments. A fair argument is that only the landlord collecting rent is benefiting from OPM.

However, quite a few years back, it occurred to me that paying rent can cost considerably less than mortgage payments, and also has far fewer associated expenses. Knowing something about how small amounts can yield huge returns in the right circumstances, I decided to dig a little deeper.

Here's a fun little hypothetical.

How much money could we save in 30 years if we chose to just rent a modest home or apartment, paying a single flat rate that often includes our utilities? What if we based our savings plan on the same model that we know we can afford from the aggressive strategy on a $250,000 mortgage in our example, i.e, $19,638.06 a year? Except now, instead of making monthly payments of $1,188.80 and putting the additional $447.70 into our investment savings, we're only paying $950 in rent and putting away $686.50(5) a month, or $8,238.06 a year. Over 30 years, we contribute a total of $247,141.80 to our investment funds.

Our combined fund balance is $940,141.95.

And that's not counting the additional utility payments, home insurance, renovations, and property taxes associated with the homeowner's mortgage. Let's conservatively say that those average out to around $4,000 a year. Factor those into our plan, and now we're paying $950 in rent and putting away $1,019.84 a month. $12,238.06 a year.

In both of these rental scenarios, we exceed our $6,000 Roth/TFSA contribution cap for the year, so we may have to put some of our investments into back-end tax funds. In the second example, where we factor in the additional $4,000 in homeowner payments, we would end up owing the most tax in Canada, but even that worst-case scenario is far more manageable. Let's assume that we manage to invest the full amount of $12,238.06 across a variety of funds every year, again at an average rate of return of 8%: We put $6,000 a year into a

Roth/TFSA and $6,238.06 a year into a Roth 401(k) or RRSP, both of which have high contribution caps, although the RRSP will have back-end taxes owing. For the sake of a worst-case scenario, we will set the back-end taxes at 40%. ($19,500 can be paid annually into a Roth 401(k) and $27,830 into an RRSP.)

In 30 years, we'd have invested a total of $367,141.80, and we'd have $1,396,631.30: Well over one million dollars more than we invested. Minus $284,760.28 in back-end tax if we're in Canada.

Even the Canadians still end up with a net total of $1,111,871.02.

Don't believe everyone who says that renting does nothing but shovel your money into a bottomless pit.

**The Takeaways**

The most important thing to note from the preceding examples—the family who chose aggressive mortgage payments, the family who opted for the full amortization of their mortgage, and the family who chose a modest rental property—is that all three families utilized the same amount of money, budgeted from the same household income, over the same 30-year time-span: In both of the mortgage scenarios, the families paid $19,636.06, divided between their mortgage and investments, plus $4,000 in associated homeowner costs. In the rental scenario, the same total of $23,636.06 was divided only between rental payments and investments.

The aggressive "I'll pay it off in 18 years" family invested $19,638.06 into growth accounts for 12 years after their primary debt was cleared, putting in a total of $235,656.72. After-tax, their fund values totaled less than $300,000. In fact, the Canadian couple who only utilized their RRSP *lost* $12,053.03 after-tax, because they did not have sufficient growth time to offset their tax rate. ($235,656.72 - $223,603.69 = $12,053.03) By 53 years old, they didn't have any meaningful growth to show for their investment despite investing so much. This is because they started late.

Our alternative couple who said, "They gave us 30 years, so we'll use 30 years" wound up much better. They always had a little leftover to contribute to growth from the very beginning.

At an investment rate of only $447.70 per month, they only invested $161,172 in total over 30 years. They got over $600,000 to show for it by the time they turned 53, despite their accounts having the same interest rate as the first family. They simply started earlier. This meant that they more than doubled the returns of the aggressive family while investing just a little more than half as much.

The real moment of cognitive recalibration comes when we learn to handle debt: Use Other People's Money. Now, does getting this long-term reward of doubled savings make an extra 12 years of mortgage payments look worthwhile, or do I need to pick up a bigger rock?

However, both families who took out mortgages also incurred the associated costs of homeownership. They paid an additional $120,000 over 30 years.

And the family who chose to rent a property for the same time could hypothetically see more than twice the investment growth of the homeowners.

Even if the renters eventually decided to buy a $250,000 home, using only their three decades worth of investment returns, they would still have more free cash left over than either of the families who took out a mortgage 30 years earlier: Anywhere between $861,871.02 and $1,146,631.30... whereas the best-case scenario of a mortgage holder was

$608,605.44. That's a difference of at least $253,266.58, and at most $538,025.86. I don't know about you, but I wouldn't mind staying in a rental property for a while. Not if I end the day with a fully-paid off home and half a million dollars *more* than everyone else who just finished paying off their long-term mortgage.

To quote that infamous rock from so many decades ago... *"BONK!"*

Slamming huge amounts of money to clear off all our debts early can feel good, but the thinking that inspires it is short-term, not long-term. It is impatient, seeking relatively immediate gratification and relief. In the long-term, this behavior leaves us woefully unprepared and can force us to contribute to taxable accounts which can shave off hundreds of thousands of dollars from our savings and retirement plans.

Long-term success comes neither from paying off all our debts immediately nor from ignoring them entirely. It comes from finding the right balance. This begins with realizing the best way to grow our money early on, and the best help we can seek to assist us in that. It also begins with realizing that not all debts are created equal: APR determines primacy.

While I never suggest letting a high-interest card go unpaid or run untethered, I cannot stress enough that there's no sense in rushing to pay off a good mortgage, either. Let yourself be comfortable with smaller-interest debts, no matter how big and scary their total may seem. It will take a few calculations jotted onto a few napkins, but the rewards can be staggering.

Even if you end up renting your home from a smug landlady who honestly believes that she is the only one benefiting from OPM.

# 5

# ALBERT EINSTEIN VS THE HIGH-INTEREST SAVINGS ACCOUNT: THE RULE OF 72, AND WHY YOUR BEST BANK ACCOUNT WILL NEVER GET YOU THERE IN TIME.

Frankly, a standard bank account opened early is little better than contributing to a growth account opened late. There's also a reason I mentioned Roth/TFSAs as part of our OPM strategy and not just our regular old savings account. Inflation, low returns, and high tax are simply prohibitive to long-term financial success.

This is probably why some people choose to be aggressive when paying off things like mortgages. They don't always know about good growth accounts until they've already committed several years into their 18-year plan.

**Step 3: Learn the Rule of 72.**

*Brief Backstory Time*

As a young man straight out of high school, I had little interest in investment. In my mind, finding a good job with a decent pension, plus a little frugality and savings was enough. However, I didn't quite want to rush off a mortgage in 18 years, either. I wanted to contribute to something, a rainy-day nest egg that could increase in size with manageable contributions over the years.

My first step was to look up a few different High-Interest Savings Accounts in local banks. Some of these accounts offered as much as 2% in annual interest rates, so it seemed like a safe way to grow my money with monthly contributions. As I'd always been taught, a bank's savings account is always a safe place to store and grow my money. The best rate was found in a bank that was not my regular one, so I opened an account there as well: I now had my day-to-day bank, and what I called my "no-touchy" bank. If I had an extra $50 or $100, I threw it into my HISA. By taking even that brief foray beyond my regular bank, I felt a sense of "I'm an adult now!" because I hadn't allowed sentimentality or a meaningless sense of loyalty to hold me back.

Little did I know at the time that the growth rate of an HISA was barely even enough to keep up with inflation, let alone generate additional value for me in the long term. Inflation will regularly outpace the interest of an HISA.

This thought didn't even cross my mind. You see, it wasn't just friends and neighbors saying the bank is a safe place to store my money. The banks were naturally saying the same thing, too. To their credit, they make a compelling argument for the safety and long-term value of their HISAs. An argument that, again, falls flat on its face when we remember that their growth barely keeps up with inflation.

Banks can preserve the value of our money to some extent, but, again, they're not necessarily the best at growing it for us. Their advertising can be brutal though. I remember that, even when I learned I was being charged $5 each time I made a withdrawal, I just shrugged it off and accepted it. I thought the withdrawal fee would teach me discipline, and I felt pretty smug that I was making the so-called responsible choice.

At the time of this writing, my single remaining HISA has exactly $0.50 in it, has maintained that balance for many years, and I frequently forget that it exists. I've moved my money on to greener pastures and left my HISA with the bare minimum needed to stay alive, just in case. And, by "just in case," I mean "just in case I manage to max out the annual contribution cap of literally every other savings option available to me, and still have something left over."

### How Does This Relate to the Rule of 72?

A couple of years before the innovation of microwaveable pizza, there lived a man who was a little bit smarter than me. His name was Albert Einstein. Famous for his groundbreaking work in physics,—which remains the intimidating standard for scientists around the world today—his formidable mathematical skills also made him something of a whiz at finance.

He valued and popularized the Rule of 72, which is an easy math tool used to find out how quickly our initial investment or contribution will double in size. All we need to know is our annual interest rate. Our contribution also needs to be benefiting from compounding interest for this tool to work, but compounding interest is by far the most common form in any case. It's what mortgages, car loans, and personal loans use, for instance.

If we aren't sure, just ask what our return rate is based on: Is it just based on the money we initially put in? Or is it based on that initial money plus the interest it earned in previous years? If it's the latter, then we've got compound interest. Most forms of investment give a return rate in compounded interest.

Now, my story relates to the Rule of 72 because, if I'd known this rule, and if I'd used it, I'd have been able to quickly tell that my HISAs were no good for what I wanted them to do: Secure my future.

It's such a great finance tool for the average worker, and it can transform so many financial futures if more people only knew about it.

There is a rumor that Einstein called the Rule of 72 even greater than his discovery of $E=MC^2$. I haven't verified that, but, whether he said it or not, it's certainly had a huge impact on making economics more accessible to the working class.

To use the Rule of 72, we first consider our average annual rate of return. For example, when putting our Roth/TFSA into a growth account, it should have an interest rate of at least 6-8%. These returns are rarely guaranteed, but it is easy for our advisor to backtrack a fund's progress over several years and read its annual report, to find the annual average. Some years will be higher, some lower, and every year will have hills and valleys, but finding an average of 8% or more over 5-10 years means that it is a fund well-worth considering.

We then divide the magical number of 72 by the interest rate. The answer we get is equal to the number of years it will take for our initial contribution to double.

This means we can work out how quickly our money will multiply without even knowing what amount we're putting in yet, so long as we know the interest rate. Because interest is percentage-based, how much money we get scales based on how much we put in. It could be $5 or $500, but it would still take the same amount of time to double based on the same rate.

Now, for a practical example, let's assume we have a basic HISA with an interest rate of 1.5%. That's fairly normal. I was pretty smug with my 2% back in the day, but 1.5% is still decent by HISA standards.

What's 72 divided by 1.5? 48.

If we deposit $100 in that HISA, we'll have a whopping total of $200 waiting for us in the account 48 years later, provided that we never make a withdrawal, since we'll lose $5 in transaction fees each time, and also remembering that inflation will transform that $200 into a fraction of its current value in half a century, perhaps even lower than its initial $100 value. 48 years ago, penny candies were still a thing. You can't get a dang handful of jelly beans out of the dispenser for less than $0.25 now.

Taking things year by year, our deposit of $100 will become $101.50 in 1 year, then $103.02 in the year after that. If our two-year financial review showed a total return on investment of $3.02, we would be firing our advisor and considering legal action.

Now, what if we take another much larger sum, such as the $161,172 invested by our 30-year-mortgage couple in the last chapter? Well, it'll become a respectable $322,344… in 48 years. And we'll be charged for withdrawing it. And it'll be worth less than that because the interest earned is taxed annually at our marginal rate, which means we pay higher income taxes with each passing year. And it will also be even less than that, because, in reality, we're far more likely to deposit the total in small, manageable increments—in this case, $442.70 a month—over 48 years, as opposed to having that full lump sum available all at once, so our annual totals and returns will both be much lower. And, finally, we'll be kicking ourselves anyway, because, thanks to the last chapter, we know that instead of having $322,344 in 48 years, we could've had $608,605.44 in only 30 years by adapting a better strategy from the exact same amount of money.

We know that compound interest can be a truly sexy thing, but it should now be clear beyond rebuttal that HISAs simply aren't fast enough. Just how many 48-year doubling periods do we have in life? A lucky person gets two, and, even then, only if their parents opened the fund for them on the day they were born. Even if we're super-duper lucky like I was and get us some of that sweet, sweet 2% action... our doubling period is still 36 years, and we're only going to get three of those if we live to age 108.

There's never a good reason to store our money in an HISA for very long when our goal is long-term growth. Higher returns are mandatory for a pros-perous retirement and a relatively stress-free life leading up to that point. Our HISAs are nothing more than a holding pond while we look for something better.

### *Make Compound Interest Great Again*

Thanks to the Rule of 72, we'll now be able to see at a glance if a contribution we make will be worthwhile, or if it'll grow fast enough to be compatible with our retirement plan. The higher our annual interest, the shorter our doubling period, so let's seek that high-interest sweetness.

A famous comedian once described his long-time faithfulness to his wife by saying, "When you're married to a filet, you don't run around with green baloney." Of course, he ended up having multiple affairs which led to him getting divorced and remarried 3 or 4 times, so he didn't necessarily take his own punchline to heart. But, whatever. It's a great quote that applies equally to both marriage and finding the best investment fund: Your HISA is green baloney.

The next two chapters will be devoted to explaining investment accounts in-depth. Roth/TFSAs are some of the sexiest places to put our money right now, and they're quite easy to understand. But that doesn't mean they don't have a lot of depth to them that needs covering.

Before we go deep, however, let's take another look at just how sexy compound interest in a good investment account can be. Let's take that same $100 we were going to store with the green baloney, and instead, place it into a Roth IRA with an impressive annual return rate of 10%.

After 1 year, our one-time deposit of $100 suddenly becomes $110.

After a total of only 7.2 years, our initial investment will have grown to $200. So, our money can either double in half a century using an HISA, or it can double in less than a decade using a well-invested Roth/TFSA. If we were to let that one-time contribution of $100 sit in our Roth/TFSA for the same 48 years it would have had to sit in our HISA, it would grow to a total of $9,701.72.

So again, our options are $200 after nearly half a century in an HISA, only $100 of which is profit... or we could have $9,701.72 after 48 years in a Roth IRA, $9,601.72 of which will be profit. That's over 96 times the profit because we put our money in a dedicated growth and retirement account instead of just handing it over to our bank. The difference is night and day, and that's just if we put in a single $100 deposit.

But what if, instead of only making one lump payment, we instead deposit $100 once a month, which is still an incredibly easy sacrifice for most of us?

After 48 years, we'd have contributed a total of $57,600. And our fund balance would be $1,161,908.53.

I had several large debts when I first began faithfully investing every month, but, even then, I was easily able to begin contributions of $500 per month. Utilizing methods such as the Debt Snowball, Debt Avalanche, and others at the same time helped me to eliminate a considerable amount of debt quickly, freeing up an additional $1,706.38 a month.

However, even if I had only continued to make the $500 payments to my fund in exchange for consistent returns of 10% interest, in 48 years I would have paid a total of $288,000, but my fund balance would be $5,809,542.64. Just goes to show how amazing compound interest is, and how ridiculously exponential its growth becomes the longer we can leave it running.

Of course, a lot of people aren't even in the workplace for 48 years, so the idea of making any kind of consistent contribution for that long can still seem daunting or ridiculous. However, in the next chapter, we'll cover strategies for making meaningful contributions and cash returns well into old age. How awesome would it be to take our standard retirement after around 30 years in the workplace, but still be able to easily invest $500 a month well into a comfortable retirement of 20-30 years?

Even if that doesn't interest you, I can promise you that it interests your beneficiaries.

### But, No Matter How Simple It Seems...

It never hurts to have an expert advisor on hand. While Roth/TFSAs can, and do, have return rates of 10%, it isn't always easy to find one with consistent returns that high. 10% is just an easy number for the sake of examples, and we might have to make do with less. As I mentioned earlier, a return of 6-8% should be our base.

It's easy to settle for less when we can't find the best, and that's when a good advisor comes in. For more advanced strategies that we'll cover a little later, such as active-managed mutual funds or segregated funds, advisors are a must and a God-send.

### *But if That Seems a Bit Much*

Know that a return rate of 6-8% is still enough for most people to obtain a very comfortable retirement. Just look at what 8% did to our hypothetical scenario in the last chapter. If our growth averages to around 6-7% each year, that's already fantastic, especially if we get started early. It doesn't all have to be about our retirement, either. While I put a lot of emphasis on that, since no one likes doing back-breaking work when they're elderly, growth accounts like this are also great for developing money that we can then divert into shorter-term investments. Do we want to buy that nice little fishing boat? These strategies can help us get there as well.

Just be aware that it always pays to have a strong goal or reason when making a short-term decision. Common short-term investments include saving up for a sorely-needed vacation or upgrading the tools of our trade. Other examples could be saving up enough to host a wedding our partner will never forget, or to clear off a high-interest debt as quickly as possible.

**Now, For a Helpful Tool**

What should we do if we aren't sure a 6-8% growth rate will be enough for us? We log into a computer. There's a free online tool sponsored by the US government made to answer exactly that kind of question. To run our financial projections, please visit www.investor.gov. Then, look at their *Financial Tools & Calculators* tab, and, finally, search for and click on their compound interest calculator. This is the one I like best, but you could just as easily run a Google search for "compound interest calculator" and find any amount of free versions online.

It's great for not only running projections on contribution plans we're seriously considering but also for having fun messing around with numbers. Since we can plug in any numbers we like for our initial investment, monthly contribution, time, and more, it's a great tool to experiment with, and we'll find that it hammers home a lot of the strategies I've shared in this book: Seeing the growth we can accumulate from very reasonable monthly contributions is another rock that should bonk us all into action.

For a more serious projection, all we need to do is estimate how much money we'll be able to contribute monthly to our growth account. Then, plug in the account's interest rate, variance, and compounding frequency. We should be able to request this information from whoever is offering us the account if we don't already have it.

Once we've plugged the relevant info in, all we need to do is input how long in years we plan to continue these contributions, and calculate. This is an easy way to discover the exciting possibilities our growth account might have. It can also tell us quickly if the growth rate is sufficient for what we're able to contribute.

Here's another fun one, which my advisor first told me about: Plugin $25 as our monthly contribution. Give a varying interest rate of 5-8%. Run the contribution from our current age to our ideal retirement age, for instance, the number of years it'd take us to reach 50 or 60 if we aren't already there. Maybe even 40 if we're feeling ambitious and thrifty at the same time.

Even people who understand how compound interest works on a rational level are always amazed to see how far we can go on so little if we just start from a young age. A 16-year-old flipping hamburgers could easily contribute $25 a month for 30 years, at a variance of 5-8%. Their total contribution is $9,000, but their fund balance would total...

I'm not going to tell you. That's your really easy homework assignment.

### Hope For the Aging

To make the most of our growth, we ideally want to start investing as early as possible, between 18 and 23 years old. Or even earlier, if parents can do so in their child's name: We will discuss much more on that exciting option later on, which should be extremely interesting to both young readers, and parents who want to give their child the best possible head-start long before they're even old enough to enter the full-time workplace.

I, on the other hand, only wised up enough to start meaningful investing at the age of 36. So, yes, that $5,809,542.64 retirement projection is likely just a very pretty number on paper, since I don't feel like being in the workplace until age 84. That being said, I learned not to underestimate any possibilities in the world of investing after the first time a fund which I had an active role in selecting saw 14%

growth in a single quarter. I mention this because, if you find you're in the same boat, don't despair. Earlier I said I was putting $500 a month into one of my primary growth accounts. That affordable contribution rate is still more than enough to ensure a comfortable retirement for almost anyone.

The point is that even if we start late, or are even feeling panicky as we near retirement age, late is still far better than never. While not ideal, older people can have some distinct advantages in beginning late-life investments. For example, many of them have reached their full earning potential in their company, they no longer have the expense of children living at home and may have fully paid off their mortgage. Just those three things can mean that older people often have hundreds or even thousands of dollars in available funds every month which they can begin putting into growth accounts. They'll have to pay more per month if they want to see meaningful growth for their retirement, or for leaving an inheritance to their family, but I am not exaggerating when I say this: It is NEVER too late.

### Final Note on High-Interest Savings Accounts

While I don't use my HISA at all these days, and I keep it primarily because it amuses me to run the clock on how long an account can stay alive with $0.50 in it, they do have their uses.

HISA growth rates, while not spectacular, are still good enough to protect our money from the entropies of inflation, or at least to minimize the damage. This is far more than can be said of a basic savings or checking account, or the 4-gallon water jug full of change on the kitchen counter. The growth is steady, and some people feel it's more predictable than what they'd see in a growth account with higher rates, where interest is more likely to have degrees of variance. A particularly good use for HISAs is short-term spending goals separate from our long-term investments: Because I want to invest for retirement, but I also might want that nice little fishing boat one day.

However, unless we're already stinking rich, we can't expect the growth from an HISA to ever generate enough money for us to comfortably live on. What we put in is more or less what we'll get out, even if we're highly patient, motivated, and disciplined in regular contributions.

Our most financially viable plan by far is to use our HISA only as a temporary holding area for our money until we find a better place to send it. Think of our HISA like the nexus of a railway, like Grand Central Terminal. It's a great place to put our money until we've figured out how to split it between our various growth accounts. Even when we are looking at short-term goals like the fishing boat, talk to an advisor about a short-term fund with no penalties for early withdrawal. As soon as we find one, it's time to take that HISA balance back down to $0.50.

The only other recommendation I can make for an HISA is to use it as a growth option once all better choices have been maxed out, or become non-viable: If contributing an extra $1,000 into our Roth/TFSA would put us over the annual contribution cap and incur extra fees, we're probably better off putting it into our HISA instead. Or, if our advisor lets us know that a growth fund is in serious peril, we might want to pull it out and put it in holding in the HISA until they can find us a more secure option: Minimal growth is better than none in the meantime. Even then, we might be better off looking towards other options not discussed in this book, such as stocks, crypto, small-business startups, or precious metals.

All in all, the HISA has its place. It's a great first pick until we know how to divvy up our contributions, and it's a great last pick for any money we may have leftover after that.

However, at no point is it the place for us to grow long-term savings, even when we're young. It's the last resort. Feeling like we need to make this account a high priority for savings is just part of the hierarchical model of thinking which we must smash, or train ourselves to reverse.

# 6

## ROTH IRA TRUMPS TRADITIONAL IRA: PAYING THE EXTRA TAX NOW CAN SAVE A TON OF TAX LATER

Back in Chapter 1, we started touching on how Roth/TFSAs should be a higher priority than traditional IRA/RRSPs. In Chapter 4, we elaborated on this a little more and, in both Chapters 4 and 5, we began digging into the deliciousness of the math behind the potential growth rates of these accounts.

Now, as promised, we're going to dive into Roth/TFSAs, and explain how we can manage them properly at every stage of life. Saddle up.

**Step 4: Open Your Roth IRA or Tax-Free Savings Account First.**

Before we go further, I think it'll help if I first explain what a basic IRA is, as compared to its Canadian counterpart, the basic RRSP.

At the time of this writing, the biggest difference we need to bear in mind is that a normal IRA only allows us to contribute $6,000 into our account each year. Once the owner of the account turns 50 years old, this limit increases to $7,000 a year.

By contrast, the RRSP allows 18% of a Canadian's annual income to be deposited each year instead but also has a hard upper limit. In 2021, this limit is a rather impressive $27,830 per year, almost 4x the maximum allowable in an American IRA.

For this reason, many people in the US are calling for banking reforms to more closely mirror the Canadian model. Should you be interested in this, the best option is to contact your local or state representative and petition for a similar change, as it is a huge advantage for Canadian investors. However, even if those changes are distant or not forthcoming, similar investment strategies can still be used to maximize the potential of the IRA's annual $6,000 contribution.

Compared to an HISA, IRA/RRSPs can seem like quite attractive options. That said, if we still remember the rough road of Roy and Annie, we'll also remember that just because an option seems great, that doesn't mean it's the one we should prioritize. I need to stress this, since too often a young person will learn the truth about HISAs only to settle for an option that isn't necessarily a whole lot better, and find themselves the target of constant adverts and banking pressures: A promise the adverts love to make is that their options will help the account holder reach certain tax-advantages, such as reducing short-term tax or even pushing them down to a lower tax bracket.

This one kid I knew figured out the inefficacy of HISAs while he was still in high school, but he also refused to look beyond the IRA/RRSP options. I don't know why a kid spraying disinfectant into rental shoes at a bowling alley felt such a strong need to knock himself down by one tax bracket rather than frantically scrambling up toward the next one,—although he did mention the hair color and cup-size of the bank teller he was working with multiple times—but I also don't stand in severe judgment of those who demonstrate ambitious economic prerogatives early in life.

### The Pros and Cons

Possibly the biggest disadvantage of the US investment model is that the maximum contribution to a traditional IRA is not stackable with the maximum contribution to a Roth IRA: We can either contribute the full amount to an IRA or Roth IRA, or we can contribute a portion to each one not exceeding the maximum, but we cannot contribute the full amount to both.

Earlier, I mentioned how a Canadian TFSA can only have a max of $6,000 put into it each year, while an IRA or Roth IRA can have $6,000 at first, which then rises to $7,000 when the account holder turns 50. In isolation, this makes the US model look better, but, in reality, Canada in 2021 has a much easier strategy because its accounts are stackable, which means a Canadian investor can sink a total of $33,380 into tax-deferred or tax-free growth accounts each year: $27,830 into their RRSP, and $6,000 into their TFSA.

The US investor, meanwhile, must choose between $6-7,000 in a Roth IRA, $6-7,000 in a traditional IRA, or a $6-7,000 split between both. While the difference between the two models isn't that huge when we're low-income, it does mean that, once we're looking to break past a certain growth threshold, the US investor will have little choice but to move on to 401(k)s or invest in the risky world of stock markets if they want an even more comfortable retirement.

Canadian investors, if they're clever, may go through their entire working lives and never need to invest in much more than their TFSA and RRSP. Even with the back-end taxes that plague RRSPs, combined with a good TFSA the total growth would still be more than enough to live comfortably for a long time by the time the investor hits retirement age.

As if that weren't enough, TFSAs offer a little more leeway in the way Canadians make their contributions. For example, if we could put in $6,000 in our first year, but couldn't afford to put in anything the next year, we could contribute up to $12,000 in the year after that. In comparison, an IRA, or even a Roth IRA, doesn't care if we missed a year. If we cannot contribute the maximum amount each year, and miss out on potential growth because of it, tough beans.

There's even a little trick Canadians can use right now if they turned 18 in or before 2009, the year when the TFSA was first implemented: They can backdate their contributions back to that year. (TFSAs can only be purchased by adults over the age of 18.)

What do I mean by that? I mean that the maximum contribution isn't just $6,000. It's $6,000 plus the maximum TFSA value of every preceding year going back to 2009. So, if we've never contributed to a TFSA before 2021, we could kickstart our growth into a brand new one with an impressive initial investment of $75,500 if we have that available. (It's noteworthy that the contribution cap has varied in previous years, i.e., some years allowed only $5,000 while other years allowed up to $10,000. The current total of $75,500 is the sum of each of the total allowable contributions from all previous years: If the sum was based on only $6,000 for each previous year, the total allowable in 2021 would only be $72,000.)

This is an amazing feature for those who start investing late, particularly those who have been ineffectually saving large amounts of money in basic bank accounts or HISAs. Even if we're only beginning our savings journey well into adulthood, we won't be too badly punished for tardiness thanks to that backdating feature. An absolute blessing for those who need more time, while those who were too young to backdate very far—say a kid who turned 19 or 20 in 2009—still had plenty of time to build up contributions in the slow and steady way instead. Likewise, young people who recently turned 18 cannot backdate contributions, but this is less of a problem as they have their entire adult life ahead of them.

If I'm being totally honest, if you live in Canada, you're going to have a relatively easy time getting your savings off the starting blocks compared to someone trying to grow investments in the USA, so don't ever take that for granted. However, it is also noteworthy that Canadian youth of today are just as plagued by debt and uncertainty as American kids, and for the exact same reason: These strategies are not taught in school.

By contrast, those in the US of A who want to prepare for a secure retirement must start young, scrappy, and hungry if they don't want to waste their shot.

### *Understanding the Roth IRA and Tax-Free Savings Accounts*

One of the most important things to remember about Roth/TFSAs is that we can withdraw the money we put in it at any time, for any reason we like, and, unlike an HISA, we won't be charged a penalty. We won't even be taxed retroactively. This means the money we put in is still easily accessible if an emergency comes up and we suddenly need it for food, hospitalization, or something else.

Fees may start to be charged once we withdraw the money we grew, however. The only part that's truly liquid is the money we put in ourselves. Any interest we earn in those accounts can have a charge associated with the withdrawal. However, unlike an IRA/RRSP, our withdrawals are never taxable even in these circumstances.

Roth/TFSAs are thus great tax-shelters, allowing us to effectively make powerful investments without experiencing the massive tax hits that so often come with trying to grow our wealth. When contributing to these accounts, we'll typically have a choice of assets to put the money in. A financial advisor will say great growth potential, high turnover, or large dividends are signs of a great asset, but as long as the account we choose has a high return rate, we'll generally be okay.

We also don't have to worry about overkill with our growth, as we can typically transfer our account to a beneficiary, meaning we can leave all the money we accumulated to a loved one in our will.

The reason Roth/TFSAs are referred to as after-tax accounts is not what people often mistakenly think: That the contributions themselves are subject to a front-end tax when initially paid, but the remainder can then grow-tax free up til and including withdrawal. That is a common misconception that even I failed to realize at first, which is why—along with the seemingly ridiculous $6,000 contribution cap—I once thought Roth/TFSAs were pointless.

Lately, I've begun to suspect that this is exactly what banks and the government wanted me to think.

The actual reason they are called after-tax accounts relates to our income tax. Roth/TFSAs cannot be used for income tax deductions, which is another reason that IRA/RRSPs initially sound so good: They reduce the amount of income tax we pay each year, and the full amount contributed then grows tax-free. Which sounds fantastic until we try to, you know, withdraw and use it.

So, when we contribute to a Roth/TFSA our taxable income for the year remains the same, and we pay the same amount of income tax. That is why the accounts can exist and grow tax-free: The money in them was already taxed years ago.

## Why Are Roth IRAs and TFSAs Underrated, and Why Is This Backwards?

There are a few reasons why this idea is taking so long to catch on, but most of them come down to advertising. Aside from that, the biggest reason why Roth/TFSAs get ignored is that we can't contribute any money into them that hasn't already been taxed, and most people who think "in the now" will do just about anything to maximize that year's income tax return or pay less tax. With an IRA/RRSP, as mentioned earlier, we can theoretically knock ourselves down into a lower tax bracket just by making our annual contribution into them, meaning we can lower the tax we get hit with in the short term.

A fact of life is that many families need $100,000 a year just to survive in modern times, but don't necessarily have a lot of income to meet that mark comfortably. Life has gotten better in many ways, but that doesn't mean we're living in luxury yet.

When a family is not especially rich, but one year finds that they have just barely edged into a higher tax bracket by a few dollars, they might try to preserve the value of those extra few dollars as best they can by tucking them into an IRA/RRSP, in the hopes that this will help make ends meet later on. If we want or need bigger tax returns in the short term, it can be difficult to choose anything besides a traditional IRA/RRSP. This can then lead to contribution habits and an unwillingness to change as people stick with what is most familiar to them, regardless of what is best for them in the long run.

Thanks to emotional complications getting the better of us, the idea of less tax right now—or a nice, fat tax return—is always tempting. It's a way of appealing to our want for instant gratification while still looking like we're being responsible on the surface. Just put our money into a normal IRA/RRSP, and the tax gets deferred off into the sunset. Out of sight and mind.

In contrast, with the Roth/TFSA, we always have to deal with the full brunt of the "here and now" taxman. However, there's a reason I recommend them so strongly, despite coming from a working-class family that could have always stood to benefit from paying less immediate tax.

The reason is this: Paying a little extra tax now can save you a heck of a lot of extra tax later. In the US, tax brackets currently vary from 10-37%. In Canada, the range goes from 15-33%. On top of that, in both countries, the tax rate can jump to 40% when factoring in supplemental income and capital gains.

All that being understood, the very nature of growth accounts means being willing to lose around 20-40% of the money we have now. And we willingly do this, because that amount is absolutely nothing when compared to losing 20-40% of a nest egg we spent 30 years or more growing at a compounding interest rate of 8-10%.

To draw from one of our earlier examples, 20-40% of $100 is only $20-$40. Not a huge loss, and realistically, there's a good chance we're only going to lose $20 or $30 from that hundred, not $40, although 40% will be most frequently mentioned as a worst-case scenario... which a whole lot of real people are currently living in.

So, we'd lose maybe $30 of tax before we contribute $100 to a Roth/TFSA. That stings a little bit.

Now imagine, instead of the Roth/TFSA, we instead withdraw from a traditional IRA/RRSP. Using the example from the last chapter, we put in our $100 without tax, enjoy the tax break for that year, and over the next 48 years it grows into a lovely $9,701.72. We try to withdraw it, the withdrawal tax kicks in, and now instead of losing 20-40% of $100, we're losing 20-40% of $9,701.72.

I ask you, would you rather lose a maximum of $40 in tax now, or anywhere from $1,940.35 to $3,880.69 in tax later? (For the record, my editor keeps telling me to round off my figures, but the thought of my audiobook narrator having to repeatedly recite these exact figures in a sound booth while not letting *any* frustration creep into their voice is amusing to me. If we can't have fun, what is all the money in the world really worth?)

Repeat that cost for each time we prioritize a traditional IRA/RRSP over contributions to a Roth/TFSA. For instance, if we want to withdraw $60,000 from a traditional IRA/RRSP, we'd need to withdraw $100,000, since $40,000 of that $100,000 would disappear into the netherworld of tax. That's a heck of a lot of money to lose after a lifetime of hard labor went into earning it, and it's probably even frustrating if you've spent your life as a lazy worthless Commie freeloader or as a blue-haired equity-driven social justice activist. Even if we're being more lenient and saying we're getting taxed 20%, rather than 40% like Roy and Annie, we'd still be losing tens of thousands of dollars to tax at a time when there's probably not a lot of income incoming anymore.

I hope I've made my point. Even if we can benefit from having an immediate tax reduction, I must stress that if we can afford to rather cut corners on non-essentials somewhere—*anywhere*—to put money into a Roth/TFSA first, that's what we should do. If most of our contributions are sitting in a traditional IRA/RRSP, we're going to get the same shock Roy and Annie did. (And even if we are now prepared for it, I still can't see how that back-end tax is something that anyone would eagerly look forward to.) It's important to internalize that even if we're in a fairly low tax bracket now, withdrawals from an IRA/RRSP later in life are often given the full tax rate of over 40%. Realistically, our choice isn't between saving $40 now or almost $4,000 later. (There, I rounded for once. Happy now, Narrators Union?) If our current income is truly the lowest of the low, the choice might even be a $10 to $15 loss on our $100 investment now... or a $4,000 loss later. When we consider that, as well as the fact that IRA/RRSP withdrawals are more likely to be made at a time when we no longer have the same peak level of income to offset the losses, it really is no contest as to which type of account we should contribute to first.

It's a huge problem that, when people do have extra money to save, aggressive advertising means they're often putting it into an IRA/RRSP. Particularly in Canada, for example, the RRSP's large contribution limit is a boon to the savvy, but it's also a trap for the desperate. A surprising amount of people, desperate to make more money for later in life, think that the way to save is to get more raises, earn bigger salaries, work longer hours, and therefore make bigger contributions into their RRSP, with the tax reductions and higher tax returns being the cherry on top that clinches it.

As mentioned earlier, contributing as much money as possible into the IRA/RRSP often becomes a habit for those who don't have a lot of financial curiosity, leading to a situation where people will max it out year after year, leaving themselves barely anything for what will keep them well-off later in life: Their Roth/TFSAs. The hungrier they are, the more they feed the IRA/RRSP, and the more they will eventually find themselves owing to the most-patient-of-all-foes, the taxman.

Again, we go back to our example of the couple who paid their mortgage off over the entire 30-year amortization period. They didn't even need to maximize their contributions to a Roth/TFSA, let alone a maxed-out IRA or hungry, hungry RRSP. They paid $442.7o a month for 30 years, and they were sitting pretty darn pretty just from that.

**Other Advantages of Roth IRAs and TFSAs**

Aside from losing us far less money in the future, Roths/TFSAs have several other distinct advantages over their traditional counterparts.

For instance, a traditional IRA/RRSP can only be used until we turn 71 years old. Then, like a scene out of *Logan's Run,* the government decides we've officially become non-contributing old farts and hand us an ultimatum. Like all ultimatums, it has two outcomes, neither of which are that great:

1. Withdraw all our money, stopping its growth cold, and just hope there's still enough leftovers after the taxman takes his hefty bite out of it. And, just for the record, this is the choice which the government will make for us if we don't make our own choice in time.

2. Convert our account into a Registered Retirement Income Fund (RRIF) in Canada, or a variety of US equivalents. Although these still allow growth, this account type mandates that we withdraw a minimum percentage each year, even if it's far more than we need. They also don't allow us to make contributions, so hopefully, we've budgeted how many years we plan to live as well as we budgeted our cash.

On the flip side, a Roth/TFSA does not have any restrictions like this. We can use it freely until the day we die. A common choice for many Canadians who had to convert their RRSP into an RRIF is to put the excess of their forced withdrawals into a TFSA. Sadly, by that time they're over the age of 71, and it's way too late to see a lot of meaningful growth from even the best TFSAs. But it still beats the alternative.

The relative flexibility of Roth/TFSAs in our withdrawals is important, as the 71-year age limit on traditional growth accounts makes a rather dangerous assumption, namely that our bucket is about to be kicked. I understand that the blue-haired people recently decreed it racist to make jokes about certain cultures setting their elderly populace adrift on an ice flow, but I can't get that image out of my head every time I think about the IRA/RRSP age limit and mandatory minimum withdrawals. (Also, I'm too damn old to care what the blue-haired people designate as racist anymore, because I honestly can't keep up with it all, and, full disclosure, I never actually watched the entirety of *Logan's Run*. I got the gist: *Blade Runner* is better.)

There's another dangerous assumption that comes with the 71-year age limit: That we've already retired. This isn't necessarily the case for lower-income geriatrics, who often have to work full-time as mechanics, consultants, or more to get by, to say nothing of those who are still getting up at 5 a.m. to milk cows and thresh corn on the family farm. Especially if they've been using an inferior growth account such as an IRA/RRSP. People who sell traditional IRA/RRSPs typically suggest that, by the time we make our withdrawals, our marginal tax will be lower, implying that maybe we won't be hit as hard as our earlier calculations suggested.

The people who sell the IRA/RRSPs may even suggest that federal tax rates across the board may have lowered nationwide by the time we retire.

Sometimes they even manage to say it with a straight face.

While people do tend to be in a lower tax bracket as they ease into retirement by often having a smaller income stream than when they were in their prime, it doesn't change the fact that traditional growth accounts will still apply tax to every withdrawal we make. And, again, withdrawals from these traditional accounts become compulsory once we're 71, even when we're forced by circumstance to still be working full-time, sitting in a higher tax bracket in our old age because of misfortunes earlier in life. And, of course, Heaven help us if we run into the same issue as Roy and Annie, where our withdrawal is also counted as supplemental income, giving us the highest tax rate of all.

Oh, and one more thing: Because that withdrawal counts as income, it is used by the Canadian government as an excuse to claw back Old Age Security (OAS) entitlements. Really makes the seniors feel validated after decades of, you know, building the country and whatnot.

So, that's one advantage Roth/TFSAs have over traditional accounts. Another advantage is that, unlike traditional accounts, they also allow us to look beyond our bank, just like we should be doing. We are typically able to direct the way we fund our contributions into Roth/TFSAs. If we have an advisor on board, then we truly do have the big picture in mind. We are in a much better position to make advantageous decisions, allowing us to seek better deals if we feel our initial investments aren't paying off. In contrast, a traditional account is more or less bound to the bank and the investments it is interested in, limiting our ability to easily navigate into a better spot if we aren't happy with our current growth.

**How Much Does It Pay to Have an Advisor?**

Simply put, it pays a heck of a lot. Roth/TFSAs are a great choice we can make for long-term growth, but there does come a point when a traditional IRA/RRSP can become useful. They are generally most valuable for those who already earn a higher-than-average income or have already established sufficient retirement security. Being able to see where this fine line exists between unnecessary expense and prudent investing is the financial advisor's specialty.

Even if we aren't high-income or already retirement-protected, we can still benefit from an advisor. Not everyone is great at math, so having someone look over the money we're contributing can be a lifesaver. For example, the annual contribution limits on Roth/TFSAs don't outright block us from accidentally going over: If we're not careful, we can contribute as much as we want, and may not even know it. However, if we bypass the hard limit, we will experience much slower growth as penalties start to kick in, such as a monthly deduction made off our account's balance every month, or even having our account's tax-exemption waived... at which point we're basically sitting on an IRA/RRSP with a less impressive annual limit. Accidentally surpassing that is something we want to avoid at all costs. Otherwise, we've negated the entire purpose of an after-tax account. Having a trained, qualified professional look after our investments is not a weakness. It's wise to seek guidance from the experts when we find ourselves out of our depth.

True story, I once got a phone call from local police officers, not because I was in trouble, but because they had encountered stray cows on the highway outside of town and had no idea how to get rid of them. Let's just say that I had to arrange for several hours of mid-shift coverage for my non-ranch job, and dust off the cowboy boots and cattle cane which had become nostalgia pieces by that point in my life.

All over the country, police commissioners are installing special red phones to be used only in the event of cow-related crises: "I need somebody who can crack these cloven-hoofed wiseguys, McMann! *Get me Finnegan!*"

Advisors are also all but a necessity for those who want the benefits of active-managed funds, as we'll discuss in Chapter 7. The funds we put into a Roth/TFSA don't have to just sit there. They can be used for other things, namely funds beyond our own bank. In the hands of an accredited financial advisor, —or even a life agent, as we will also discuss later— the money in our Roth/TFSA can become carefully managed funds, which go by different regional names. In the US, they are less clearly defined and more confusing nationally, and may require a little digging to find at all: Again, this is why advisor's may be needed. In some regions, these managed funds are known as Separate Accounts or simply managed mutual funds. However, in other regions the name Separate Account refers to a far more cost-prohibitive method requiring a minimum investment of $100,000, making it all but useless to a lower-to-middle income investor. In Canada, the funds are a much-more developed tool and referred to exclusively as Segregated Funds.

My opinion, and heartfelt recommendation, is that this is another issue that should be brought to US state representatives and fund managers. The streamlined Canadian model of Segregated Funds is one of the fastest-growing investment alternatives to stocks and mutual funds. Their popularity stems from both the earning potential and the additional investment security provided by fund managers.

Of course, that higher reward isn't without risk, and our growth becomes a lot more vulnerable to the market hills and valleys when it's going into a segregated fund. That 14% quarterly growth I experienced definitely wasn't the perpetual norm, and many readers may prefer sticking with 7-10% growth instead, as that is already more than enough for those starting young, while also being consistent with their risk tolerance. However, having an advisor minimizes the risk and can even prevent serious losses that we'd almost certainly run into if we were to attempt high-risk strategies on our own. Why? Because the majority of us have day-jobs beyond round-the-clock monitoring of our investments' market trends. We don't have time to be looking two quarters down the road to project future fund values. Even if we're well on our way to becoming professional investors, we still benefit from the mentorship of an advisor.

Advisors also play a key role for investors who start late. Naturally, the later we start, the fewer doubling periods our money will go through before retirement. We all know by now how big an impact starting even 12 years later can have on your ability to enjoy tax-free growth, thanks to our mortgage illustration from Chapter 4. A good many Americans end up kicking themselves and wishing they were taught about Roth IRAs in school. A great many more end up going their whole lives without even knowing what a Roth IRA is. All this, despite living in an age where it is now more important than ever for all young people in America, especially those from lower-income families, to know about such simple investment tips.

In any case, those who start their investment journey late have to work extremely hard to adequately make up for lost time, which can mean opening up a 401(k) account as a supplement. Advisors are invaluable in this situation, as they can help us run the numbers and double-check the math to help us decide where we should focus our contributions. Unless we have enough money to max out both our Roth IRA and 401(k), it pays to have an advisor to help optimize our investing.

When we have the choice between two or more growth investment platforms, precisely where we should focus our contributions can fluctuate a lot depending on market conditions, so we'll need someone with inside knowledge or understanding of the system to accurately tell whether our 401(k) or Roth IRA will save us the most in tax and give us the most growth in return for our contributions. This can save us a great deal of time and stress. Although starting early on a Roth IRA will save us that same time and stress for much less cost and effort, it would be imprudent of me to suggest that everyone reading this book invested in a DeLorean.

### Learning A Little More About 401(k)s

Normally, a 401(k) is given not through an institution or advisor, but rather through an employer. For those who feel an advisor isn't necessary to help them run their 401(k) account, please note that whether or not we should prioritize it over our Roth IRA can vary according to all sorts of trends. In the

US, even politics can determine the viability of one account over the other, and to make a 401(k) consistently work for us, we must be willing to change our plans completely every few years as economic policies change with each administration. While we tend to give in to our biases when looking at political matters, there is never a more important time to shut off the emotion and turn to the economy with a purely analytical eye. If nothing else, we need to be able to pivot our financial planning on short notice, dependant not so much on who's leading the country, but rather the economic policies most likely to be legislated during that administrative term, at both the state and federal level.

For example, in 2012, during President Barack Obama's second term, many experts were led to believe, quite reasonably in the wake of a crippling economic crisis, that income tax rates would continue to rise until they were on the same level as most of Europe's, and they made their investment choices accordingly. Deferring tax was considered to be an especially bad idea compared to just eating it and investing in a Roth IRA.

However, these same experts saw their projections change drastically when 2017 rolled around and

President Donald Trump enacted the Tax Cuts and Job Act, which gave substantial tax breaks to 80% of American workers as well as small businesses. The median household income saw an average increase of $5,000 nationwide. This meant people had a greater ability to make meaningful contributions to growth investments, and gave smaller businesses more room to expand and hire additional employees. While the Roth IRA was still arguably the better option, the distinction was not so clear as it had been 5 years earlier. Even those who were just entering into retirement at this time found they weren't bitten as badly by having chosen traditional accounts.

The lower taxes also meant people were more comfortable with prioritizing Roth IRAs since being limited to contributing only with after-tax income suddenly didn't feel like such a big hit to blue-collar workers all over the US.

However, at the time of this writing during the Biden administration, serious consideration is being given to repealing this act, in which case income tax rates will likely return to levels seen a decade earlier. If this happens, traditional IRAs are likely to see a surge in popularity once more, as they will seem more attractive on a surface level. A consistent trend is that people experiencing rising tax rates will want to defer or reduce their income tax payments whenever possible, in the hope that future legislation enacted closer to their planned retirement drops the tax rate back down again. Long-term plans are often abandoned during times of seeming crisis. It takes courage and a lot of planning to hold fast to the best course of retirement investing when times are lean. Especially when our banks are still telling us how much tax deductions we can claim *right now* by taking out an IRA with them. That gets tempting.

Since our employer often has to match a percentage of what we contribute into a 401(k), this growth account generates more value for us compared to the money we put into it vs a traditional IRA, making it more viable as a way to reduce the impact of immediate tax on us now, as the larger tax later won't hurt so much.

There also exists, of course, the Roth 401(k) for those who still prefer to be taxed more now in exchange for being taxed much less later. However, which version of 401(k) we should focus on isn't as clear-cut as which version of IRA we should prioritize.

When deciding how to contribute to a traditional 401(k), it also pays to think about what state we're living in, and whether or not we want our retirement to be in that same state. This is because not all states have the same tax rates on income, so while a traditional 401(k) may seem better in one state, a Roth 401(k) would be much better in another. Whether we move from a state with low-income tax to one with high, or high to low, we need to anticipate our investment strategies changing a bit.

In cases where we expect our tax rate to be low now, but much higher towards retirement, the Roth 401(k) is the way to go. In cases where our rate is currently high, but we know for a fact it'll be much lower once we retire, the regular 401(k) can work well.

### *The First Great American Equalizer: The Roth 401(k)*

As a rule of thumb, I still say eating the tax now is worth not having to worry about being taxed later. If we don't have an advisor with us to crunch the numbers and see whether a traditional or Roth 401(k) will be better for you, go with the Roth.

But what if we now have to choose between a Roth 401(k) and a Roth IRA? If we don't have the money to maximize contributions to both, this can be an agonizing decision.

Which is better depends on a few factors. However, in many ways, the Roth 401(k) is one of the biggest advantages for someone in the US, acting as a better IRA while still having some of the perks of a traditional 401(k).

While a Roth IRA can only accept $6,000-7,000 in contributions each year, a Roth 401(k) can accept $19,500 each year, with some allowances for catch-up contributions. While it's never ideal to start late, this is one of the better ways to catch up once we've maxed out our Roth IRA.

An important question to consider is this: Does our employer support Roth 401(k)s? Do they match a percentage of our contributions into them, like they would for a traditional 401(k)? If so, then the Roth 401(k) can seem more appealing. Are we extremely high in income? If we can max out our Roth 401(k)'s contribution limit, even after tax, that's another point in its favor. However, employers won't normally match us all the way on that unless our salary is already in the high-income range. Even so, we can still contribute a respectable amount every year.

Another point in the Roth 401(k)'s favor is that, unlike the Roth IRA, it doesn't have an income limit. Each year the Roth IRA is either restricted, or outright closed, to those earning above a certain limit, such as more than $125,000-140,000 each year after modifications and adjustments. This limit is higher for those who are married. In a country where the average person earns between $50,000 and $75,000 a year, this limit rarely comes up, but it is something that high-income earners must factor into their retirement planning as well. Again, the strategies in this book are designed to be utilized by anyone who wants to try a new method, regardless of location, age, education, or income level. My goal is for this book to be a unification for every investor: No matter what amount of money or income we start with, we can all follow the same basic steps to success or greater success.

Unlike a Roth IRA, the Roth 401(k) doesn't let us take our money back out very easily when we aren't retired. If we're already bringing in a high enough income for the Roth 401(k) to be warranted, it's less likely that we'd need to make a sudden withdrawal from it anyway, but, as always, there will be exceptions. Speaking from personal experience, my highest annual earnings put me into the income range where a Roth 401(k) was a better option. However, that was also the time of my life when my monthly expenses hit an all-time high, which meant that the smartest move for me was the options with greater liquidity. I cannot emphasize it enough: Your personal and financial circumstances are as unique as your fingerprints. Any plan you make must be personalized, and that is why an advisor will almost always be your best option.

Another point against the Roth 401(k) is that, like a traditional IRA/RRSP, we can't keep it open forever. At the age of 72, we must withdraw. Fortunately, this account type is more flexible than the traditional ones, because we don't need to withdraw if we're still in the workplace, and the withdrawals we do make can be rolled right over into a Roth IRA with little fuss.

Overall, the Roth 401(k) is less flexible, but it can be a great equalizer for US investors who may be feeling frustrated, especially when they have learned the advantages of their Canadian counterparts. Since a Roth 401(k) has some distinct advantages over an RRSP in any case, America still has a lot to cheer about.

Before we move on, here are some important tips on using 401(k)s and Roth IRAs together:

1. If our income qualifies as too high for a Roth IRA, contributing into a traditional 401(k) first can help, since the normal 401(k) contribution happens before tax, while the Roth IRA checks our income after-tax.

2. If our 401(k) is already maxed, we can instead place the contribution into a traditional IRA, then roll it into a Roth IRA. However, be aware that this will come with a penalty since we'll be moving deferred-tax money into an after-tax account. Think of this penalty as a retroactive tax.

3. If we can contribute to both the 401(k) and the Roth IRA fully without penalties, and we're using a Roth 401(k) instead of a traditional one, we could instead look at the investment fees, and focus on the one that charges us the least for what we put into it. 1% is what I consider too high, 0.5% is just fine.

4. Social Security benefits can, and will, be taxed if our income is seen as high enough. Withdrawals from a 401(k) may be read as

income, but withdrawals from a Roth IRA won't. It still pays to maximize contributions to our Roth IRA each year if we can.

5. Building up a strong Roth 401(k) is a great way to have income to roll over into our Roth IRA later, allowing it to continue growing faster for longer as we hit the impressive milestone of 70+ years old.

### *The Second Great American Equalizer: Your Child's Roth IRA*

Saddle up, America, because we're about to delve into possibly the greatest investing advantage exclusive to the US of A. As we discussed earlier, Canadians who start investing later in life can backdate TFSA contributions back to 2009, but American investors do not have that luxury. They must start young, ideally by the time they're 18.

But here's where the story changes. In the US we can, as parents, decide that our kid can start even earlier than that: Roth IRAs can be purchased for children by their parents.

There are a few rules to this, though:

1. Our child must be earning some form of verifiable income. This can include babysitting, farm and ranch work, dog-walking, yard work or landscaping, newspaper delivery, washing cars, fast-food and retail jobs, or even lifeguarding and first aid if they qualify.

2. The child cannot contribute more to their Roth IRA than their total earnings. This is to prevent parents from fraudulently using their children to own multiple Roth IRAs.

3. The allowance that we give to our kids doesn't count as income for their IRA. The upper limit for our child's Roth IRA still caps at $6,000 per year, but only if they are earning at least that amount from an actual job.

However, as we've demonstrated repeatedly, these contribution caps are barely an impediment, especially for young investors. Contributions of only a few thousand dollars a year at this age could easily translate into millions of dollars by the time our kid is ready to retire, even if this Roth IRA is the only investing tool they ever use.

For instance, if we have a 15-year-old daughter, Li'l Sue, who starts investing only $500 a year—around $41.67 a month—into a Roth IRA with an average 8% growth rate, by the time she reaches 70 years old, she'd have a tax-free $427,367.20 waiting for her. Not bad considering that she only contributed $27,500 over 55 years.

More lucratively, let's say she contributes $1,000 a year. That's still only 88.33 a month, with a total lifetime contribution of $55,000. She'd have $854,631.84 by age 70.

Now imagine she decides to go big and contribute $3,000 a year. That's still only $250 a month, for a lifetime total of $165,000.

By age 70, she'd have $2,563,998.07.

Contributions of this level would be very manageable even just from utilizing the concepts in this book when combined with a modicum of self-discipline.

The low income the girl would generally earn during her teen years isn't as much of a drawback as we might expect, for three reasons:

1. Because her tax rate is either very low or absolute zero, almost all her earnings can go directly into her Roth IRA, although it's still wise for us to keep a logbook somewhere with all of her income truthfully recorded in case the IRS wants to ask questions later. The primacy of a paper trail is something we should all aspire to throughout our lives, and teach to our kids.

2. What Li'l Sue puts into her Roth IRA, we can match. If she puts in $500 in a given year, we can put $500 on top of that in that same year as well. This total still can't exceed their income for the year or the annual $6,000 maximum: She would need to have earned a total of $1,000 that year for us to add our $500, and our matching funds cannot exceed $3,000—half of the annual cap—if she earns $6,000 or more.

3. She can be free to enjoy some of her earnings on games, movies, food, and social events

while still dutifully setting a percentage aside for her future. It can be difficult to convince our child to think about old age. It's hard enough to even get adults to do that, but if we show them the value of compound interest, it gets easier: Hundreds of dollars can become hundreds of thousands, and thousands of dollars can become millions. If she's motivated enough to consistently earn an income, she'll be motivated enough to spare some of it for later.

4. If Li'l Sue can get in the habit of putting away an average of $16 a day, she can look forward to becoming a tax-free millionaire.

## Final Notes

When we can afford to, diversifying between our Roth/TFSA along with either a traditional IRA/RRSP or 401(k) is a fantastic idea. For all the grief I give the more traditional methods, they do have the one big perk of having protection against insolvency. It's unlikely we'd need to file for bankruptcy when we've eliminated all our high-interest debts, but knowing we have a nest egg that'll stick by us even if we lose everything else can feel reassuring, even if it means having to eat extra tax later in life.

However, the chances of that worst-case scenario are tiny compared to our chances of reaching retirement and needing to make a withdrawal. When in doubt, or without an advisor to enhance our insight with situational nuances, it's smart to always focus on our Roth/TFSA first, kind of like a reverse Debt Snowball: Maxing out our growth accounts with the smallest cap first. It doesn't hurt that they tend to have some of the best rates of return, either. When making forced withdrawals from traditional accounts later in life, always place a portion of those withdrawals straight back into our Roth/TFSA, as this will help us keep it growing even once we're technically no longer earning an income. We might alternatively decide to withdraw from our traditional accounts first before even touching the contents of our Roth/TFSA, which again is made easier by the mandatory withdrawal age.

This is a great way to keep ourselves comfortable as we enter into our seventies: Keep our Roth/TFSA going and growing for as long as we can. We always benefit from having something in it, and never benefit from leaving it low or empty.

From now on, I would recommend this type of account as the first one we contribute to, and the last one we withdraw from once we retire. However, no matter how we go about using our accounts, remember we'll always benefit from an advisor: Their job is to help protect our gains and maximize our earnings.

Be aware of differences from state to state, and how they can impact the way and rates at which we're taxed. This can influence whether it's better to focus on our Roth IRA or a traditional 401(k), though, as always, go for the Roth first if we're in doubt. For those with higher income, never forget we can open a Roth 401(k) too, allowing us to do a "double-Roth," investing large amounts of our money into future growth. The 401(k) is the best friend not only of the late starter, but also of high-income earners in general: They can frequently use it, have their employers match part of it, and then use the fact that their after-tax income is technically lower now to fill up their Roth IRA without penalty.

With a little bit of careful management like this, we can safeguard our future, and teach our kids to do the same.

# 7

# PULLING THE OL' SWITCHEROO: HOW INVESTING IN AN ACTIVE-MANAGED MUTUAL FUND OR SEGREGATED FUND CAN PROTECT YOUR MONEY BETTER THAN REGULAR MUTUAL FUNDS.

When handling a Roth/TFSA, we might notice many of our contributions are effectively going into mutual funds. This is typically sufficient to achieve the gains of 6-8% we've already waxed lyrical on, provided this is the return rate we were promised would be most likely.

As such, this is a passive, comfortable form of growth. However, there is an advantage to shifting our Roth/TFSA contributions into actively managed segregated funds. Although it might seem a little pricier to the untrained eye, there are key advantages to consider, such as better protection of our money and its overall earnings.

This brings us to…

## Step 5: Put an Active-Managed Mutual Fund Into Your Roth IRA, or put an Insurance-Based Segregated Fund Into Your TFSA.

Once we've looked beyond our bank, embraced the concept of OPM, learned the Rule of 72, and opened our Roth/TFSA first, we'll find ourselves in a great position to dip our toes into Step 5: Getting into active-managed funds.

Before we jump in though, it's important we ask a few questions.

### What Is a Mutual Fund?

Stacy's story already covered the basics, but let's dig a little deeper. Multiple investors coming together and pooling their funds for a group of managers to handle means that a mutual fund isn't just an investment. It's a company. Everyone pooling money together would be the shareholders. The chief fund manager or financial advisor would effectively be the CEO. The chief manager could then hire under-managers and financial analysts as employees, but this isn't always the case. The first modern mutual fund was launched in the US in 1924, but remained obscure until they achieved extreme gains for their shareholders in the 1980s and 90s. In large part, they survived and grew as they could survive massive market crashes, like the Great Depression, whereas more volatile, close-ended funds often had to shut down.

Today, active-managed mutual funds exist but are relatively overlooked in favor of the passive model. This is because active-managed funds are difficult to run properly without a skilled team of analysts, researchers, or economists, which drives up their costs. It also detracts a bit from the main caveman-brain perks of the mutual fund: That it's both cheap and simple to buy into and usually generates returns with minimal fuss.

It's no surprise that the passive model is much more popular. Traditional IRA/RRSPs are still much more popular than Roth/TFSAs, but we've demonstrated how that popularity doesn't conflate to the wisest of investments. A passive mutual fund means our fund manager, the person we're trusting our money to, doesn't need to maintain much care or involvement other than making sure they have a bot or an app tracking how different stocks are performing in the market.

This tracking tends to be good, as it strictly sticks to what the math says will be the best outcome, but it's not as good at tracking changes that could alter the equation entirely. Our money is still vulnerable to market fluctuations. The lack of active involvement can also mean struggles to get consistent customer support when these fluctuations become worrying, as Stacy found to her detriment.

The average worker like Stacy has more urgent things to do than keeping eyes on a string of accounts while keeping up with market variations just to figure out why she's seeing losses in her fund. In her case, she was a single parent working long hours to provide for a child who requires additional time and care due to physical and learning disabilities. It's easy to burn ourselves out with incredible stress if we try to take on the fund manager's job in addition to balancing our work and family responsibilities.

I wouldn't recommend Roths/TFSAs if most of their investments ended up this way, but, for the sake of friends like Stacy, I must mention that, when deciding what to do with the money we put in those accounts, we have better options than passive mutual funds.

Even simple active mutual funds are much better in Roth IRAs. Active mutual funds tend to generate a lot more money in the short term but are traditionally held back by the higher tax. In a Roth IRA, they don't get taxed. We get to have our cake and eat it, too. But we can even do one better than that.

### Segregated Funds & Active Accounts

Segregated Funds, or SFs, are a Canadian investment tool that is similar to a mutual fund in that we're paying money into a collected pool that is then managed by professionals.

However, it's also similar to the US Active-Managed Separate Account, or SA, as both of them are insurance-based investment funds. They also both require, by law, that the customer's invested assets be kept separate from the assets of the insurance company itself, hence the names "separate" or "segregated."

The service is offered by insurance companies but isn't used by them to fuel their policies. For this reason, we can be confident our money will stay in that pool, or else go towards an investment that will generate returns.

Note that the SA should not be confused with the Separately Managed Account, or SMA, which is what may even happen if you try to look up either of them on the Internet. As I mentioned earlier, the US variation of these accounts is less clearly defined, so it is imperative to talk directly with the insurance companies to know exactly what they can offer us.

Unlike the SA, the SMA requires a minimum investment of $100,000 and so isn't the best option for the average working-class investor. These SMAs are also so-named because, instead of our money going into a pool, it's just ours on its own. Quite a drastic difference, so we need to be careful when planning our investment. In some circles, the terms SA and SMA are used interchangeably even by industry professionals, so it can be even more confusing: Be sure to clearly define our fund before we attempt to invest in it.

From now on, the SA and SF will be referred to collectively as an SA/SF.

In some US regions, SA/SFs might even be completely unavailable. Traditional mutual funds are still just fine, but if we're worried we might wind up like Stacy from Chicago, there are still a few things we can try.

The first thing we can do is contact the relevant insurance companies directly, and ask them if they offer separate account options. If that doesn't work, we can be a little more creative and ask them if they'd instead be willing to create similar funds based on the Canadian model.

A good business loves to innovate when it smells opportunity. Just ask acclaimed US fund manager Michael Burry: If the financial service we need doesn't exist, ask if they'll create it for us. In his case, the innovation was credit default swap options which made him a billionaire after he accurately foresaw the inevitability of the 2007 Subprime Mortgage Crisis. If you don't know what I'm talking about, go watch *The Big Short*. After studying the crisis in greater detail, I suspect it overlooked a few key factors which contributed to the advent of the crisis, but it's still a great film that humorously breaks down complicated investment matters to an understandable level for an everyday viewing audience.

In any case, while it might seem daunting to request a service instated just for us, remember that, while most of us are learning our finances backward, the people running insurance companies, especially long-established ones, tend to know exactly what they're doing. They will be aware of how satisfied Canadian investors are with their segregated funds, which have superior protections compared to regular mutual funds, ultimately benefiting both the investor and the brokering insurance company.

Even in 2021, people are still going through the fresh trauma of the 2007 crisis, meaning consumers and creators are both looking for ways not only to grow their money but also to protect it in case another major upset occurs.

Before moving on, there are a few important things to note about the Canadian model:

1. A segregated fund is a contract. Always read a contract carefully before agreeing.
2. One of their terms will likely be a penalty if we withdraw too early. Know all specifics of minimum investment periods.
3. Even in an absolute worst-case scenario, such as the company being reduced to atoms, we'll still get back 75-100% of the money we put in due to legally mandated investment protections.
4. Since the service is often offered by

insurance companies, many segregated funds come with a death benefit. If we pass away while our contract is still active, the money we put in will instead be given tax-free to the beneficiary of our choice.

5. Depending on our contract, we can keep our contributions protected from bankruptcy, insolvency, or even lawsuits. In difficult financial times, our funds cannot be seized. This is like having the benefits of a traditional IRA/RRSP through our Roth/TFSA. It's also one of the biggest upsides to this kind of fund, so make sure our contract includes it! The peace of mind this offers can be incredible in hard times.

Now, as US economic policies and even tax rates can vary from state to state, I must once again urge that we get an advisor on board, particularly one who is well-versed in the way our state's economy works. Individual states can often be compared to countries due to their size and output. However, for segregated funds, we aren't necessarily looking for a general finance advisor, but rather for a life insurance agent who can be invaluable in any insurance-based investment fund.

Some financial service companies have even developed an entire model wherein life agents function as brokers, providing overarching insurance coverage and ideal investment opportunities, and it would be well worth your while to investigate which companies exist in your region. *World Financial Group* is one such company that operates in both the US and Canada, and has been showing very promising growth for several decades. However, the old mindset regarding these types of companies dies hard, and many of them will still be dismissed, even in online searches, as nothing more than a new variation on the Multi-Level Marketing scheme, or MLM. Do your research, and pay particular attention to verifiable long-term customer satisfaction. It's also important to note that few MLMs can last more than a very few years. Longevity is just as important for confirmation as happy customers.

There's a pervading stereotype that life agents are the modern-day door-to-door vacuum cleaner salesman. Much like insurance, vacuum cleaners are a great innovation, but the stigma attached to the most vigorous proponents of both products has been hard to shake off. Of course, if the agent who pitches to us turns out to be just a salesman who fast-talks and skims over their qualifications, then we should be prepared to refuse any offer until we have gotten every detail of the contracts and policies from someone who helps us feel confident in our decision, not just pressured into it.

I cannot overstate the difference that has been made in my own life by utilizing the services of fully qualified advisors and accredited life agents. I once even gave serious consideration to pursuing insurance brokering as a career, going so far as completing my licensing exams before deciding that other opportunities were better suited for me. However, the preceding course material alone was enough to open my eyes to countless opportunities which most people remain unaware of, and led me to continue researching obscure methods of investing which could change peoples' lives for the better. Doing the job of a life agent was not my final calling, but I never hesitate to refer anyone to those for whom it was.

Had I not considered a career as a life agent, I never would have written this book. The things I learned were that much of a wake-up call for my own life that I decided to continue developing strategies in a simple-to-understand format that could be shared with the world.

Insurance-based investing is still a relatively unknown and obscure area, which many people can readily admit to being confused by. In these situations, a qualified life agent can help us to look beyond our insurance company in the same way that a general finance advisor or mortgage broker would help us to look beyond our bank. For example, many of the financial companies who specialize in insurance-based investing train their life agents based on strong broker models developed by top-performing real estate companies.

The practical upshot of this is an astonishing impact on both savings and retirement plans, as strategies that might not be so viable before now have a chance to be the bee's knees. Having a great agent or advisor here is vital. Since SA/SFs are actively managed, they will, on average, have higher manager fees and, thus, slightly lower base returns compared to more passive funds, so the last thing we want is to settle for the first option we're given from a company that already offers these funds. Just like when looking for the best mortgage, the key is to find not just a strong company, but a reputable brokerage.

Likewise, for a company that doesn't yet offer these funds, the last thing we want is to try negotiating a better deal on our own. Just getting them to create the service already takes a bit of tact, and skewing the service away from favoring the parent company creating it would require even more.

A great broker or life agent will ensure we find an SA/SF comparable in returns to a good mutual fund, which will set us up for success as an individual before we even reach Step 6.

### *The Manager's Role in Active Accounts*

While passive mutual fund managers are usually more than content to simply have an automated index reader to tick over, active managers are much more hands-on and much easier to speak to regularly. Just like it's a great idea to have a good agent or advisor, it's also a fantastic plan to find a good manager and to negotiate upfront around what their fees should be, as well as how often we'll be talking to them in non-emergency situations. The clearer the understanding before we start, the better our relationship with them will be going forward.

Historically, active investing only generates slightly better returns compared to any investment's passive counterpart but takes much more work. Since we have a manager on board, however, they're the ones who take on the work for us.

Although no one can truly see the future, their experience allows them to behave like our own personal tea-leaf reader. While a passive manager's virtual tools will be limited to the market's trends and indexes, the active manager is unconstrained in that sense, letting skilled managers perform above and beyond projected outcomes time and again.

Even the less skilled active managers, so long as they're at least competent, will have a much better ability at seeing sudden changes on the horizon compared to busy day-job investors such as ourselves and will be able to account for the irrationality of their fellow humans in ways a bot never will.

It can be quite risky working a nine-to-five job while also actively managing our growth investments. A manager makes this possible. This not only lets us enjoy the protection offered by the more actively managed SA/SFs, but the manager's vigilance will boost this protection even further through their actions.

For instance, a passive manager relies almost wholly on automated processes. The processes will then run according to projections and historical data. But what if the majority of our investments are now under threat, and these processes do not pick it up? An active manager, on the other hand, can swap our money between funds within our Roth/TFSA, giving us more protection through diversification by ensuring the majority of our money will always be in the safest place it can before an impending crisis hits.

Now, it's never fun to lose any amount of our investments. Stacy can attest to that. But imagine our money is split 20% and 80% between mutual funds and SA/SFs, a fairly common proportional split for investors. Let's say that we and all our friends are investing our 80% portions in mutual funds in the same market or industry. Theirs are passive, but ours are active.

How grateful would we feel if those portions we've invested take a huge nosedive in value, and we learn that our manager had already sold off and reinvested most of the money from the bad active funds into much better ones?

Even by swapping the 20% portion in a safe fund with the 80% which may be in a jeopardized fund, our losses will be greatly minimized: Whereas most people we know would've taken a severe hit to around 80% of their investment, we've only taken a hit to 20%.

A good active manager is like a form of investment insurance. It costs a little bit more to hire them, but they'll help to minimize our losses should something unexpected occur.

**Questions to Ask Your Manager, Agent, and Advisor**

When speaking to any of these three individuals, it always helps to ask the following questions, which I've numbered in no particular order of importance:

1. "I'm thinking of making X-dollars in contributions each month, and I want them to go first into my Roth/TFSA. Anything leftover can go into a traditional IRA/RRSP, or 401(k). What kind of investment markets should I look at for each account?"
2. "Within each of my accounts, how should the money I put in them be split by

percentage between their constituent investments?"

3. "I want to achieve a comfortable retirement while maintaining a reasonable standard of living. With the time I have left, what should my risk tolerance be?"

4. "What level of risk does my current plan need, and is there a way to reduce it?"

Every investor is different, and managers, advisors, and agents help find the crucial balance needed for us to achieve enough growth for our goals while keeping risk at a comfortable level.

Something else worth noting is that many managers and advisors are just as traditional as most investors, i.e., they are not aware of the benefits outlined in this 6-step guide I've put together for you. That is another reason why life agents are more necessary than ever, as many of the strategies we've discussed are optimal for insurance-based investing which a life agent is far more likely to be familiar with. Your life agent is more likely to run like a Thoroughbred with these strategies, while an old-school advisor is more likely to balk like an old mule. It is again best for us to look for financial service companies specializing in insurance-based investing: They will be the ones who are most aware of the newer strategies because their entire company is based on them.

We've mentioned risk tolerance before, which is one more aspect that only our unique financial fingerprint can be used to identify. We all have different levels of risk that we are comfortable with.

To help gauge our comfort with risk, we can also ask ourselves questions like, "Do I feel the urge to check in on my investments every day?" If the answer is yes, then it's a sign that we get nervous over investing easily and would be better off emotionally with a lower-risk option.

Another self-reflection would be, "How much money am I willing to lose?" In other words, how many times would our contributions have to suffer massive losses in a row before money feels tight and we get cold feet about investing at all? The lower this number, the safer we'll have to play, as it's no good to push too hard and then lose out on such powerful growth because of a conditioned fear response.

Overall, it's good to know how nervous we are about investing before going in, as we'll have an easier time communicating our concerns to our agent when we meet. They can only personalize a plan for us if we give them *all* the information they need to do so successfully, and that includes information on an emotional level.

However, in the large majority of cases, we won't need to be particularly nervous at all. An active manager who we can actively correspond with is a fantastic extra layer of security for our Roth/TFSA, especially when it's put into a separate account, segregated fund, or active-managed mutual fund as we've discussed.

As trust is built between us and our manager, there's no reason they can't handle ETFs and Index funds for us as well, especially if done through our Roth/TFSA. In all cases, they render a valuable service that lets us live our own lives without keeping a constant eye on markets.

# 8

# FILLING THE BUCKET BEFORE YOU KICK IT: ADVANTAGES OF INVESTING IN A CASH-VALUE LIFE INSURANCE POLICY, AND OTHER INSURANCE PRODUCTS.

Insurance can be an important form of tax-sheltered cash to protect our savings and help out in times of crisis throughout our lives. When we have people to look out for, it's also good to make sure we have coverage on our life so that any extra savings we might have can be bequeathed to them in a will, rather than disappearing into a funeral.

Any extra earnings we have from our contributions at the end of life should ideally be allowed to continue growing, making things easier for the next generation of our family, and allowing life to continue improving in at least our small corner of the world.

Creating this buffer of insurance for our savings brings us to our final step.

**Step 6: Invest in Cash-Value Insurance Products.**

Way back in Chapter 3, we went over how mortgage life insurance is a bad idea, for reasons such as low chance of a payout, and the fact that the coverage goes to paying off one very specific kind of debt, rather than handing out cash to our loved ones for their free use once we're gone.

As a working person, there are two aspects of finance I deeply cherish. The one is a well-planned retirement and the other is knowing that my family will still be secure should something happen to me.

Steps 1-5 were all about us. At first glance, Step 6 would seem to be about what goes on in our immediate family's world after we're gone. However, that is not the case. Those types of insurance which carry a cash value can be of great value to us during our own lifetime, which is the primary reason I decided to include them in this book: They're just too dang beneficial at all stages to be overlooked as an investment tool.

*What Kind of Insurance Should You Get?*

Many of the options mentioned in Chapter 3 are good choices, but I'd like to briefly touch on a few more here.

**Universal or Whole Life Insurance**

This is the primary form of cash-value insurance, and is also one of the most popular forms, as we pay the same rate to keep it going each month. In return, we not only get a respectable-sized benefit for our beneficiaries, but we also build up cash in an investment portion, which grows tax-deferred interest. We are then able to make withdrawals from that cash-value while we're still alive, using it for whatever we wish.

The two primary types of cash-value policy are Whole Life Insurance and Universal Life Insurance, which are quite similar but with a couple of key differences.

With Whole Life Insurance, the investment portion offers annual dividends which can be used in a variety of ways: Cash payouts directly into our pockets, continued fund value and interest growth, reduced premium payments, or even increased coverage of the policy. Additionally, the cash-value is guaranteed: Should we choose to cancel the policy, we receive the accumulated fund value that we have contributed plus interest, although cancellation fees may apply. (For the sake of clarity, the cash payout to our beneficiaries is called a death benefit, while the portion of funds we can use in our lifetime is referred to as the policy's living benefits.)

Universal Life Insurance is also called adjustable insurance, as it can be altered by the policyholder as their circumstances dictate: The amount of the premiums paid can be changed as well as the payment schedule, and the death benefit can be increased or reduced. This flexibility is primarily what differentiates it from a Whole Life policy, and also what makes it a little riskier: If the investment fund is not generating sufficient growth or if the premiums are not kept at a maintainable rate, the policy may lapse. This is why an advisor or managing life agent is strongly recommended for those who choose this option, as they can monitor the fund value and select the best investments to keep the policy in good standing.

Because the available cash from either a Whole Life or Universal policy is technically an insurance payout, it doesn't get taxed while it's growing, making it yet another way to build wealth at a modest rate tax-free. However, generally, this cash-value is only loaned, meaning it's taken away from our coverage unless we pay it back.

As another personal example, my company was impacted by the COVID-19 pandemic just like the rest of the world and forced to institute temporary layoffs. For two months, I was out of work. Thanks to the investing I had done, this time without a paycheck was much easier to manage. During this time, I was able to use the built-up cash-value within my personal Universal Life Insurance policy—which I selected over the Whole Life Insurance option for a variety of reasons unique to my circumstances, as will be the case for any of us—to continue paying my premiums. Once I was back at work, I immediately paid the amount of those two premium payments back to replenish my fund's cash-value. This prevented the overall face value/death benefit of the policy from being impacted. By contrast, this was a far better scenario than that of many people who immediately canceled their insurance policies as soon as they got into a similar financial bind: Like Roth/TFSAs, insurance sadly tends to be viewed as an unnecessary luxury when we're suddenly worried about affording food and mortgage payments.

Overall, cash-value insurance is flexible in that we can effectively use part of it for all sorts of things while we're still alive and well, but the downside of this flexibility is the policies tend to be more expensive. On the other hand, the policy lasts for as long as we live, so long as we keep meeting our payments. This means, if we get a policy with conditions we like, we can look forward to enjoying those benefits for the rest of our lives, and don't have to worry about re-qualifying 10 or 20 years later when we are older and may be in poorer health, as is often the case if someone wants to renew a Term Life policy.

Note that life insurance doesn't get paid out automatically in most cases: Our beneficiary needs to know about it. They need to file a claim before receiving a payout, and they'll need a certified death certificate to do so. *Always* let your loved ones know the details of your life insurance provider. The provider can provide help in submitting insurance claims, taking the burden of confusion off our loved ones during an already difficult time.

**Term Life Insurance**

Another popular form of life insurance, this is also known as 'pure' life insurance. We can't take loans out of it as we can with cash-value insurance, but it is generally much cheaper. So, while not the best choice for building wealth or deferring taxes, it is still an affordable option that's good for our peace of mind. Note that Term Life Insurance only lasts for a certain amount of time, during which we must make our monthly payments.

When its time is up, we'll have to apply for term life insurance again if we still want it. Some people may decide that they no longer need it as they are older and may have fewer expenses, i.e., they may have taken out the insurance policy primarily for peace of mind while they were still making home and vehicle payments. If those debts have since been eliminated, and they have sufficient retirement savings which can be left to a beneficiary, the need for life insurance may have been rendered moot.

So, how is this different from just having a non-term policy that lasts forever so long as we keep up on our payments?

An insurance policy, or an insurance contract, generally cannot be changed while it's active. If we agree to a policy that lasts 20 years, the company can't change that policy's conditions. But, when it runs out and we have to get re-insured, the company is free to remove that policy type and offer a new version instead, with different costs or duration. For example, we may be ineligible for the same insurance coverage we had before due to changes in health, occupation, habits, and even our age.

**Health Insurance**

A bread-and-butter form of insurance for pretty much everyone in the US, health insurance will either pay our doctor or pharmacist directly, or it will reimburse us for what we paid. This insurance covers pretty much every medical, surgical, or prescription-related cost we can imagine. However, the coverage is only up to a certain preset amount, and usually only if we got our treatment from an associate of the insurance company.

This makes it good for consistent medical prescriptions and regular health checkups, potentially saving us a lot of money depending on where we live. Some health insurance policies even cover dental work.

The US has had a history of increasing taxes on those who don't have health insurance. This isn't the case at the time of this writing, but it's worth bearing in mind for those who hope to save their money in the future, in case those laws make a return. Again, we need to be aware of the intentions of our current government administration when planning our finances.

**Disability Insurance**

Disability insurance kicks in whenever an accident or sickness prevents us from working at our regular job. The amount we pay is between 1.5-3% of our gross income for the year, and the payout amount is about 45-65% of our gross income, tax-free. The policy intends to help tide us over while we have limited or no access to our regular income as a result of being debilitated for a long period. For this reason, the money will be paid to us in a monthly allowance until we get better, rather than as a lump sum for us to spend all at once.

We usually need to be older than 18 and younger than 60 to qualify for this coverage.

Because the company wants to be sure our disability is a long-term debilitation, they tend to have a very long waiting period before they payout. This is an unfortunate necessity for the insurance companies, as fraudulent claims in this area are some of the most prevalent forms of insurance fraud: It's a lot easier for a dishonest person to fake a back injury than it is to fake death or terminal cancer. This means we can't use disability insurance in place of normal health coverage or critical illness insurance. However, it is still a very wise investment. It gives us financial oxygen as we recover from a long-term injury or illness, and can give us the extra time we need to find new work if the disability is permanent.

**Critical Illness Insurance**

Critical illness insurance protects us from the financial costs incurred from the onset of cancer, heart attacks, strokes, and other similar health conditions. In the USA, the costs required for dealing with these critical illnesses can be far beyond what any normal health insurance plan is willing to cover.

They also tend to pay out directly in cash. This is because the initial estimated cost of our treatment is probably lower than what the actual cost will be, so the company would rather hand us what they promised and trust us to use it to pay off the costs as they mount.

This insurance form is surprisingly cheap, mostly because it only covers a very narrow array of medical issues. Always double-check insurance contracts to make sure the issues we want to be covered are actually covered. Most forms of critical illness insurance also cover some forms of surgery, like organ transplants and coronary bypasses, in addition to the conditions mentioned above.

The money can be used rather flexibly once paid out, but we still need to satisfy the above stipulations to receive it.

## Estate Planning Insurance

Simply put, when a person moves on or is on the cusp of doing so, their family needs to make the difficult decision as to how to divide up their estate. This can be quite a complicated procedure, made even more difficult during times of grief, so a lawyer almost always has to be called in to help take stock of everything, as well as to carry out the will of the deceased as intended.

Estate planning insurance is a specialized form of life insurance that helps our will be enacted. Mortgages and owed taxes can be paid off by this insurance so that possessions that would normally have to be sold can instead be gifted to loved ones. This insurance can also be used to establish a support fund for a loved one, or even to make donations to a charity we support once we're gone, should we

choose to make a charitable organization our beneficiary rather than a loved one or family member.

This is one of the most meaningful forms of insurance but is probably also the most commonly overlooked. However, the premiums are very reasonable,
and it can be of invaluable assistance to a bereaved
family.

All of the above insurance types are useful, but one,
in particular, stands out for the purposes of this
book…

### *Whole Life Insurance and Universal Life Insurance, aka Cash-Value Insurance*

The flexibility of Whole Life and Universal Insurance, as well as their willingness to give us OPM
through the form of temporarily withdrawing the
money while we're still alive, has historically seen
great use as a tax shelter for the wealthy, and some
experts have even suggested without irony that this
was the primary reason for which it was created.

This fact alone should make cash-value insurance a
desirable option for the savvy everyday investor, as
many others may erroneously still associate the
policy with "rich people insurance," dismiss it, and
then move on to a term life policy instead. They

even feel financially validated in their decision, as term life premiums are generally lower. But the truth is, a cash-value policy with a death benefit into the high six-figures can be acquired with payments of only a couple hundred dollars a month. That is an easy amount for the average family to budget for, and the benefits for the whole family, in life and death, can be huge.

The money we put into our insurance policy's cash-value doesn't get taxed. At the time of this writing, it isn't usually taxed even after we withdraw it unless the withdrawal exceeds a certain amount, in which case it is counted as income again. This is what typically happens the moment we start withdrawing the interest our cash-value has accrued, so be careful.

Generally speaking, the longer we've held our insurance policy, the more we're able to safely withdraw. We can make these withdrawals at any time, for any reason, and the money can go to anything. As mentioned earlier, we don't even have to pay it all back so long as we're willing to accept a lower death benefit for our loved ones once we're gone. Since the death benefit is normally quite large as well as tax-free, this isn't usually a huge problem. Going back to my example, had I chosen to not pay back the two premiums which I allowed to be paid from out of the fund value during the two months when I was out of work, the total impact to my death benefit or fund value would have been less than $500. Not much of a hit when we're dealing with a payout in the hundreds of thousands or even millions of dollars.

Such a choice can also be well worth it for our loved ones, depending on what we're planning. For instance, these withdrawals could help us pay for Li'l Sue's education, or even invest in other forms of growth while still having peace of mind that our family will be okay should the worst happen. We can also use these withdrawals to supplement our retirement fund, allowing a more comfortable life. Finally, using the fund value for paying premiums is not just reserved for lean times such as my two months when I was not working, either. This strategy can also be used by retirees.

For example, elderly people who have paid for the upkeep of their policy over many years can likewise use this "recycling" of their cash withdrawals right back into their premium payments in exchange for a gradual reduction in their cash-value or death benefit. Particularly if they have sufficient other investments and retirement savings bequeathed to loved ones,—as mentioned earlier, investment tools such as Roth/TFSAs also offer tax-free payouts to a beneficiary—this is a great way for people in retirement to keep their policies active with virtually no out-of-pocket expense and very little long-term impact: The cash-value they can borrow against will be a considerable amount, as they have been building it up for decades, and they may never use up all of it in their lifetimes.

Under differing circumstances, we can instead invest the money we withdraw into our Roth/TFSA once we're retired, giving us another way to keep it growing even when we're technically no longer earning an income. This is one of the best ways to use the money from this life insurance policy even before we're retired, provided it allows us to contribute more to our best growth accounts than we otherwise could.

Some people in retirement even manage to continue payments to both their cash-value insurance policy *and* their Roth/TFSAs... using only the withdrawals from their policy's cash-value! Since their growth accounts will have accrued substantially through ongoing compound interest by this time, the impact on their policy's face value is lessened even further.

Building on that, getting a cash-value insurance policy like this works very well when we're young: The younger we are, the lower our monthly rates for life insurance are, and, remember, our monthly rates don't change under this policy, unlike when we try to renew a term life insurance policy. Normally this wouldn't be a huge advantage, since lower rates don't mean much when we're paying them for longer, but the fact that we're building up usable cash-value at the same time makes this fantastic. Compound interest in our favor is just as sexy as ever, even through insurance.

Many advisors I've spoken to recommend that we let our cash-value build for at least 10 to 15 years before we try to withdraw it, to get a sizeable amount. So if we want to use it earlier, we need to start building it earlier.

If we don't want to make withdrawals from our life insurance directly, we could alternatively use the amount we've built up as a security promise when taking out loans elsewhere, which can be helpful when getting the equipment we need to start a new job, or even our own small business. We can also choose to take a loan from the insurance company itself, using our policy as security. Because we're essentially borrowing against our own money, the company typically offers much lower interest rates than banks do, making this kind of life insurance a way to access credit relatively cheaply.

Even with a relatively new cash-value policy with little built-up value, this can be an option: The loan simply becomes covered by a portion of our death benefit. Should we die before repaying the loan, the loan is automatically paid back to our creditor, and the remainder goes to our beneficiary.

In fact, some types of business loans require the applicant to take out a life insurance policy for the additional security of the lender. This is particularly true in cases of "key-man" insurance, wherein a business venture is largely or fully contingent on the survival of one person: No matter how delicious his secret brine-and-spice recipe may be, *Pop Gherkins' Pickle Emporium* may not thrive so well if Pop Gherkins himself isn't greeting the customers every day, or if he dies and leaves the business to a sulky nephew who won't even wear Pops' iconic straw boater hat. That's the kind of thing that business investors need to consider, which is one more reason to have a good insurance policy with usable cash-value in place well ahead of time, particularly if you have an entrepreneurial spirit.

In some cases,—although this can be more difficult —the death benefit of a life insurance policy can even be used as collateral for personal loans from a bank. Again, in the event of the policyholder's death before the repayment of the loan, the balance owing is repaid from the death benefit before the beneficiary receives the remainder. However, this often requires negotiating with our loan officer, and the bank will generally prefer that our policy's investment fund already have several years of built-up cash-value before agreeing to its use as loan collateral.

The only caveat I must give is to consult with an advisor before making sudden moves. It is recommended that we keep track of our insurance policies, as well as how much we can withdraw from a Whole Life, Universal, or other cash-value policy. If we are ever uncertain, ask our advisor.

Withdrawing too much too early can trigger penalties on top of the deferred tax that often comes with withdrawing our interest. Get too greedy, and we can even endanger our death benefit or render it useless, so we need to keep careful track of what we withdraw and how it impacts the remaining death benefit, similarly to how we would check the balance of any other account when we withdraw from it.

Recklessness is never a sound financial plan. Take care in our planning, and don't spend more than we need to. All of the positives listed above are just to let us know what's possible, and what strategies a cash-value insurance policy can help us fulfill.

### *Final Word*

Insurance, when we personalize the policy to our unique needs, can be a wonderful source of relief in times of strife, debt, emergency, and death. Cash-value insurance is one of the most powerful ways to insure our death while still building some extra personal wealth on the side. However, this account isn't as core to our strategy as the Roth/TFSA. If one of those two accounts is mandatory for a comfortable life later on, cash-value insurance is more what I'd call 'recommended.' Strongly consider it, but make sure that we and our loved ones are getting more out of it than we're paying to keep it. And, now more than ever, make sure that the life agent we're working with has a strong track record of customer satisfaction.

No matter what insurance type we take out, its value ultimately comes down to how its policy is structured. There's a reason extremely wealthy people love to use cash-value insurance: It's a great financial tool that can "interact" well with our debts, payments, and other investments. However, if chosen poorly, or if we have no clear plan for using the cash-value to contribute to our other investments or a loved one's future, then we might be better off just using a regular term life policy.

# CONCLUSION

All things being understood, we're now equipped to reevaluate the way we look at long-term prosperity. Life goes on, the world changes, and it pays to adapt to it. While many things are best left to full-time professionals, I hope that you've taken away enough from what I've shared to make some great decisions for your future and your family.

Remember the six steps.

**Step One:** Learn to look beyond your bank. All you need to do is put that learning into action. If you're perpetually frustrated paying off a mortgage, seek out a broker and get a better deal. If you can't find a growth account with a satisfying interest rate, call an advisor or life agent. It'll save a lot of agony later on.

**Step Two:** Embrace the concept of using Other Peoples' Money. Some debts need to be paid off quickly to avoid mounting interest. Other debts have such low-interest rates that it's better to focus on investing even before the debt is fully paid off. You've seen how powerful it can be to invest in financial growth early on. Whether you're in a mort-gaged house or even just a long-derided rental prop-erty, you can have incredible long-term investment options attached to your home.

**Step Three:** Learn the Rule of 72. This is a hard and fast rule that'll help you tell at a glance if the growth account you're looking at will generate enough interest for the goals you wish to achieve. Don't forget the compound interest calculator from Chapter 5, either!

**Step Four:** Open your Roth IRA or TFSA first, espe-cially if you live in the USA. You can only contribute so much to these accounts each year, but they can have great return rates, fewer traps down the road, creditor protections, no term limits or mandatory withdrawal dates, and can be easily left to a benefi-ciary as a tax-free payout. The sooner you open this account, the sooner you can capitalize on that posi-tive while minimizing its negative. Also, strongly consider getting a Roth IRA for your child as soon as they begin any form of verifiable employment.

**Step Five:** Put some sort of actively managed or segregated fund into your Roth IRA or TFSA. It can cost a little more, but what you get is a more active and attentive manager, along with more protections, which can result in exponentially greater investment returns.

**Step Six:** Invest in cash-value insurance. This is a great way to not only open up another source of OPM but also to give yourself peace of mind. Your family is depending on you.

Put these steps into action, remember the caveats we've covered, and I'm confident you'll succeed.

If you enjoyed this book, the best "Thank you!" I can ask for is a detailed review and recommendation on Amazon or another online bookseller of your choice. For additional value and financial insights, you can subscribe for free to my website at www.paxtonsfinnegan.com. There, you will receive a free online copy of my in-depth guide, *The Law-Abiding Pirate*, to learn further strategies for maximizing your investments while protecting your money from the omnipresent ravages of inflation. That's just a couple of the ways that the Internet can truly benefit small businesses and freelance workers such as myself in our ever-changing technological landscape.

Finally, please consider this book to be your invitation to join our Facebook group, *You Can't Have My Money!* It's a great place to share financial ideas, tips, and discussions with a large community of everyday investors from around the world, as well as getting the inside scoop on my upcoming projects. We all have a thought no one else has thought of, and we all have something to share for the financial benefit of all. I look forward to chatting with you. (No, I don't farm out my Facebook obligations to some patsy.)

Happy trails, and don't let *anyone* undeserving have your money.

REFERENCES

Anspach, D. (2021, April 15). *9 things people don't know about Roth IRAs*. The Balance.

https://www.thebalance.com/surprising-roth-ira-facts-2388898

Banks Editorial Team. (2020, May 11). *Are there any tax-free savings accounts in the USA?* Banks.com.

https://www.banks.com/articles/banking/savings-accounts/tax-free-savings-accounts/

Bell, A. (2021, February 24). *6 ways to capture the cash value in life insurance.* Investopedia.

https://www.investopedia.com/articles/personal-finance/082114/6-ways-capture-cash-value-life-insurance.asp

Bieber, C. (2018, May 24). *Pay your mortgage early or invest?* The Motley Fool.

https://www.fool.com/mortgages/2018/05/24/pay-your-mortgage-early-or-invest.aspx

Bieber, C., Backman, M., & Brockman, K. (2021, March 6). *Retirement battle royale: 401(k) vs. IRA vs. Roth.* The Motley Fool.

https://www.fool.com/investing/2021/03/06/retirement-battle-royale-401k-vs-ira-vs-roth/

BravoPolicy. (2021, June 14). *Underfunded universal life insurance: Everything you need to know.* BravoPolicy.

https://bravopolicy.com/life-insurance/underfunded-universal-life-insurance/

Canada Revenue Agency. (2021, January 18). *Canadian income tax rates for individuals - current and previous years.* Canada.ca.

https://www.canada.ca/en/revenue-agency/services/tax/individuals/frequently-asked-questions-individuals/canadian-income-tax-rates-individuals-current-previous-years.html

Chase. (2021). *How to consolidate your credit card debt.* Chase.

https://www.chase.com/personal/credit-cards/education/basics/how-to-consolidate-your-credit-card-debt

Connett, W. (2020, October 20). *The best Roth IRA investments.* Investopedia.

https://www.investopedia.com/articles/personal-finance/110614/most-common-roth-ira-investments.asp

Dave, P. (2020, December 27). Whole Life vs. Universal Life Insurance. Investopedia. https://www.investopedia.com/articles/pf/07/whole_universal.asp

Eneriz, A. (2021, April 28). *Debt avalanche vs. debt snowball: What's the difference?* Investopedia.

https://www.investopedia.com/articles/personal-finance/080716/debt-avalanche-vs-debt-snowball-which-best-you.asp

Hayes, A. (2020, October 3). *Mutual fund.* Investopedia.

https://www.investopedia.com/
terms/m/mutualfund.asp

HowToSaveMoney Team. (2021, March 29). *Segregated funds Canada: The pros, cons, and alternatives.* HowToSaveMoney.ca.

https://www.howtosavemoney.ca/segregated-funds

Investment Executive Staff. (2010, February 4). *91% of Canadians have retirement worries: Poll.* Investment Executive.

https://www.investmentexecutive.com/building-your-business/financial-planning/91-of-canadians-have-retirement-worries-poll/

Kagan, J. (2021a, April 30). *Complete guide to estate planning.* Investopedia.

https://www.investopedia.com/
terms/e/estateplanning.asp

Kagan, J. (2021b, July 9). *Disability Income (DI) insurance.* Investopedia.

https://www.investopedia.com/
terms/d/diinsurance.asp

Kilroy, A. (2020, May 20). *What to know about cash value life insurance.* Forbes Advisor.

https://www.forbes.com/advisor/life-insurance/cash-value-life-insurance/

Kumok, Z. (2021, June 28). *Critical illness insurance: What is it and who needs it?* Investopedia.

https://www.investopedia.com/articles/personal-finance/010416/critical-illness-insurance-who-needs-it.asp

Lanctot, P. (2019, December 12). *Insurance that will pay the mortgage if a spouse dies.* PocketSense.

https://pocketsense.com/insurance-pay-mortgage-spouse-dies-3255.html

McClelland, C. (2019, September 30). *More than a third of Canadians have no retirement savings, half live paycheque to paycheque, poll finds.* Financial Post. https://financialpost.com/personal-finance/more-than-a-third-of-canadians-have-no-retirement-savings-half-live-paycheque-to-paycheque-poll-finds

McWhinney, J. (2018, February 6). *A brief history of the mutual fund.* Investopedia.

https://www.investopedia.com/articles/mutualfund/05/mfhistory.asp

Ng, K. (2021, February 11). *TFSA investors: 1 top growth stock to buy and hold forever.* The Motley Fool Canada.

https://www.fool.ca/2021/02/11/tfsa-investors-1-top-growth-stock-to-buy-and-hold-forever/

Pant, P. (2020, July 13). *Actively vs. passively managed funds.* The Balance.

https://www.thebalance.com/actively-vs-passively-managed-funds-453773

Phung, A. (2020, March 7). *How do segregated funds differ from mutual funds?* Investopedia.

https://www.investopedia.com/ask/answers/06/segfundsvsmutualfunds.asp

Resendiz, J. (2021, January 28). *How credit card companies make and earn money.* ValuePenguin.

https://www.valuepenguin.com/how-do-credit-card-companies-make-money

Richmond, S. (2021, March 30). *Roth 401(k) vs. Roth IRA: What's the difference?* Investopedia.

https://www.investopedia.com/articles/personal-finance/063015/roth-401k-vs-roth-ira-one-better.asp

Rotter, K. (2021, March 30). *What to do after maxing out your 401(k) plan.* Investopedia.

https://www.investopedia.com/articles/personal-finance/070615/i-maxed-out-my-401k-now-what.asp

Sato, G. (2020, November 26). *Is it better to use a mortgage broker or bank?* Experian.

https://www.experian.com/blogs/ask-experian/is-it-better-to-use-a-mortgage-broker-or-bank/

The Investopedia Team. (2021a, January 10). Savings account vs. Roth IRA: Knowing the difference (E. Howard, Ed.). Investopedia.

https://www.investopedia.com/ask/answers/06/savingsvs.ira.asp

The Investopedia Team. (2021b, January 18). *Baby Boomer* (B. Barnier, Ed.).

Investopedia.

https://www.investopedia.com/terms/b/baby_boomer.asp

Thorp, B. (2021, April 20). *What are active ETFs?* Wealthtender.

https://wealthtender.com/insights/investing/etfs/actively-managed-etfs

U.S. Securities and Exchange Commission. (2021). *Compound interest calculator.* Investor.gov.

https://www.investor.gov/financial-tools-calculators/calculators/compound-interest-calculator

Wathen, J. (2017, October 5). 3 benefits of an actively managed fund. The Motley Fool;

https://www.fool.com/investing/2017/10/05/3-benefits-of-an-actively-managed-fund.aspx

Wilhoit, T. (2014, May 11). Accumulate wealth with the Rule of 72. YourFriend4Life.

https://www.yourfriend4life.com/accumulate-wealth-with-the-rule-of-72/

# HUNTING PURPLE ELEPHANTS

### A 7-STEP, 7-WEEK PLAN TO ELIMINATE UNNECESSARY SPENDING, INCREASE HOME INCOME, AND INVEST THE SAVINGS

**Paxton S. Finnegan**

# INTRODUCTION

Living paycheck to paycheck is the new norm, or at least that is what it seems for so many citizens of the western world today. Each pay period, we have to decide which bills to pay this time and which ones can be held off until the next payday. This is a common occurrence for most families, and, most ironically, it's happening to people living in the most thriving, luxurious, and convenient lands that mankind has ever hoisted a flag over. Our car seats warm our butts on cold days, for Pete's sake! Do we honestly think ancient emperors and dictators had it anywhere near as good as we do now?

Sure, most of us still have enough pioneer grit left in our souls to doggedly soldier on if our butt-heater shorts out... at least for a couple of days until we can get it to the shop and pay a guy in greasy coveralls to get it fixed. (Seriously, it's like a tea-cozy for your butt! What are we, cavemen?) But what about when something more crucial is jeopardized? What happens if the refrigerator goes? What if we need new tires or a new transmission? Heck, what if things that are a little more internal start to short out? Like, say, what if someone needs a new hip? Or a new kidney? Do we have a reserve fund saved or adequate insurance paid for these types of purchases, repairs, and medical emergencies?

The answer from most people would be, "I guess I'd just have to put it on my credit card," or "I'll get a store credit card when I buy the refrigerator." Heck, a shocking number of people still publicly admit that their financial plan involves some form of large inheritance or lottery winnings. However, that is not a plan, just as a credit card is not a reserve fund to pay for purchases. Opening a new credit card to resolve existing debt is not unlike a desperate farmer manually digging out an old storm drain with a shovel while he's already waist-deep in raging flood-water. He may be giving the excess water some-where to go, but he's still in the hole, and suddenly the water's up to his neck and moving a lot faster. That's credit card debt in a nutshell.

Sometimes we feel defeated because we don't know how we will pay for these needed items. It is not uncommon for people to buy a new car because it's legitimately easier than coming up with the thousands of dollars needed to fix a shot transmission on short notice. We do what we have to do, gulping just enough oxygen to keep floundering for a few more months, but we know it is not helping our long-term goals.

Other times, we think we are making headway because we get a new credit card with a 0% introductory interest rate. To be fair, this can be a good strategy if used wisely, and I myself have used it successfully. However, oftentimes we get so excited at the possibility of transferring all the balances from our other cards to this one that we don't read the fine print. In many cases, it turns out that only certain cards qualify for balance transfers, and when the introductory period is over, the interest rate can be in the double digits. Some people have ended up paying as much as 25% or more annually on credit cards. Do just a couple of basic calculations with that number on a multi-thousand dollar balance, and then get back to me about how many of your hairs turned white.

We all want an easy fix because we dread the thought of sacrificing our happiness with a complex fix. This is an unfortunate mindset because the reality is that much of our happiness is based on how strong our financial foundation is. The love of money may truly be the root of all evil, but the abject need for money can easily jockey into position for a pretty close runner-up.

Most of us don't learn how to be financially secure unless our parents taught us considerably more than most public schools ever will. However, although many of our parents grew up in far leaner times when frugality was considered a virtue, even twenty years ago they couldn't have possibly foreseen a time when paying multiple monthly subscriptions for a variety of streaming services would be considered part of everyday life. The revolutionary advancements in technology are exploding, and our wallets are imploding from trying to keep up without a plan.

Being financially secure is a comfort to us, yet most of us live in an economically insecure world. The

20th century saw incredible advancements in technology and production that brought prosperity to hundreds of millions of people. However, that growth is never unhindered by global circumstances, even in comparatively wealthy western nations such as the United States, the United Kingdom, and Canada. Oil pricing caused skyrocketing gas prices in the 1970s. There were major financial crises with worldwide impacts in the 1980s, the late 2000s, and at the time of this writing in the early 2020s. And, yet, most of us, particularly in North America, can still adapt and thrive in uncertainty. We can change our world and make it more financially sound no matter our age. Then we can help our children or grandchildren learn the lesson earlier so they don't have to worry about the same traps we fell into so willingly.

There are many, many ways to eliminate unnecessary costs from our lives, and there is no single one-size-fits-all solution. We definitely want to begin smart investing early on, a topic which I covered more thoroughly in my first book, *You Can't Have My Money!*, which we can consider to be a companion guide to this book. However, many people are living in such dire financial straits, even on a middle-to-upper-class income, that they need to make major financial changes before investing is even a wise option. Sometimes tearing down must precede building up.

Sometimes, we just need to kill some purple elephants.

When we struggle to cover monthly expenses, our long-term investment allotment, which ideally should be the one chunk of change we keep a death-grip on until the end, is often viewed as the first cost to cut. I won't lie. That's a decision I've had to make in my own life, in times when I found myself in a major shortfall or unexpectedly out of work. My first call was to my financial adviser: "Put a hold on my PAD until I get back on my feet!" That could have been avoided, and quite easily, if I had kept a better definition of the word "essential" in my daily life.

Here's the main takeaway from this book: We can build a primarily debt-free existence now, and then use the money we had been spending on so many unnecessary things for investing and an all-around better life. It doesn't have to be about knowing the right stocks to buy, or getting a better-paying job, or being on the ground floor of some miraculous start-up company that's going to replace the Internet. All of those things are great, but they are rarely feasible, especially if we're living with excessive debt. The good news is, those lofty ideals don't need to be feasible. The life you are living now has opportunities to transform the life you are living now.

Did reading that frustrate you? Absolutely. Half of the people who read that last paragraph just said what I had said many times in the past: "I can't just drop my debt! It's latched on like a freakin' vampire, and it's bleeding me dry!" And that's true. The solution doesn't come in the form of some magical evaporation of all debt. It comes in the form of debt restructuring, with some basic and not-so-basic cost-cutting which will enable us to pay off our debt more efficiently and even increase household income. It's time to ice the blood in our veins because we now have to dispatch the same purple elephants which we have unknowingly been fattening up out of our own pockets for years.

Using this seven-step, seven-week plan will help us find our purple elephants. Heck, in the next chapter, I'll even tell you what those are. (Come on, I have to titillate you a little bit in the intro.) It will help us better understand our financial foundation and where we need to strengthen it, which will better prepare us to begin investing in the future, and the future of our families.

If you purchased this book, then you are ready to get out of this cycle of continued growing debt. You are ready to take control of your financial health and make it stronger. This plan will help you make those first steps to end the debt cycle. It will not always be comfortable, and not every option will be compatible with or even applicable to your unique financial situation. For that reason, it is my job to provide you with as many feasible options as possible, to give you a path forward that's right for you.

First and foremost, get a journal. We'll need that from day one. I don't care if it's an online document, or if we jot it down on loose-leaf sheets, or if we have to dig out that old diary from middle school with the glitter-pen unicorns and magazine clippings of your heart-throb *du jour*. I recommend two journals which we will keep for 30 to 45 days, and even assign something as simple as a notebook and pen to each member of the family with strict instructions to carry it with them at all times. A notebook is my strongest recommendation, and the journal format I use almost exclusively. (Forget analog: I'm still wishing that quill and ink and wax seals would make a comeback.)

If anyone in the family makes any purchase in their daily lives, even so much as feeding a quarter into a jelly bean machine, they write it down and keep the receipts. Just looking at last month's statements isn't going to give us an accurate look at our daily expenses, even if we pay almost everything on cards. Only writing down and keeping receipts will provide us with a realistic perspective on a typical month.

Also, if we don't track our time for those 30 to 45 days, we won't realize how much time we are wasting doing nothing more than reading posts on Facebook or watching the Reels section on Instagram. Most of us don't realize how much time goes toward useless activity. If you don't believe me, try doing a mandatory online training course for work while keeping even one other tab open on your computer while you do it. Or try keeping your journal in your phone while TikTok still exists.

The next thing to consider is that we cannot do this alone if we have more than just one person in the household. If we are single, then it is all on us. However, if we live in a household with a partner—married or not—and if there are children, especially ones that are old enough to want to earn and spend money, then they should be keeping their own journals, expenses, and time management. It is 100% essential that we make this a household effort, or we are going to crumble alone. Call a family meeting. Lay the grim reality of our financial situation out to them in no uncertain terms. And then start our family plan.

This book lays out a foundational plan. At the end of the seven weeks, we will know what our purple elephants are and have a plan to start removing them from our lives. Some will be as easy as canceling a service, but others will require research, restructuring, careful calculations, and some footwork. In addition, we will need to reevaluate our debt regularly to ensure no new purple elephants are creeping into our world, because that is how it happens. Free trials. Teaser interest rates. Special occasions to go out to the movie theater. Paying a freakin' buck-and-a-half extra for extra butter on the popcorn at the movie theater. These and so many other excuses are how debt creeps into our lives.

We've all heard of the elephant in the room. Once we're done with this plan, we're going to be amazed at how we didn't spot our elephants before. Because they're a bioluminescent purple that glows in the dark, and they smell bad.

# 1

## SEEING THE FOOTPRINTS AND THE PURPLE POOP: THE DAWNING REALIZATION THAT YOU ABSOLUTELY HAVE A SPENDING PROBLEM.

**Step 1: Prepare your Purple Elephant Hit List. Be ruthless.**

A while back, I saw a skinny dude in skinny jeans, holding an even skinnier latte, complaining to a very patient barista that he had lost or broken three iPhones so far that year. A single thought went through my head.

"Men used to hunt mammoths."

Growing up on a cattle ranch means that I will always be aware of how much better my butt looks whilst decked out in a pair of boot-cut Wranglers, but it also means that I am predisposed to giggle like a little girl at men in skinny jeans whining about their multiple dearly-departed iPhones. Dude, seriously, you'll have to miss out on your precious *Candy Crush* for a couple of days, or posting photos of your quinoa/cardboard salad on Instagram, but... men used to hunt mammoths.

The only problem with my bemused judgments was that I was standing in the same lineup behind him, fully intending to get an extra-large, creme brulee macchiato with maple flakes, salted-caramel drizzle, and extra whip the very second that his whiny butt and protractor legs weren't blocking the cash register. My impatiently-anticipated myocardial infarction in a to-go cup wasn't even on the menu, but I knew from past experience that they could assemble it if I threw an extra $5.00 at them. I wasn't exactly chipping a spearhead from a flint rock, myself.

My fiery-eyed mammoths had turned into purple elephants, and, even worse, they were hunting *me*.

My delicious maple-flaked, whip-topped, caramel-flavored coffee (that probably had some actual coffee inside it somewhere) was my purple elephant. Not the only one. And definitely not the first one. Just one.

Many people live paycheck to paycheck and often couldn't tell anyone where the money goes. They pay their bills before they indulge in some items, but it shouldn't leave them broke until next payday, right?

Wrong, bucko!

The fact is most people have no idea where the money not associated with scheduled monthly bills actually goes. For example, there's no possible way in the fiery pits of unholy heck that they maybe spent over $300 on coffee last month. That would be ridiculous.

People spend money without thinking. End of discussion. They pay their bills and account for the bill money, but once the necessities are paid for, the accounting stops, and the purple elephants start surging the southern border.

This chapter is going to explain why this missing money is so important. It will also show why we should be able to account for it and give us an example of how this money is lost without anyone even realizing that it is being siphoned off. This is where we learn what our purple elephants are.

**Definition of a Purple Elephant**

A purple elephant is an expense in our lives which may or may not be important or even used, but when we got it, we thought it was wonderful, essential, non-habit-forming, or, worst of all, forgettable.

There are two main purple elephants. Let's think of them as an evil Bonnie and Clyde-esque duo, and call them Amethyst and Tyrian.

Amethyst is the show-pony of the two. She is every expense we excuse as self-care or once-in-awhile indulgences. She is all the pretty things that we need to feel pretty, or satiated, or entertained, or maple-flaked, or of acceptable social standing in the public eye. We don't think about how often we indulge her shameless desires, and Amethyst's costs rack up in surprising parallel to our belt notches being let out. Also, she wants to eat your kids.

Nobody on the glitzy-yet-cynical red carpet wants to take photos of Tyrian's ugly mug, so he operates behind the scenes, primarily in the form of monthly subscriptions that we may or may not use. What subscriptions? They come in many forms, for both work and recreational use. These include business and office software, online gaming, stock images, website administration, food and cooking sites, arts and craft sites, video-editing and photoshop software, plus countless others. We don't think we have that many, and some people if asked would say they don't have any at all. They may even honestly believe it.

We sign up for something like a paid or free trial for a week or a month, sometimes planning to use it regularly, sometimes out of curiosity heightened by a successful click-bait strategy, and sometimes because we just have a one-time need for the product. We use the app or service for the trial period, but we almost inevitably forget to cancel and BLAMMO! We're subscribed. Even worse, we say, "Hey, look, there's a discount if you sign up for the full year! Holy horse crap, that's only like $8.00 a month!" and then we click the little button that says, "Renew annually." It's weird that we don't remember that button: Instead of going *"Beep!"*, it let out a guttural demonic laugh and wafted a slight odor of sulfur.

Then we use the app twice, decide that *Fruit Ninja* was more fun, and forget about it.

Other subscriptions we are fully aware of, such as streaming services for music, TV shows, movies, podcasts, and online news. We just consider these bills and account for them, but they are not necessities, and depending on how many subscriptions we have, that overlap can be part of Tyrian's murderous plot of hidden expenses and accumulated debt. Yes, a lot of them are only about $8.00 a month. But suddenly we have six or ten of them, and Tyrian just offered another one of his own kids as a burnt sacrifice on a brazen altar dedicated to the ancient Canaanite god Baal. (I have to use horrifying visuals for Tyrian and Amethyst, because a reader's instinct is to adorably anthropomorphize them, and then you'll feel bad later on when we start hacking them into chunks of bloody stew meat with the Sacred Golden Cleaver of Financial Self-Control. Maybe I should have gone with purple tarantulas...)

Let's take a look at a real-life scenario.

**Example of a Real-Life Scenario**

We have an all-American family living in Dallas, Texas. Meet the Chowders: Dad Clem, mom Tottie, elder daughter Rosemary, and younger son Herb. Clem and Tottie both work full-time while the kids are in school. They live in a nice home in a safe neighborhood. Clem and Tottie each earn about $4,083 a month, so they have a very respectable combined household income of $98,000 a year. This is roughly $40-45,000 above the national household average.

Every morning, Clem and Tottie each get a gourmet coffee on their separate work commutes. If they are hungry, they may also grab a sandwich or pastry while there. The coffee/pastry combo is at least $12 each, while a coffee alone is still at least half of that. There are four 5-day work weeks each month. Three days a week, Clem and Tottie get coffee only, while two days a week they're a bit peckish and grab the croissant, too. They are more than satiated on the remainder of the drive to work, they are invigorated to start each new day, and they just spent $336 a month on coffee.

Instead of packing lunches for the family, everyone pays for lunches. The children's lunches each average $2.64 daily, while each of the parent's lunches run about $12 daily. This means the family spends almost $30 a day on lunches or $146 for the week—about $584 a month.

The children are in extracurricular activities, which means takeout food is purchased at least two days a week, sometimes more, and then, as a special family tradition, they all go out to eat at an upscale restaurant one night each weekend. The takeout for a family of four can run around $50, while a meal at a nice restaurant can be up to $120 or more. Sometimes they decide to skip the risotto and scallops appetizer to spend a little less money at the restaurant, but that's usually because they had takeout three times that week instead of the usual two. Regardless of the circumstance, it still averages out to about $880 a month. In the summer months, this food cost goes up considerably on account of vacations, day trips, friends visiting, and general child-at-home boredom which can apparently only be satiated by ice cream.

For entertainment and electronics, the family also has an Internet connection, TV and movie subscriptions—yes, that's pluralized—cell phones, music subscriptions, video game subscriptions, and more.

I guarantee most people do not sit down and add up all these subscriptions, so let's do that now:

Cell phone(s): $140
Internet/phone/TV: $200
Video game console subscription: $60
Amazon Prime (Monthly average, paid annually for $119): $10

HBO/Starz/Etc. (3 average): $45
Netflix: $18
Other miscellaneous streaming (Verve, Crunchyroll, Youtube): $75
Music subscription (SiriusXM): $22
Other music subscriptions (Spotify/Pandora): $16
**Total per month:** $586

Most people don't think about the fact they are spending almost $600 on these types of subscriptions. To be clear, these estimates are conservative, and we're not even done yet.

How many times have we signed up for a trial service and forgot to cancel? For example, many times we are sent documents to sign, so we sign up for the software trial, sign the document, and close it down. The trial and upcoming subscription are forgotten, except for a slight waft of sulfur that we can't quite pinpoint.

Subscriptions range anywhere from $10 to $100 or more, with the average being about $40 a month. To be conservative, let's estimate there are only four of these forgotten subscriptions, which adds another $160 to the monthly expenses.

This family has now spent about $2,546 in one month outside of the required bills. We may say breakfast and lunches are necessary because people have to eat. Yes, people have to eat, but eating out and buying lunches every day is a purple elephant, especially for the parents.

Let's break this down. Buying school-provided lunches for both children run the family $106 a month. In that same month, the parents spent $480 on their lunches. This is a difference of $374. The parents spend more on lunches in a week—$120 for the two of them—than for a month of the school-provided lunches for the children. Buying lunches as the everyday norm—instead of packing most of the time and only purchasing lunch occasionally—is why Amethyst is more aggressively hunting the parents in this situation. Clem and Tottie slogged through twelve publicly-educated years of peanut butter and cafeteria beans, thank you very much, and they have zero intention of going back to that particular misery after tossing their graduation caps in the air... and moving on to the equally-depressing world of laundry-scented college dorms and $0.50 ramen noodles.

While earnestly trying to teach their kids life lessons in responsibility, Clem and Tottie are unknowingly spending more than 4x the kids' lunch budget on their own lunches. Not to mention that they spend more than 3x the kids' lunch budget on coffee.

Not every family's case will be as extreme as that of the Chowder's, and, if that statement applies to you, congratulations. But the truth is that for many real families across the modern world, the numbers are far worse. People simply do not think about their spending once they pay their monthly bills covering home, food, fuel, and utilities. And the absolute worst part of Tyrian's subscriptions is that virtually all of them are linked to a credit card. They get paid automatically, quietly digging a deeper hole every month. When we factor in the hard reality that many families even opt to receive their credit card statements online, it becomes quite easy for them to spend months doing nothing more than taking a glance at the bottom line, and some will even skip that part and say, "I think I used the credit card a couple times, we'll pay a couple hundred to that this month." Almost without fail, they underestimate their monthly spending. That can quickly lead to a financial catastrophe which can tear a once-loving family apart.

The Chowder parents were undoubtedly pleased to shed their ramen and climb their respective work ladders after college to get where they are now, earning a respectable $98,000.00 a year. But we just conservatively carved $30,540.00 out of that, a huge annual chunk of change to which they have barely given a second thought.

Be under no candy-coated illusion: Debt has destroyed countless families, and debt can destroy your family.

So let's hunt.

### Release the Hounds! Track Down Your Purple Elephants

Some of the following activities may be familiar, some may not. However, they all work, and when they are used together, we will not miss any purple elephants. Diligence is our ally. From now on, let's make the decision that every year, either in January when the new year starts or when we are doing our taxes, we will review our finances and find any new purple elephants.

Let's take a moment to acknowledge that sometimes our lives or tastes change. What we deemed as essential one year may not be the following year.

This change in what we feel is important in our lives is both legitimate and fine. Don't beat yourself up and feel like you missed a purple elephant the year before because it probably was not the case.

We can take the time to think about it and remember why we kept it, or we can just accept that as we mature, our lives change, and what we need is not always the same. The good thing is we can get rid of it now, and if we decide we want it back, we can bring it back.

Hunting purple elephants is never a one-and-done type of activity. Our lives change, which can change what we deem as purple elephants. An unacceptable expense this year may be completely justifiable next year when we're back on track and have a solid financial plan. So don't despair over losing something that you loved with every subscription cancellation. It might only be gone for a year or a few months, and then come back but in a more disciplined form. And this plan is nothing without discipline.

Before we set off on our grand safari, murdering purple elephants until it makes Jimmy Kimmel cry, let's quickly use the previous example from above to better understand how this works. Just to see how much it can save us now and help us in the future.

### Changing Status of Real-Life Debt Example

Fast forward a few years. Both of the Chowder kids are now over 18 years old and have moved out of the family home. Herb is in college, while Rosemary has completed it, started working, and rented an apartment of her own.

Several of the subscriptions that were previously considered a necessity are no longer needed. In many cases, when the kids move out, then the video game console subscription is no longer needed. They can also remove some of the streaming, TV, and movie subscriptions because they are no longer being used. However, the subscriptions are not all that is gone from their expenses. Let's look at what the Chowder parents are paying now:

Cell phone: $140

Internet/phone/TV: $200

~~Video Game console Subscription: $60~~

Amazon Prime (average, paid annually for $119): $10

HBO/Starz/Etc. (3 average): $45

~~Netflix: $18~~

~~Other miscellaneous streaming (Verve, Crunchyroll, YouTube): $75~~

Music subscription (SiriusXM): $22

~~Music subscriptions (Spotify/Pandora): $16~~

**New total per month:** $417

They have eliminated their video game subscriptions, Netflix, miscellaneous streaming services, and one of their two music subscriptions. That is a difference of $169 a month which is now back in the pockets of Clem and Tottie. They are saving $2,028 per year.

When the children graduated from high school, the school lunch expense of $106 a month also disappeared. Eating out three nights a week dropped to twice a month. This means that the eating out expense has decreased from $880 to around $160 a month. They are still spending $336 a month for their morning coffee because they enjoy it and don't want to give it up. However, they have started packing lunch most days and only ate lunch out about four times a month each. This change decreased their part of the lunch expense from $584 to around $192 a month. In addition, they have removed $160 of forgotten subscriptions.

Now, instead of spending $2,546 a month in expenses outside of the necessities, they are spending about $1,105 each month. That is a savings of about $1,441 each month, and at least $17,292 per year. Most important to note is that the changes in this example happened more or less organically. Think of how much more could have been saved, both now and in the past, if they'd buckled down and done a little financial homework.

You may have similar results, better results, or you may even be one of the blessed few who finds that you don't have a lot of purple elephants to begin with. The point is if we can find and eliminate purple elephants,—which might even mean reclassifying them from obsolete expenses that were once legitimately essential,—then we are going to put more money in our pockets to invest for the future.

How did the Chowder family gauge their expenses so well that first time and each time thereafter? They each completed a finance journal. Tottie isn't as primitive as me and my notebook, so she created a spreadsheet for each person to use on their phones, making tracking expenses easy without costing extra. They each agreed to log their expenses every day for a month. At the end of that time, they would come together as a family with their receipts and start the hunt.

Each year the family reevaluated their spending and reevaluated the purple elephants they were willing to feed and manage. When the children left home, they had a solid understanding of being financially stable and what it would take to maintain that. From above, we can see that Clem and Tottie figured it out, too, and they weren't even being half as vicious as I would have liked them to be. But I'm working on it.

This activity is never over. It just looks a little different every year as things in our lives change. Never stop hunting.

### Finding the Purple Elephants: One-Month Journal Activity

There are several ways to find those invasive purple buggers, and they can all work to some extent individually. Most people only use one, if any, of these options, but, when used together, we will be able to root out all the purple elephants and then gleefully move onto the culling stage. (Remember: They're not cute. They're a bunch of kid-cookin' Baal worshippers. No mercy!)

This activity takes about one month to six weeks to complete. By following along for this amount of time, it will help us not only find the purple elephants that come by every month but will also show us those that sneak in and out quickly without being noticed. Finding every single purple elephant is the endgame, whether they be hiding behind skinny trees or quivering on our living room floor beneath a comically-undersized throw rug.

Whoops, there I go, putting adorable imagery in your head again! We are gonna cleave them suckers SO hard...

With focus, discipline, and full family cooperation, we will easily find them all with this finance journal activity. Please note that the activities outlined in chapters 1 and 2 are designed to be completed together, so be sure to read both before we get started.

### Financial Journal

The first step is to keep a daily journal of all our expenses. ALL OF THEM. What does this mean? It means that whether we spend cash, use a debit card, write a check (I'm reasonably certain that those still exist), or use a credit card, we write the expense down.

Yes, that includes the morning coffee. Yes, it includes the newspaper. Yes, it includes the jelly beans from the candy machine. Big or small, everything gets written down.

We may be asking why, so let's think about why this journal is essential.

Many of us keep a journal either to write down our feelings, what we need to do, what we did at work, etc... Keeping a journal of our finances will help us find our purple elephants and will also help us decide which of these we will be keeping and feeding for a while longer.

It will show us each little expense that is feeding a purple elephant. Now we need to decide how we will journal.

I still prefer my notebook, but many people today prefer to use electronics. We can create a document on the computer, we can use a spreadsheet, we can use an accounting ledger, and we can save our files to the cloud.

The "what" really doesn't matter as long as we enter things daily and have a place to make notes about the purchases and our feelings about them. There are even apps for our phones. Just search "expense tracker," and we'll find tons. This is the best option in many cases because most city slickers have their dang phone in hand 24/7, even when they somehow manage to forget their wallet and keys.

Buy or set up our financial journal and be ready to start ASAP. Remember, we will be recording every time we make a purchase, even if it is only a few cents, and I know that particular scourge because I still have a hard time walking past those jelly beans if I've got the quarter in my pocket. We'll see at the end of this activity in 30 to 45 days how much those little expenses we ignore are actually costing us.

### Keeping Receipts

Keeping receipts for a business is essential. Whether we own a business, have a side hustle, or any other form of income, we should always keep our printed receipts. Yes, have the store print out the receipt for us. If we purchase something online, print out the receipt. Don't just save it to a file and forget about it. If we can't get a receipt, be sure to note that in our journal next to the purchase so we can still balance our columns at the end of the month. (The reception lady at the tire shop gave me weird looks when I walked up to her, munching on a handful of freshly-dispensed jelly beans, and asked if it was possible to get a receipt.)

At the end of each day, make sure our receipts match our daily entries in the finance journal. There will probably be discrepancies when we are just starting, such as an entry without a receipt or a receipt without an entry.

By the end of the activity, we will be accustomed to always asking for a receipt, and the entries will line up with receipts much more accurately.

The importance of keeping receipts is twofold. First, keeping receipts helps us account for the money we spend. Second, the receipts will help us at the end of the month or year, and we will be better able to budget and set goals for our financial future.

Through receipts, we can see patterns emerge in our spending so we can better identify necessary expenses vs purple elephants. When we find these patterns, we can budget for them, so we always know when they are coming if they are a necessity.

Let's use the example of filling the car up with gas. We need the gas, but have we looked at how much we spend on gas each week, month, and year? It is a necessity but it is an often ignored expense. Do we make quick runs to the convenience store for a gallon of milk or to the beer store to grab a six-pack of beer on the weekend? Each trek with our vehicle is gas usage and requires us to buy gas more often. By watching how often we purchase gas, we can find patterns, such as less spent on gas in the winter as compared to the summer.

### Statements

Monthly billing statements are just as important as receipts, whether they arrive by email or on paper to our post office box. In today's world, statements are increasingly less likely to be sent to our homes. To save the environment—because a Swedish kid yelled at the UN, and then for some reason sat on a COVID-19 panel—we opted out of receiving a paper statement. Rarely do we go into the website and check it, or even fully read the monthly summary sent to us, but this is where we will find more purple elephants.

Think of our monthly credit card statement. Do we look at the transactions for the month, or do we just pay the bill? The majority of people cannot honestly say they looked at it. Most will just pay whatever balance is owing on the bottom line. A tragic number of us will even just "take a guess" and make a payment without even looking at the statement for several months. Underestimating that balance is almost a certainty, as we have shown in our journaling exercises.

The fact is our lives are so automated, we may not even see a bill because we are set up on automatic payment plans. Living in this state of ignorance of what we are spending is a problem, and we need to step back and take a look at our statements.

Regarding bills, we need to look at statements because most of us do not read the emails they send to us. We either file them in a folder in our email, or we delete them. However, do we know if any of the subscriptions that send us notices have increased monthly subscription fees lately?

If we have Netflix, for example, did we realize that they have recently raised their prices twice in less than a year, and may be raising them again soon (Levy, 2021)? Most of us set up our auto payment and ignore it as long as we still have our movies, TV, or other entertainment. Even my trusty financial notebook has betrayed me in situations such as these, as the hard copy breakdown of my monthly expenses may be out of date within a few months.

It is for this reason and others that we need to look at our statements every month. Even if we don't receive them in the mail, we can log in to our account and get our monthly bill and statement. Our bank and credit card provider generally tabulate our payments online as they are processed, so we can check on our spending at any time rather than waiting for the month-end statement. Debit purchases are tabulated almost immediately, whereas credit card expenses may take a few days to be processed and accounted for online, so be aware that our running credit card statement may not be up to date every time we log into our account.

For our journaling activity, we need to print these statements out. Print out every statement for each subscription and service we have. Print out the statements for every credit card and bank account. Have I mentioned that most people have multiple credit cards, multiple bank accounts, and many are even clients with multiple banks?

We will want to print out the previous month and the month in which we are doing the activity to see a range of expenses and debts we may not remember or have missed in our expense tracker. Also, we will be able to see how many purchases may not ever be trackable if we don't hunt it down ourselves, such as those made with cash that was never put into the bank.

It is probably safe to say none of our automatic payments went into our finance journal, which is, unfortunately, expected. We set up the auto payments and forget them. They just come out of our account or get placed on our credit card, and we never even think about them again. Some of these could be purple elephants.

Before the advent of online banking and bill payment options, we always received statements. We had to balance our checkbooks and look at our credit card transactions.

We didn't necessarily track every cent, but we tracked our finances better 20 years ago than people do today. However, all is not lost, and we can easily get those statements to complete this activity.

**Pulling Out the Purple Elephant Gun**

So, let's jump ahead in time again. We have spent the last 30 to 45 days keeping track of every cent we spent. We have saved all our receipts. We have printed out two months of all our statements, bills, and banks, and now it is time to get down and dirty.

The first thing we will do is review all our credit card statements. For every transaction on the statement, verify the expense in our finance journal. If it is not there, add it into the journal at the end with the date, store, and reason for purchase. If it is in the journal, put a check by it and move to the next purchase. Do this for every credit card or line of credit statement that we printed.

Once we are done with the bill statements, move on to the bank statements. Make sure we have ALL accounts—checking, savings, and money market—that we pull money from each month. Check each debit transaction against our finance journal. If we missed a transaction, put it in our journal after our missed credit card transactions. If it is in the journal, put a check by it and move on to the next.

Once we have completed this, take a look at the statements again. Are there patterns in the transactions? Do we remember each transaction, or was it blind spending? Is it a subscription we forgot we set up or was it intentional? We then need to decide if the transaction is necessary, a splurge, an impulse, or a purple elephant.

Once we have reviewed our statements, check our finance journal and analyze it. How much cash did we use to purchase items? Were these items necessities or blind spending? Were they intentional? How many transactions were missed? All our receipts should match up to our credit card and bank statements, as well as journal entries. How many are we still missing that we forgot about or forgot to ask for? Decide how well we are using our money and how intentionally we are spending it.

Regulating our spending doesn't mean we can't splurge occasionally. Remember, an occasional splurge is acceptable, but they have to be under control. It is wisest to remember that most splurges should require compensation, i.e., "A treat because I've been good" actually has to mean something: We can have that rare gourmet coffee, but it will feel more earned if we can account for several other expenses, necessary or otherwise, which we deliberately skipped this week to afford that luxury. Not only does this compensation create a healthier balance in our spending, but it also gives us a greater appreciation for the luxuries we were dismissive of only a month ago.

For many of us, this activity is one of the biggest eye-openers of our lives, and it can be a little scary. We don't want to admit our spending habits, and yet here they are in our face. It shows us why we are living from paycheck to paycheck and have nothing left to invest or save.

In just one cursory culling of statements, I found three monthly subscriptions totaling over $80 a month which I had unknowingly been paying for quite a while. What I did is our next and final step in this activity: I got out my purple elephant gun and showed no mercy. The elephant gun in this case was that wonderful "unsubscribe" or "cancel my subscription" button. With three web searches and three button presses over about 15 minutes, I saved myself over $960 a year. That's a moderately luxurious week-long vacation or new major appliance right there.

Get the whole family involved. Have everyone set up their journal and expense tracker. If the children don't have phones or laptops, give them each a notebook to keep track of their spending. Maybe even spend a little extra to get notebooks with zippered pockets to keep the receipts in so they aren't lost. Explain to everyone exactly what they are doing for the next few weeks and what they will do at the end. Maybe have a weekly check-in to make sure everyone is still on task. It may take some creativity to keep the children motivated, but we need to remind ourselves that it is setting them up for financial success. Once we have our first journal all set up, we will start looking for the next hiding places that purple elephants love. This is why we need a second journal in the next chapter.

# 2

# HOUSEHOLD INCOME IS A FAMILY AFFAIR: TRACK YOUR TIME USAGE AND HELP THE KIDS MAKE THEIR OWN CASH.

**Step 2: Budget your time to increase your income.**

We've all heard the saying, "Time is money," and it has never been more true. Whether the time is spent at work or home, it can be used to make money.

Purple elephants often dig a hole we need to climb out of financially. We may not be at rock bottom yet, but we have no safety net if there is an emergency.

Many people do not have health insurance because they can't afford it—or so they think. Others have too little insurance on their cars, homes, and life. If there were an actual emergency requiring a hospital stay, many people would be drowning in debt. If an accident occurred and their car was totaled, their home burned down, or they died, it would not only be emotionally but financially devastating for the family.

Most of us don't want to live like that anymore— afraid of the financial devastation from the unknown. We want to know how to increase our monthly household income, and, if we have children, we'll want to understand how to teach them financial security for their futures at the same time.

Let's face it: We didn't learn this stuff in school and our kids won't either. It is a problem that no school system is addressing. If any were, there wouldn't be so many memes on social media sarcastically stating how much algebra we use because it is much more relevant than understanding taxes. In addition, they didn't bother teaching us about real-life finances, and they never taught us about time management and how time is equal to money. But, on a more positive note, you can now get university degrees in underwater basket-weaving, Afro-lesbian studies, and interpretive dance. I'm confident that their graduates will be bringing home the bacon in no time, and that their parents will never consider university tuition to be the single largest and hungriest purple elephant into whose gaping maw they ever shoveled their hard-earned cash.

But I digress.

We have had to learn about finances and time management on our own, or maybe we are still learning it. It doesn't matter where we were at, because the first chapter got us started on an excellent foundation for finances, and this chapter will help us learn to schedule and manage our time to make it work for us and provide more household income to our family.

This chapter works for single people, married people, people in domestic relationships, and single parents. It works for people with or without children or people who want children in the future. If we have children, we can start teaching them time management now, so they have an advantage in the future. We can use the ideas in this chapter to help them contribute to the household income.

That last sentence may have had you slam on the brakes and have you asking why your kids need to help contribute to the household income. We were taught to provide for our kids. Well, both ideas are true. However, when we look into history, teenage children and sometimes younger have always helped and contributed to household finances. Particularly in rural areas such as farms, ranches, and dairies, unpaid family labor is such an expected part of life that it is even required to be accounted for on our tax returns as a smart way of reducing taxable income. Whether our kid is mowing the lawn, washing dishes, or gathering eggs from a chicken coop, their chores can significantly contribute to household income.

No, I'm not talking about sending our kids to make sneakers in a squalid sweatshop in China. When children are babies and toddlers, just starting to learn the complexities of life, yes, we should provide for them completely. They need us, but we should also be teaching them. They need to learn the value of money and the value of earning money. Think about it: Did we have to do chores to earn an allowance? Most of us did. Some of us hoarded our money as kids, and sometimes our parents even came to us for loans in difficult times. This saving of money didn't mean we understood finances better. It just meant that we liked having cash around, and knew what was required to acquire it.

Having teenagers contribute to the family income is also about teens having summer or part-time jobs, or maybe helping out on the farm, to make money for buying the things that they want. Did we have to clean out gutters, babysit, or do other odd jobs as a teenager to earn spending money so we didn't have to ask our parents for it? Yes, we did, and those gutters were really gross.

When children do chores and we pay them an allowance—or teenagers get jobs and have their own spending money—they are contributing to the household finances. No, they aren't paying us rent or contributing to the bills with cash in most cases, but they are contributing. They are giving us more time by doing chores. Teens are earning money to buy their video games, pay for their subscriptions, or other items they want outside of what is necessary or what we are willing to pay. In both cases, we save money and have time to make more money. Plus, by having them do chores or make their own spending money, we are in the perfect place to teach them about being financially healthy, how to decide to use money wisely, and maybe even start investing at a very young age.

Since we are trying to learn to be financially healthier and want the same for our children, the whole family should participate in the activities outlined in these first two chapters. What better way to learn and support one another than to do it together? We can create a family goal to celebrate the destruction of the family's purple elephants and gain better financial health. If we complete the exercises and do the work, we will not only be rid of more purple elephants but will be on our way to meeting some of our long-term financial goals.

Remember, it is our everyday spending that determines the future of our long-term savings.

**Household Income Is a Family Affair Activity**

Whether your family is just you or includes a partner and children, this activity will help you create a firm financial foundation and will help you continue if your status changes in the future. There may be some sections that do not pertain to everyone at this time, but if there is a chance of children in your future, at least read the sections explaining how they can contribute to the household finances for future reference. I have seven weeks to get you on track, but the lessons can be naturally expanded upon and utilized in synchronicity with the expansion of your family for the rest of your life.

Household income is a family affair because everyone in the family uses the family income. It is used for paying rent or mortgage, food, utilities, gas for the car, and many other necessities. It is also used for extracurricular activities, nights out, movies, vacations, and more. When we think about the household income, everyone in the household should be contributing in their own way.

As mentioned in the last chapter, this activity should be done simultaneously with the financial journaling portion of our purple elephant hunt. We will each have two journals working in tandem with one another. Time is money, and we need to start viewing it that way. Utilizing our time better can help us make more money and help us get out of the hole our purple elephants have dug us into.

### Daily Journal

If we were using an expense tracking phone app for our finance journal, we would need a separate journal for this part. However, if we were using an electronic journal on a laptop or tablet, we can keep the two together in one file or even in one document. If we have a hard copy journal, that is also fine. Try one or two pages per day, depending on our daily spending and tasks.

We will keep this journal for the next month to six weeks, just like the financial journal. Each day, we will list everything we have done for that day and the time spent on that task. If we drove 30 minutes to work, we would enter on that day "Drive to work: 30 minutes." If we watched TV with the family that evening, the entry might say, "Watched TV with family: two hours."

It also means that if we spend 15 minutes on our cell phone, we add the entry. If we spent 30 minutes watching TikTok videos, we would add it. We need to account for every minute of every day, including sleeping and eating, walking or driving to a location, riding a bike, or whatever else the day might bring. Everything we and each member of our family do needs to be written down. Now, don't expect toddlers to participate, but for children in first grade, this would be an excellent place to start. Tweens and teens should be required to participate.

Why? Teaching children at a young age about time management and how to use their time wisely will give them a strong foundation for their future academic and professional careers. Also, children naturally begin to cost more in a modern household as they get older. The more they cost, especially for their hobbies, the more usage of household income they should be required to assume responsibility for. This is particularly true once they have their own phones and become interested in extracurricular activities which come with regular fees or paid subscriptions. The Barbie doll that cost Clem and Tottie $10 was an excellent investment at the time, as it kept little Rosemary entertained for the next six years. But now she is older, and her interests are leaning toward an anime streaming service that costs them $20 a month. Get her a journal. Make her use it.

Everyone in the family will track their time in this way. If the kids ride the bus for 45 minutes, they track it. While in school for eight hours, they track it, just as the parents track their commute to work and the time spent there.

**Important note:** We do not have to list everything we do at work and the time spent on each task while there, just as the kids don't have to track individual classes and assignments at school. It is actually important to simplify this journal quite a bit, to avoid mounting frustrations from family members who feel they are being ordered to account for every pair of socks they throw in the laundry bin. This exercise is more about where our time is spent daily, so just specifying that we were at work and the total number of hours spent there is fine. However, we should include the time away from work for lunch, especially if we are on the phone for any reason: All work-related and recreational screen-time must be tracked.

Now that the entries have been explained, we can see how having one journal and incorporating the financial and daily tasks on one or two pages will help us at the end of the 30 to 45 days better. We'll be able to more easily analyze our finances and time usage to find ways to get rid of purple elephants who no longer serve a purpose, and also to better finance those purple elephants that we want to keep. The more important something is to us, the more likely we are to consider it a necessity, and that sentimentality is not necessarily a bad thing. By using the journals, the things which are most important to us will become evident, and it will be easier to sacrifice the expenses that don't hold the same place in our hearts. It's about finding and redefining our priorities.

*Example of Daily Journal of Parent*

**September 15th**

- Woke up and got ready for work, checked phone: 5:30 a.m.–7:00 a.m.
- Drove to work: 7:00 a.m.–7:45 a.m.
- Work day-computer and phone: 7:45 a.m.–5:15 p.m.
- Drove home: 5:15 p.m.–6:00 p.m.
- Checked phone, changed, and helped with dinner: 6:00 p.m.–6:40 p.m.
- Dinner with family and cleanup: 6:40 p.m.–7:30 p.m.
- Phone and TV time: 7:30 p.m.–10:00 p.m.
- Last check of phone: 10:00 p.m.–10:30 p.m.
- Sleep: 10:30 p.m.–5:30 a.m.

*Example of Daily Journal of Child/Teen*

**September 15th**

- Woke up and got ready for work: 7:00 a.m.–7:45 a.m.
- Caught the bus to school/ checked social media: 7:45 a.m.–8:10 a.m.
- Locker/phone: 8:10 a.m.–8:30 a.m.

- Morning classes: 8:30 a.m.–12:15 p.m.
- Lunch and checked phone/games: 12:15 p.m.–1:00 p.m.
- Afternoon classes: 1:00 p.m.–3:20 p.m.
- Bus ride home and phone time: 3:20 p.m.–3:45 p.m.
- Video games and phone: 3:45 p.m.–4:55 p.m.
- Homework: 4:55 p.m.–6:40 p.m.
- Set the table and dinner with family/cleanup: 6:40 p.m.–7:30 p.m.
- Watched TV and phone: 7:30 p.m.–10:00 p.m.
- Got ready for bed and phone: 10:00 p.m.–11:00 p.m.
- Sleep: 11:00 p.m.–7:00 a.m.

### Side Hustle or Part-Time Job

You probably noticed in the examples above how much our phone usage overlaps the time of almost any other daily activity, which is what makes it one of the most difficult time-spenders to account for, yet almost certainly the most prevalent. The next time we sit down at a crowded coffee shop, particularly one populated by teens or young people, take a cursory glance around and note how many are holding conversations vs how many are holding their phones. The greater the number of people per table may reduce the amount of actual conversation: The couple on a date at table six is far more likely to be engaging in conversation and direct eye contact than the group of five teenage girls populating table nine.

Twenty years ago, this statement would have been obvious, but today it may very well leave us branded by society as a web-footed backwoods nutjob: Your kid doesn't need a damn phone.

For those who worry about contact in an emergency, we can rephrase slightly: Your kid doesn't need a damn smartphone. Talk. Text. Maybe GPS. Good enough.

Since it's become necessary to go back to the forgotten obvious to save our financial future, let's blow our minds with some elementary-level math.

The way to make more money is to work more hours.

Now, before we start ranting about not having enough time to spend time with our family as it is, think about it this way. Working more hours is not necessarily a permanent aspect of this plan to become financially secure. Depending on the depth of our debt pit, it may be only a short-term plan to get us on more solid footing. But the irrefutable fact remains: Studies show that, on average, people who work 10% more hours will earn 40% more income. That is a figure we cannot afford to ignore.

Some of us earn salaries, so working extra hours at our regular job does nothing for us financially, unless a lucrative promotion is being worked toward based on exemplary job performance. We don't get overtime even if we work more hours. Others work an hourly job and can get some overtime money for working more hours each week, and may even have benefits/bonuses which are paid according to hours worked. Still others work hourly, but the company refuses to give overtime by classifying any hours as part-time. However, even this can work to our advantage when we are in a tight spot. As an emergency response worker, I used to be assigned standby shift patterns which were technically classified as part-time but also required round-the-clock staffing. In this case, I didn't get paid overtime rates if my twelve-hour shift turned into sixteen or even twenty-four. However, it meant that there were plenty of regularly paid hours available if I felt like working a double. At the time, I was young and single. I took the money and was one of the highest-paid employees in my company while still operating at a grunt level. I took a hit to my social life for a few years, but the rewards were considerable. The only secret is showing a willingness to work, and extra work will be offered.

No matter what everyday job we may hold, we also need to consider a side hustle or part-time job.

It is often assumed that a side hustle and a part-time job are the same, but they are not. A side hustle may be a job that we can only do part of the time, but a part-time job is not a side hustle.

An employed part-time job is when we work for a company or store part-time after our primary job. A part-time job is often performed in the evenings or on weekends, depending on what hours we work in our primary job. As part-time workers, we show up, do the tasks assigned to us, and leave when our shift is over. For teens and students with limited work hours outside of their studies, a traditionally part-time position is likely to be their primary job.

A side hustle is when we work for ourselves outside of our main job hours. Technically, it is still a part-time job, but we are both boss and employee. A side hustle usually comes out of a hobby or preexisting knowledge base which can be used to earn money. Maybe we make crafts, clothes, or jewelry that can be sold on Etsy, eBay, or similar sites. Perhaps we are marketing wizards, so we start to do some freelance marketing work. Maybe we play around with graphic design, so we freelance as a graphic designer. Even downloading a simple video-editing software can bring value to our lives if we have artistic friends who are interested in turning their new song into a music video or who regularly create original content on YouTube.

With a side hustle, we bear the brunt of the work in terms of paying ourselves, paying taxes, buying supplies, and such. However, most of the time, we already have the materials and software, because they tend to stem naturally from our favorite hobbies. As for getting started as a freelancer, we can start for free on any number of freelance websites, such as Fiverr, Upwork, and others. The hard part of these sites is setting up and getting our first client. However, once we have everything ready and priced competitively, the floodgates open. Never underestimate the value of a few positive online reviews.

The best part of a side hustle is that we work from home, and we set our fees, prices, and hours. If we are working part-time for someone else, they decide our location, hours, and pay. A side hustle can be profitable while being much less rigidly structured, particularly in regards to time, which works to our advantage: If our main job requires us to stay late, we are in a better position to change our schedule at a moment's notice than we would be if we had to get to a part-time job immediately after our first shift ends.

The bad part about the side hustle is it can take time to get set up, to say nothing of getting consistent sales or projects. However, many people have eventually been able to quit their primary jobs because their side hustles start making more money, which gives them more freedom while doing something they already enjoyed.

Please don't assume it is not hard work, because it is. But, whether we start a side hustle or get a part-time job, our extra hours spent there will help us stabilize our financial foundation.

During the six weeks we are journaling our time, start looking at what we can do for a side hustle or what type of part-time job we would like. Don't try to work a full-time job and part-time job while working on a side hustle because that particular burnout is real and long-lasting. Look at our different options. Look at what we need to start our side hustle. We may already have everything needed for a startup, but we may also be missing some crucial items for monetization.

Don't start our side hustle or apply for part-time jobs yet. Just think about each and figure out which one will fit our life better and if we have something that we can use for an easy startup.

If we have a partner, have them do the same thing. Can they get a part-time job or start a side hustle to help out more? When we review everything at the end of the 30 to 45-day journaling, we may decide that our partner doesn't need to contribute in this way, and that's fine. However, have them complete this exercise, because, when we sit down with our family and analyze everything, we want all the options open.

At the end of the six weeks, we'll make the final decision based on all the factors shown in our journals.

### Getting the Kids Involved

Teenagers often want pretty expensive extras in their lives—video game consoles, games, and subscriptions to play with others online. They may collect items that are expensive, or want to go see their favorite band live in concert. They may also just want to be teenagers and go out on the weekend shopping, to the movies, or out for dinner with friends... all of which cost them/us extra money. And don't forget prom, school dances, class rings, and buying yearbooks.

All of these items are types of purple elephants. Yes, there are some that we will make sure our children have if they want them. If a teen participates in a school sport or activity, we will make sure they have the uniforms and items needed to participate. If the teen wants a class ring, then most of us who are sentimental over our own class rings will make sure they get it.

However, we do not have to pay for all their activities. As they get older, they need to be able to pick up the slack. If they want a yearbook every year that they are in high school, they can pay for that. If they want to go to prom, they can pay for the dress, rent the tuxedo, and buy the tickets. If they are taking a date to the prom, they can buy dinner.

As parents, it is our job to teach them to be responsible with money because we know from experience that schools do not teach them about financial stability. This means we need to help them find their first jobs to contribute to their spending.

We need to give them the necessities and some of the purple elephants, but going to the movies every Friday night with a group of friends should be paid for by them. They should pay for a new video game. A video game subscription or streaming service to watch anime that only they watch should be paid for by them. We are not responsible for these items. This is why teenagers need to get a job and learn how to have a solid financial foundation before leaving their parents' homes. Teaching financial responsibility and time management is what we as parents are most responsible for, outside of imparting strong moral values. If we can teach our kids those three things, we have succeeded as parents.

Teenagers that are too young to get a part-time job at a store or restaurant can do odd jobs around the neighborhood. There are dozens to choose from, and some vary depending on the time of year.

In the spring, they can clean up yards and gardens. In the summer, they can mow grass and weed flower beds. In the fall, they can winterize the gardens and flower beds or rake leaves. In the winter, they can shovel snow. We can use our knowledge of the neighborhood to help the kids out in the job-hunting process. Do we have neighbors who are elderly, or may have a disability that makes it difficult for them to complete additional household tasks, renovations, or yard care on their own? Those should be the first doors our kid knocks on.

If that doesn't appeal to them, there is no shortage of options. They can do painting projects, clean out garages, wash cars, babysit, and so much more. Just because they can't work in a real job doesn't mean they can't start contributing to their spending.

Once they are old enough to have a part-time job, they should be working at least one day a week. They should not be working so much that it interferes with school, and many locations in the United States and Canada say that teens can work 20 hours a week. Many people think that is too much during the school year, so 10 to 15 hours could be the maximum our family decides on. But if our teen shows an interest in work, wants to work 20 hours, and can demonstrate that it is not interfering with their education, let them work.

If our children are too young to work around the neighborhood or have real jobs outside the home, they can work in the home. Remember allowances? Children can do chores around the house to earn that. Parents can even have the children set goals or decide on items they want. They then have to do a set number of specific chores to reach the goal or earn the item.

Their help with chores will give us more time to work our part-time job or side hustle. In fact, the children can help out with the side hustle to earn money. They can do small tasks like measure, count, organize, file, answer the phone, and take messages, or do other tasks that are not hard. This will develop a strong work ethic, reinforce the math skills they are learning in school, and learn professional skills they will use in the future.

One way to teach the family about setting financial goals and working as a team to reach that goal would be to create a family goal, such as going to a theme park, on a cruise, or some other type of vacation. As a family, we decide where we are going and what we are doing. However, if the children want a say in the vacation, they have to contribute. Have everyone contribute to the vacation fund based on a set percentage of their income. In this way, everyone is contributing the same amount in relation to how much they make. If the child does chores, then make part of their chores be their contribution. Maybe take this time to teach them a new chore, such as vacuuming, cooking, or doing laundry. Little by little, chores become more than just a way to free up more time for parents: They become a way of teaching kids how to manage the daily routine of a household. Having everyone contribute to upcoming trips in this way means that the family vacation is truly a family vacation and not just a place Mom and Dad took the kids over the holiday.

And, if history has taught us anything, it is that working towards a goal gives people focus and a greater appreciation for the reward at the end of the rainbow. Even if a child's daily chores only allow us more time for our own work, explain to them how this is benefiting the whole family by reducing our household debt. Let them know their contribution has value and is appreciated.

At this point, we should be able to see exactly why our children need to work. It is not child labor, and any job, even chores, should not interfere with their education. Use this time to help them learn about short-term and long-term financial goals. Teach them about investing wisely. Teach them how to create a monthly budget to save and build their savings to reach their goals. The little jobs have become a part of their education. Use this time in their lives to teach them financial responsibility, and it will set them up for the life we wish we'd had.

**Analyzing the Household Income and Time**

At the end of the 30 to 45 days, it will be time to analyze the household income in terms of all family members. Each person in the family should have kept a journal of what their days consisted of and how much time was used doing the task. Knowing how each person uses their time will help the whole family decide what changes can and should be made.

This doesn't mean that every moment of every day needs to be associated with making money, but every day should have elements of productivity. Maybe create one day a week to be the family day, but other days can be used for the part-time job or side hustle.

Implementing a family day allows those family members who work a second job with required hours to have the time needed to share time with the family. When other family members are working their part-time jobs, those that have side hustles can work on their extra income tasks.

**Real-Life Time Management Example**

Let's look back to our example of the Chowder family. Clem and Tottie both have full-time jobs Monday through Friday from 8:30 a.m. to 5:00 p.m. Rosemary is 15 and in high school. Herb is 12 and in middle school.

The Chowder family have just finished six weeks of journaling their expenses and time, and are now analyzing everything.

Clem does woodworking and leatherwork as a hobby. He has decided that he will start an Etsy shop and maybe have a booth at some local craft fairs as a side hustle. Other items will be listed on eBay or local buy-and-sell pages on Facebook.

Tottie loves marketing, even though that is not her primary job. She has been reading everything she can on the subject and has taken some free classes on how to do it. She decides to have a marketing side hustle, using her husband's business to learn more. She plans on offering her marketing services in a freelance capacity.

Rosemary has had several neighborhood parents reach out to her about babysitting jobs several evenings during the workweek, with additional babysitting on weekends. She decides she will do that during the school year, but in the summer, she will be able to get a part-time job at a local fast-food restaurant as well. She also loves swimming, and plans to monetize her favorite hobby part-time at local pools, swim meets, and rec centers by getting her lifeguard certification.

Herb is too young for a part-time job with an employer, but he loves working with any kind of power tool, even if it is just pushing a lawnmower. He knows several older couples and single parents in the neighborhood and decides he will start a landscaping business to help them with gardening and lawn care during the spring, summer, and fall. He also begins working at Clem's woodworking venture in an apprenticeship capacity, honing his skill with saws, chisels, routers, drills, and sanders. Finally, he offers to do laundry, pet care, and other household tasks whenever time allows, to give his parents and sister more time to work in their respective jobs.

To ensure they still have time together as a family, they decide that Sunday is the family day, and they will spend time at home with each other on these days. In this way, the family unit doesn't suffer while they are working hard to reach their goals.

It is during this analysis that the family decided on a two-week vacation in Ireland next year. They figure out how much each person has to contribute based on their conservatively estimated income or chore equivalent. Since everyone is helping to plan the vacation, they are all excited to get started.

From this example, we can see how this will work. It does require buy-in by all participants, and this may not be as easy as expected. However, when we offer the children some say in the goals, the buy-in becomes a lot easier.

Also, note that part of Tottie's side hustle is to market her husband's side hustle. This means that Clem is free to focus on producing his lawn furniture and leather overlays while Tottie does the work to brand and build his business and customer base. This simple collaboration just created more work-time for both parents, and, even if Clem and Tottie agree that Tottie should be paid a fee from Clem for her services, she is still contributing to a considerable increase in his business, which more than offsets the fee and increases the total household income.

Looking at our own time and teaching our family to look at their time can help everyone learn more about time management and the importance of hard work. It is not about working ourselves or others to death. It is about creating a strong work ethic and financial foundation. Perhaps even more importantly, it teaches our kids how to monetize their interests from a young age, which is the first step in steering away from being stuck in a dead-end job that they hate. However, these are not the only areas of life we all need to work on.

Because coffee still exists.

# 3

# CONVENIENCE STORE, LIQUOR STORE, COFFEE SHOP, AND GROCERY STORE: AN UNHOLY ALLIANCE

**Step 3: Reduce cash and card spending in-store.**

Going to the store is an essential part of our lives in many cases, yet it is one of the primary sources of indulgent and splurge spending that needs to be wrangled to be less frivolous and more time/money-saving.

We have to buy food, so we go to the grocery store. We run to a convenience store on the way home from work if we run out of milk in the morning. We stop at the liquor store to pick up a case of beer for the weekend. We stop at the coffee shop every morning on the way to work because we deserve a pick-me-up and call it self-care.

Do we realize how much these purple elephants can cost us? In the example from the first chapter, Clem and Tottie spent about $336 a month on their morning commute before they even started budgeting gasoline. When we analyze our finances, we need to look at how much we have spent on "self-care," which is usually just Amethyst doing her dirty deeds again.

In this chapter, we will be learning how to find the purple elephants in our shopping routines. It will also help us create ways to keep them from storming the breach every time our hands grip the push bar of a shopping cart.

We may already do some of these tips and tricks, but others will be new to us. Remember, this is all about finding ways to have more financial security and saving time. We may decide, however, that some of these purple elephants are worth keeping, but it's best not to decide until after we have completed our activities. Our ideas and ideals may change at the end of the next seven weeks. And, even if we see an expense that is so egregious we know we need to get rid of it immediately, be sure to notate it in our journals first. Knowing the exact amount of money we have saved in the end is half the joy of hunting purple elephants, especially when extrapolated across an entire year.

**Convenience Store**

How often do we go to the convenience store? If we're not sure, we'll know at the end of the next six weeks because every time we stop there, we'll write it down in the journal and note how long we were there.

How many hours a week are we in a convenience store? If we smoke, possibly more than other people, but the fact is that we all end up in convenience stores, and it is never a good thing.

Even if we are just going to pick up milk, do we just pick up milk? If we say yes, we are either among the blessed few who do not impulse buy, or we are lying.

People are going into convenience stores more today than ever before because many convenience stores are also gas stations. In 2019, the average amount spent during a visit to a convenience store with a gas station attached was $22 (Gaille, 2019), but factoring in staggering increases in gas prices beginning in 2021, that average has risen dramatically. In fact, the depression associated with our gas pump total often leads to increased despair spending inside the store.

"Well, crap, I'm already $75 in. What's another three bucks if I get to drown the misery in Dunkaroos?"

To alleviate impulse, pay at the pump. Do not set foot in that store. This will keep the purple elephants hidden from our eyes, our nostrils, and our wallets.

However, that is not the only reason we should avoid convenience stores. The fact is that everything we buy there that can also be bought at the grocery store or drug store is going to be priced considerably higher because of the "convenience" they offer. How do you think convenience stores can afford to stay open and pay employees 24/7 when most of their business is done during the daytime? After a month of tracking expenses, you will never have to ask that question again.

If we are stopping after work when other stores are still open, we aren't paying for convenience. We are just paying a higher price for the assumed convenience of rushing in and out. Let's review our time and see if that is true. While it is true that lineups at the grocery store tend to be longer around rush hour, that same period after work is also one of the worst times to stop in a convenience store because everyone is stopping to fill up for the next day or for the convenience of grabbing some milk on the way home. Is it really convenient?

Convenience stores are never truly convenient and are too pricey. From this point on, unless it is a dire emergency, all convenience stores should be considered a purple elephant and avoided. Pay at the pump and avoid going inside at all costs.

## Liquor Store

My first "home" after high school was a rented, 2-bedroom apartment in a block of townhouses. It was a putrid craphole. I moved out a few months later after my warring neighbors living on either side of me decided to converge for a knife fight on my deck, requiring me to call the police that night and scrub arterial spray off my front door the next morning. Although the rent was what I could afford at the time, I eventually realized that I was the only person who lived alone in any of those apartments. My neighbors even expressed amazement that I could carry on without at least the aid of a roommate while working a minimum wage job. Everyone else living in that block had distant family members or multiple roommates crashing on all of their couches.

They also had stacks of liquor cases, bags of empties, and overflowing ashtrays outside every door.

Alcohol and cigarettes are not only a problem for the families dealing with obvious cases of addiction. Many people enjoy a glass of wine or beer in the evening. During a scorching backyard barbecue in the summer months, there's nothing like refreshing margaritas, daiquiris, or piña coladas. Or maybe your relaxation of choice is a tumbler of scotch on the rocks on a Saturday night.

Over 45% of people living in the United States drink some form of alcohol weekly (Boersma et al., 2020). Many believe alcohol in any flavor helps to alleviate stress, have a good time, and forget about our problems for a while. I still dream of that $90 glass of 100-year-old Rémy Martin Louis XIII Cognac which I indulged in while on a Beverly Hills vacation, even as I still hear the sobbing of the bean-counter angels floating above my shoulder. However, does alcohol help us in the ways we want to believe? Not enough to validate the money we spend on it regularly.

It is estimated that Americans spend about $650 a month on alcoholic beverages (Brenoff, 2018). The COVID-19 lockdowns beginning in 2020 saw that number go up considerably, as people saw increases in idleness, boredom, and depression. When we complete six weeks of journaling, let's pay special attention to how much we have spent on alcohol.

Even if we disagree with the morality of drinking to excess, and agree on the associated dangers of alcohol impairment, we rarely think about alcohol in terms of its financial cost to families. Booze is just Amethyst stumbling home with a missing high heel and a black eye after a rough night out. It does virtually nothing beneficial for us.

I drove a taxi for a short time, and I was always stunned by how many regular customers would call me almost daily for a trip to the beer store, and usually tip well out of a strange sense of guilt. They were spending a minimum of $20 a day just for the cab ride, plus the cost of their booze, smokes, and tip. That's at least $600 a month, just for rides to the store.

I once joked with one of my regular fares that, while I enjoyed our daily chats, she could probably save a lot of money by stocking up on booze only once a week. She gave one of the most sincere and depressing answers I've ever heard.

"It would be gone in two days."

In her mind, she was being responsible by calling a cab every day if it meant that she was only drinking 6 to 15 beers a day.

Frankly, the best way to get rid of this purple elephant is to stop drinking completely. Most people will balk at that, and anyone with an addiction will find it all but impossible, but it comes down to putting the needs of our family first. Instead, let's decide to only drink on special occasions. Don't stop for our weekly case of beer or bottle of wine. Forgo a drink with dinner when we go out. Drinking alcohol is not a necessity and should never be treated as one. Use it as an occasional splurge to make the act of drinking alcohol more special.

And, if you need help to stop, you already knew there was help available that you should have been reaching out for long before you picked up this book. Reach for it.

**Coffee Shop**

Most people reading this will not like the following statement, and, believe me, I don't like that I have to make it.

Don't buy gourmet coffee. No coffee deserves anyone's hard-earned double digits.

Many of us stop at one of several regular coffee shops most mornings, or even all, to buy a specialty coffee. The coffee shops are even making it easier for us—that devilish convenience strikes again—by adding drive-thru windows to their stores.

The fact is that we can make the same items at home. Buying an espresso machine is not cheap, but we can purchase one for less than what we would spend on our morning coffee in a month. We can buy the milk we like, the coffee we want, and the syrups and flavorings we like. When we buy and prepare gourmet coffee for ourselves, we will be getting the same coffee for about a third of the price of the one at the store. How would it feel for that $6 coffee to become $2 instead?

Even limiting our intake to our homebrew isn't good enough. Gourmet coffee should be treated as a once-a-week treat from now on. For every other day of the week... A one-quart bottle of generic instant coffee that will last well over a month costs $2.99. Just something to think about.

Sometimes, we don't have to give up the purple elephant. We just have to rework how we access what the purple elephant represents.

**Grocery Store**

The worst place in the world to go shopping without preparation is the grocery store. In the grocery store, we are more likely than ever to splurge or impulse buy. Why? While we are there, we get hungry, or we go in hungry. We try to figure out what meals to make for that week while we are pushing the cart through the store. We go in with the anticipation of filling a large cart, unlike when we wander through a convenience store where we may splurge, but generally only on one or two unneeded items.

Worst of all, we justify every single item we buy. Because they're groceries.

Some of us actually make a shopping list, but, for the vast majority of people, that only serves as a reminder of the items we need, and then we still impulse buy any shiny item that snags us by the periphery.

The truth is that the purple elephants at the grocery store will be hidden much better because we know we need food to survive, which means we have to go to the grocery store anyway. However, we don't have to give in to those impulses with a little planning and discipline.

### Make a List

The first elephant to destroy is the impulse or splurge purchases. This means not only do we make a list but stick to it. If it is not on the list, then the item is not purchased. This does take a little time, so let's look at one of the best ways to make the shopping list.

When making our list, we need to know what meals we will be making. Plan out our breakfasts, lunches, and dinners for a week or two based on our pay periods. Make sure we include healthy snacks to avoid impulse buying at convenience stores. We should shop only once a week, on or around our payday if possible. There is no reason to go to the store daily. Generations ago, that may have been needed,—at a time when milk showed up on our doorstep every morning and wheels had wooden spokes—but since the God-given advent of these funky little things called refrigeration, canning, and vacuum-sealing, we now have the option of weekly, biweekly, or even monthly shopping trips that will help stave off our grocery store purple elephants.

Once we have our meals planned out, go through our cabinets and refrigerator to find out what items we need for these meals. Some of the meals will only need a few ingredients from the store. For example, we don't need salt every time we go to the store. We may not need salad dressing or ketchup. Find the ingredients we already have. Decide if we have enough for the time and number of meals in question, and then, if we don't think there is enough, put it on the list.

Don't add items to the list that are not needed for meals or snacks. By only adding the required ingredients to follow the meal plan, it will keep the list to a minimum and will keep the cost down.

Just as important as sticking to our list while in the store is ensuring that it only has essentials written on it before we leave the house. Years ago, I had boarders who constantly forgot which items they had already purchased, which led to our communal fridge constantly being filled with multiple bottles of mayonnaise and maple syrup. They were extremely Canadian.

## *Shop the Perimeter*

Why is shopping the perimeter of the store a good idea? It seems contrary to financial reason. Shopping the perimeter of the store is more expensive, and the purpose of this book is to do away with purple elephants.

The fact is that yes, shopping the perimeter of the grocery store is a little more expensive, but not all that much. When we shop mainly on the perimeter, we are getting unprocessed and healthier foods for our family.

When our family eats healthier, they are less likely to have physical problems. A healthy diet can also help with many physical and mental issues because the food doesn't contain chemicals and preservatives that can throw the body out of whack. Going down the potato chip aisle is going to be cheaper than grabbing a bag of potatoes, but let's not delude ourselves into thinking it is benefiting us, even from a financial viewpoint.

We may have to get some items from the aisles, such as coffee, tea, and other drinks, as well as pasta, flour, and other often-used foods, especially in the frozen section. When we do have to shop in an aisle, check the labels and get the item we need with the least amount of chemicals, preservatives, or ingredients in general. This is easy when it comes to frozen vegetables, but other items will require us to be aware of their contents. Also, for the love of all-holy horse manure, avoid those frozen pre-made meals. While they can be convenient, and generally even delicious, their chemical and caloric count is through the roof. Not to mention that their comparative price as opposed to making the same thing from fresh ingredients isn't exactly a selling point when you stop and do the math on it.

Here's a fun little game I started playing a few years back that helped my health exponentially, and probably deserves a book of its own: "Don't buy anything that has ingredients." (Insert GIF of brain exploding.)

Shopping the perimeter and making meals from fresh ingredients can save us money in the long term. How? Since our family will be healthier, they will need to see the doctor, dentist, and pharmacist less often for the treatment of illness, tooth decay, and obesity-related issues.

I also used to work in healthcare, including performing home visits and wellness-checks: There were definite trends that I noticed lining the pantry shelves of my most frequently-seen patients.

This doesn't mean that our family will never get sick, but eating a healthy and nutritious diet can definitely help our wallets. Plus, we will know that we are doing the best for our family and teaching them the importance of nutrition and taking care of themselves. Especially when we consider the cold fact that the large majority of healthcare and hospital bills paid throughout North America are related to self-inflicted conditions such as obesity, smoking, drug and alcohol abuse, etc...

Preventative measures that cost us a little money in the moment are frustrating, because, if they work, we never see the health and financial problems that we are saving ourselves from. However, a quick perusal of national health statistics, coupled with the cost of repeated hospital stays, should be enough to open our eyes.

If we aren't living a healthy and disciplined lifestyle, we become our own purple elephants. Remember the end of George Orwell's *Animal Farm*?

*Coupons*

Another way to cut costs is to cut coupons. Another example of doing it old-school, because it still works. While they do not always appear in the Sunday newspapers as they did in the past, some websites and apps help to find coupons. Also, using the store's sale flyer can help us plan meals based on what is on sale. Use these to our advantage and we save even more money.

We've seen entire reality TV series dedicated to people who thrive by knowing the science of coupons, and it's an art that we should at the very least have a cursory understanding of. Coupon use varies by state, and even by nation,—Sorry, Canada, but your lack of "stackability" means that you won't be getting a nationalized version of *Extreme Couponers* anytime soon—but if we can legally stack coupons in exchange for huge savings, it's worth our time to dig out a pair of scissors, do a little napkin-math, and put that old printer to use.

The area where many extreme couponers fail is in the purchasing of huge amounts of useless or unhealthy items. We're still going to be sticking to the shopping list we planned out at home, but also do a little flyer research before we head out the door.

It's worth switching from our preferred brand of pork and beans if the off-name brand has a stackable coupon for $0.50 off this week.

### Buy in Bulk

The last way to save money on essentials from the grocery store is to buy in bulk when we can and do it based on the storage available in our home. Purchasing certain items, such as toilet paper, laundry detergent, paper towels, etc. in bulk will save us money. If we can't buy all the items in bulk immediately, do it over time, staggering the reorder dates to allow for the extra costs at that time.

Evaluate the household and then figure out which items make sense to buy in bulk. When we know what we want to buy in bulk, then we can do it via the Internet. We can use a store like Sam's Club or Costco, but the prices will usually be cheaper online. Figure out if the shipping makes a big enough difference or if we just like going to the big stores. However, remember there will be BIG impulse items in bulk stores. It is recommended to order online to stop the purple elephants before they creep into our world again, just because we get giddy anytime we hear the words "less overhead."

Trust me, I've been there: I had no idea I could buy that awesome chili-garlic hot sauce from China with the rooster on the label in two-gallon jugs, but we're never going to finish that thing during the ten years or so that it will end up occupying my precious fridge space.

**Extra Expenditures to Evaluate**

There are always extra ways in which we spend money. So many, in fact, that I can only give the most general ideas. You're going to have to determine those which are unique to you and your family in your journaling exercises. Evaluate your own expenses, and determine how to reduce or remove them completely.

*Other Shopping*

If we have to do other types of shopping, such as clothes/shoe shopping, side hustle supply shopping, school supply shopping, etc., do it all on the same day, and before we go grocery shopping. This will save time because we will do all the shopping simultaneously and allow us more time later in the day to relax or get some extra work done.

Bundling all the shopping into one day will also save gas as we will not be making multiple car trips from home. In most cities, and even small towns, stores are located close to one another in a downtown core or central shopping district, so it only makes sense to hit them all at once. As long as we remember that grocery shopping is not the only type that requires strict adherence to a list.

### Gas for Your Car

If we own a car, we probably fill up before or after work, but is that time-efficient? No. The best time to fill up the car is after we have done all our weekly shopping for that week.

By filling up the tank while we are out doing our grocery shopping, it means that all our errands are done, and we can put the remainder of the day to productive use. Plus, it will keep us from having to do it later in the week. Additionally, it is a waste of cash to top up a fuel tank that is almost full every day: Don't run yourself dry, but use most of the other 3/4 tank first!

However, some people will end up filling up more than once a week, particularly if they have longer-than-average work commutes. If that is the case, fill up on our way home and pay at the pump. This is an easy way to save time and money and can easily be implemented into our life.

Once a regimented schedule becomes just another daily routine, we make better choices without even noticing it. Anyone who has made a concerted effort to eat right and exercise will attest to this, and the same is true for our spending habits. Habits are the best thing in the world when they're the right kind.

### *Fast Food and Takeout Options*

When life gets hectic, we often put our need for food on the sidelines. We find ourselves stopping at a fast-food restaurant, running through a drive-thru so we can eat in the car between stops, or maybe we grab takeout afterward. Americans spend about $262 per month on eating away from their home (Credit-Donkey Staff, 2020). While this does include going to restaurants, the majority of it is spent on fast food and takeout options because our lives are hectic, inconvenient, and, sometimes, just because we need a hot dog.

Grabbing fast food happens for a variety of reasons. It could be that we have an evening class after work, and we think this is the only option to eat between work and class. Maybe our kids have soccer, dance, karate, piano, or some other activity after school, so this quick stop seems like the best option for getting something in their stomachs before the lesson starts.

Ordering takeout so that we can pick it up after our class or after the kids are done with their lesson or activity is almost as easy as fast food. However, we often tell ourselves that takeout is healthier, so it's worth it. We order it while they are still in their activities, or we order it right after class and then pick it up on our way home—convenient and healthy.

However, is either of these options all that convenient or healthy?

The answer is no, and most of us know that even though we don't admit it. Whether we are buying the food for ourselves, our children, or both, we know these are not the best options.

Takeout can be full of preservatives or may have been sitting in a steam-tray or under a heat lamp for hours before it was put in takeout containers and handed to us. Chinese food is either shining with oil or wrapped in deep-fried white bread. And anyone who has ever blotted the pepperoni grease with a paper towel is deluding themselves when they justify pizza as a regular purchase for their kids by saying, "Yeah, but it's got green peppers on it, too."

We use these options because they are convenient, and that is the only reason. They're not healthier or cheaper. We know we should give the kids a home-cooked meal, but on busy evenings or weekends, that isn't always an option.

Or is it? Can a home-cooked meal be an option during these busy times?

The answer is yes. Technically, we can make home-cooked meals in preparation for these times and bring them with us. We can heat them before leaving work, eat them in the car—I said in the car, *not* on the road—before running into class, or even eat them at our desks while finishing up the day's task before we leave work.

We can heat them and hand them to the children when we pick them up and have them eat as we drive them to their next destination.

We can also leave them at home and heat them quickly after we're all at home again. It may be a little later than a normal dinner, but the whole family will be eating a home-cooked meal. Crock-pot and pressure cooker meals are great for these days as well, so don't count them out. We learned to shop in bulk, and cooking in bulk is just as good an idea for saving time and money, if not more so: We can make soups, stews, casseroles, pasta, and chili in large batches, then ladle them into portioned containers and freeze them for a good meal when needed.

The best roommate of my life had a rice cooker on a nightly timer and always made enough to share. Uncle Roger was not lying: A rice cooker is one of the best kitchen investments we can make, and raw dry goods such as rice will save *exponentially* more money than buying microwaveable pouches or other processed instant varieties.

The truth is that we can remove fast food and takeout meals from our diets, but it takes a little work. We have to decide if we want this purple elephant to continue living with us or if we want to prepare some to-go meals to help save our health and finances.

Meal planning is already a new part of our lives to rid us of purple elephants, so taking it a step further to include meal preparation is not unreasonable. We can make it part of the day our family spends together. Or, if it is decided that either or both parents will not take on a part-time job or side hustle, and instead focus their time on managing the home, meal prep can be a huge part of their contribution.

We can make this work efficiently, but it will require a commitment to meal planning and preparation. Again, once we make commitments part of our daily discipline, they become second nature, just like after we managed to slog through that first miserable week of getting back into the gym.

### *Junk Food*

Another area almost as bad as fast food and takeout meals, and in many cases even worse, is junk food— candy bars, ice cream, cookies, cake, brownies, potato chips, and the list goes on. These are the foods we munch on while reading, watching TV or movies, playing video games, or when we are bored.

Review our daily task journal and see how often we eat out of boredom. It is an activity that impacts our health and wallet, and so it should absolutely be in our journal.

Standing in front of an open refrigerator door, staring inside like there are no food options in there, and then shutting the door just to grab a bag of potato chips from the cupboard is a common occurrence in most households. We know we should be eating healthy, but that bag of chips is just so much easier. It seems to all come down to convenience, along with the brief satiation provided by salt, sugar, and fats. And it's generally delicious.

Junk food is a purple elephant. We get used to having easily accessed foods to take the edge off when we are hungry or bored. We even manage to convince ourselves that junk foods are a good investment because they are processed and packaged, and therefore have a long shelf life as opposed to fresh produce which rarely lasts the week. However, the bottom line is that these foods are more expensive, less healthy, and typically give a short boost of sugar energy which then dumps us lower than we were before.

Since we are already meal planning, include snack planning as well. This may take a few times to get the items that are preferred and the amounts needed to cover the time frame, but it will be worth it. Plus, we can use these healthy snacks to tide the family over until we can get home for dinner when we have evening or weekend activities.

Finding easy and healthy snack ideas can be found just by searching the Internet, but we probably already know some foods we had as a child and loved. Some of these could include carrot sticks, celery with peanut butter or cream cheese, raisins with almonds, dried fruits, yogurt, and a host of other options. (I'm not saying that banning peanut butter from schools has directly led to the current epidemic of childhood peanut allergies. I'm just saying that my school had an annual peanut-butter-centric "Teddy Bear Picnic Day" when I was a kid, and nobody ever exploded.)

Any items we need to cut or prep can be done at the same time we are prepping meals for a quick heat-up on those busy evenings and weekends.

One last snack tip: Make the snack its own event with its own small time-allotment. The single greatest cause of overeating and obesity is combining snacking with other activities, such as driving, working on the computer, or watching TV. If we allot five minutes for a snack, we'll eat a couple handfuls of popcorn; If we sit down in front of the TV with popcorn, we'll clean out Grandma's old mixing bowl and lick the extra butter from the bottom.

All of this sounds like a lot of time spent planning, preparing, and cooking, but in reality, it is less time than we can imagine. It may take us longer the first few times, but we'll create a routine and have a flow down before we know it. In addition, if we do this with the family, it can be time well spent with one another. Teaching our kids kitchen skills is yet another daily aspect that we know we can't rely on schools for, and nor should we.

### Cigarettes and Other Narcotics (Legal or Otherwise)

Just like drinking, smoking is a purple elephant that is stealing money from our pockets. People who smoke a pack a day spend about $188 a month (Linton, 2021). Quitting smoking is one of the best things we can do to help our wallets and physical health.

It is not easy to quit smoking, but it is well worth our time and will save us money.

In addition, any other addiction we may have should be treated and stopped. Addictions are purple elephants that are dangerous. They shorten lifespans, damage relationships, destroy families, and inflict us with diseases that we may carry for decades. If you are reading this book, and you have an addiction—whether it costs you money or not—then you know what you need to do: Find someone to help you through the process and beat your addiction. Look for the resources and organizations available in your community, online, and beyond. You *can* beat this.

At this point, we realize that purple elephants hide everywhere, even in places that are necessities. By following the instructions and tips in this chapter, we'll be able to reprioritize the purple elephants from the grocery store and avoid them altogether everywhere else.

**Real-Life Shopping Example**

Previously, when Tottie went shopping, she would take Rosemary and Herb with her. The two of them would put extra items in the cart, such as extra chips, candy, ice cream, pizzas, and so on. Tottie didn't mind because she knew the extra food would be eaten.

Clem rarely went to the grocery store, but he would pick up milk, toilet paper, and other essentials at the convenience store by his office if he knew they were needed. He knew he was paying more at the convenience store, but it saved him time, and the whole family believed that he was helping out Tottie.

After the Chowders completed their journals, they realized that the extra items at the grocery store and the convenience store trips were adding to their grocery bill by over $300 a month. This additional expense didn't account for their monthly $336 in morning coffee or the beer and wine they bought every week. They knew if they were going to get out from under purple elephants, they needed to change how they shopped.

Moving forward, Tottie went to the grocery store alone and with a list. She didn't buy an item unless it was on the list. Clem started taking the time to run into the grocery store when they were running low on essentials instead of purchasing more expensive and smaller, temporary items at the convenience store. He still didn't care for grocery shopping,—it's always been a pet peeve of his that he can't explain—but the family's increase in meticulous planning meant that he ended up going shopping far less often anyway. Both Clem and Tottie decreased their beer and wine purchases to once a month. Not only did this lower their monthly grocery and shopping bills, but it decreased their alcohol intake, making them healthier by the reduction in sugars and carbohydrates.

Remember, it is okay to splurge occasionally on a treat, so long as we don't make it a habit every time we go to the store, and so long as we try to remember to compensate for those indulgent purchases in some way, either by skipping some other expense which we can do without for that week, or by also contributing the exact cost of the treat item to our savings, credit card payment, or a holiday fund. It's not exactly Inquisition-era self-flagellation, but we do learn to respect and appreciate treats more when we can demonstrate that we have earned them.

**Hint:** Dismissively saying, "I deserve this. I worked hard this week," is NEVER good enough. That statement is far too general, which leads us to use it whenever we get the munchies or other purchase impulses. A better-formulated statement would be, "I skipped my morning coffee every day this week, which offsets the price of ingredients for Rosemary and Herb's favorite chili nachos. They both did extra chores this week to help Clem out, and they've earned a family treat for Saturday night."

Mentally rationalizing, calculating, and compensating our treat purchases may seem ludicrous, but it's a fantastic benefit of becoming a skilled purple elephant hunter. Our minds will intuitively become a set of constantly tipping balance scales. We should even extend this practice to our journaling exercise: When we buy a treat item, identify it as such with a symbol or emoji, and notate the justification or compensation relating to it.

Let's be rigorous and disciplined in our grocery store shopping, and completely avoid convenience stores, coffee shops, and liquor stores. These actions will not only teach our children how to budget and save money but will help all of us build a solid financial foundation for the whole family.

# 4

## SOME PURPLE ELEPHANTS CAN'T BE CANCELED, BUT THEY CAN BE RESTRUCTURED

**Step 4: Consolidate debts and credit cards.**

We've completed the 30 to 45 days of journaling both our time and expenses. Now, it is time to start getting rid of the purple elephants. However, we can't cancel every purple elephant, nor should we. There has to be a balance.

This means that instead of canceling some of the purple elephants that take our money and time, we need to restructure them to allow ourselves more breathing room. We need to better budget our finances, while still enjoying some of the luxuries that we are blessed with in modern nations.

Before we move on, that last sentence is a point that I need to drive home, as some readers may feel that it is the polar opposite of what I've been talking about in this book: It does us no good to be thankful for our physical blessings if we do not take the time to enjoy them. Otherwise, we've wasted a gift that many people who are living in impoverished or oppressive nations can only dream of.

To be clear, frivolous or exorbitant living without purpose is a waste of life, which is why we see so many extremely wealthy people fall hard into reckless behavior, strings of meaningless relationships, substance abuse, crippling despair, and suicide. They are blessed beyond comprehension but feel no other purpose in life beyond gratification, which eventually wears off like the diminishing hit of a drug addict.

However, on the other side of that coin, living an appreciative life with the confidence that we have given our family a work ethic, strong moral values, and the hope of a prosperous future is truly the American dream. People from around the globe do not flock to America for the promise of an easy life. They want to work, just as we all do, and they flock to America for an opportunity to build something they can truly call their own. That's the freedom that drives us all, and it's the reason that the line "life, liberty, and property" was very nearly put into the Declaration of Independence rather than the famous "life, liberty, and the pursuit of happiness." Owning something of our own,—particularly in the wake of subservience and stewardship to a monarchy—was considered by the founding fathers to be near-synonymous with the attainment of happiness, and the primacy of property ownership in the western world goes back to the Law of Moses, sometime around 3,500 BC.

So, take that, Commies!

Most of us don't think about credit cards, mortgages, loans, and other seemingly necessary monthly bills as being purple elephants, but the fact is they are—or at least they are to a point. In the infamous words of Bane, executed so memorably by Tom Hardy, "I am necessary evil!" (I don't care what the basement-dwelling keyboard warriors say: *The Dark Knight Rises* was just as good as *The Dark Knight*. Fight me.)

Other forms of loans, such as a line of credit on the equity in our homes and higher education loans, are purple elephants as well. It is normally best to do without them if possible, but, as with almost any aspect of our finances, there are exceptions, such as investment loan strategies. If we need a line of credit for an expensive repair or if we need the educational loan for college, then we have shouldered the burden of even more purple elephants. While they may have been legitimately necessary, we need a good plan in place well in advance for them to be paid off or, if possible, restructured.

In addition, we may have medical bills that weren't adequately covered by our insurance. Many people in the United States, Canada, and other developed nations do not have sufficient insurance for emergencies, or even find out that their insurance products are severely under-funded after years of devotedly making regular payments. These bills are a form of purple elephant that can't always be avoided.

What you may have noticed by this point is that your individual needs will be dependent on the stage you were at in your life when you picked up this book. Are you a single person, or do you have a large family depending on you? Are you renting a home, paying a mortgage, or still in school and living with your parents? Covering all our options can be confusing, but just remember to break every strategy down to the very basics: Get the journals, and use them to dissect our financial lives. Whatever state or stage of life we may be in, we can follow these steps to improve it.

In this chapter, we will be discussing consolidation or restructuring debts so we can pay them off faster and alleviate the crushing weight of our purple elephants. We will also discuss financial options for homes, whether those be mortgaged or rented, and which one is best for your unique situation.

**Consolidation Is the Name of the Game**

When the term consolidation is used, it usually means the action of rolling up all of our similar or excessive bills into one lump-sum debt and thenceforth making only one payment. Sometimes, this means consolidating only a surplus of credit card balances into one new credit card, but it can also mean refinancing our homes, vehicles, or other possessions, or applying for a consolidation loan to combine a variety of debts into one.

This chapter is where we break down the options and give the facts. From there, we can decide what works for our family and living situation, and cull a few more purple elephants.

Consolidating bills doesn't mean that we will be paying off everything in a couple of months. It means that we will be paying the debts off over time, but in a streamlined format that is easier to keep track of, and will often save us both time and money. Instead of having five or eight bills, or even more, that we pay sporadically across the month, we will have just one bill to pay, and often at a far lower rate of annual interest.

**Credit Cards**

Credit cards are purple elephants, plain and simple. They help us build our credit, and they are often necessary for such things as automated payment plans, airline tickets, and hotel reservations. However, despite their obvious utility and convenience, they have also been the downfall of many families, leading to extreme debt and loss of possessions. Credit cards are a necessary evil and need to be utilized wisely.

Credit card debt helps and hurts many people. It helps us build our credit history, but it can also become so overwhelming that we may feel we can never get above the debt. There are several ways to overcome that overwhelming feeling while figuring out the best way to restructure our credit card debt. Knowing these things will help us make a more informed decision.

First, it's not enough to know the names of our credit cards. We need to be familiar with the issuing bank. We also need to know our current balance, our minimum monthly payments, and the annual percentage rate (APR) for the card.

Having this information will let us know how much we need to budget each month for credit cards and how long it will take us to pay off each card while making minimum payments only. If we're not great at head/napkin math, there are free online calculators which simplify the process of working out a payment plan from debt with compounding interest.

When we start looking at that, we realize that we are paying well over the bottom-line balance because of the APR, which can be well into the double digits on many credit cards. Once we have this information, we look at options to consolidate our debt.

### *Debt Counselling Service*

One way to consolidate credit card debt is by utilizing a debt counseling service. These services help us figure out how to pay off credit card debt in the best way possible. In addition, obtaining help from an accredited debt counseling service can stave off foreclosures and repossessions in many instances. These types of services do charge fees, but, for the most part, that fee is nominal when we consider the path to financial freedom that the service offers. They will contact all the credit card companies to negotiate a payoff, collect our scheduled payments, and then disseminate the payments to the creditors on our behalf.

If we are working a full-time job and a side hustle, this may be the best option because they are doing all the legwork so we don't have to.

### *D.I.Y. Debt Consolidation*

The next option is the D.I.Y. version of the debt counseling service. The D.I.Y debt consolidation has two primary ways to focus the payout method. These include the **Debt Snowball Method** and the **Debt Avalanche Method.** We will discuss these in more detail later in the chapter.

Once we pick a method, we stick with it until we pay off all the cards. There are advantages and disadvantages to the D.I.Y. methods, so, before we choose an option, let's look at it a little more closely.

Some of the advantages:

- It will help create a budgeted payoff plan.
- It requires no new fees, lines of credit, or loans.
- It can help us to create a budget strategy that we can continue to use in the future, and even greatly increase our savings and investments after the debt is paid.
- Paying down credit card debt and keeping balances low raises our credit scores.

Some of the disadvantages:

- Budgeting payments can be hard if our income fluctuates every month.
- It doesn't work as well if we have a hard time regularly meeting monthly minimum payments, as both methods require tightening our belts to make some amount of overpayment for a time.

- It requires tenacity to continue on track and not deviate from the payoff plan.

### Balance Transfers

The next option is the balance transfer. This form of consolidation means that we open a new credit card, preferably with a lower interest rate, and move the balance of all our higher interest rate card balances to it.

However, before we run out and open up a new credit card, we need to do the research. For example, make sure the interest rate is lower. Also, review the credit card company's terms and conditions. Sometimes, there are fees associated with transferring balances from other credit cards.

The best options are credit cards with an introductory 0% interest rate for a specified length of time. These introductory offers are usually for six months to a year. This gives us that time frame to pay off the balance as much as possible before the actual APR kicks in and adds to the balance. This makes a 0% introductory rate card ideal for balance transfers concurrent with a D.I.Y. debt consolidation strategy: It keeps us motivated to get the most value from our chosen method, particularly during the teaser period. We can get a lot accomplished in six months with 0% interest if we put our minds to it, which leaves us with a lot less owing by the time we start paying the balance plus interest again.

Even if we find a card that has a 0% introductory APR, we need to research to ensure that the actual APR is less than that of our current card. This way, we are not just setting ourselves up for extra debt when the teaser rate expires. Remember, the last thing we want is a lateral move, but rather a move to a more rapidly reduced debt, which requires both a smaller balance and lower APR.

### *Mortgage*

Unless you are still a young person living at home, we all need rent or mortgage payments so that we have a place to live. Traditionally, the real purple elephant is considered to be paying rent. After all, paying a mortgage is also an expense, but, in the end, we have something to show for those payments: A home to live in forever. The consensus is that we don't have anything to show for our time and expense when we are only renting a property. If we have to rent for now, that's fine, but most people will make it their goal to buy a house, condo, or lot of land sometime soon.

HOWEVER! Pull the reins and whoa up for a moment. Buying a home is not always the joyfully tear-filled hug-fest which HGTV would lead us to believe.

Remember, it was an over-eagerness to make everyone a homeowner that primarily contributed to the 2007/2008 Subprime Mortgage and Housing Market Crisis. This burst economic bubble crippled the global economy in ways not seen since the 1970s Oil Crisis, and which would not be repeated for another 13 years until the 2020 Coronavirus pandemic. The concept of "predatory lending" has been primarily blamed for the housing crisis, possibly because blaming Wall Street is always the easiest solution. However, even this is highly controversial, as the widely crapped-upon greedy bankers seem to have been the most incompetent greedy bankers in history, which isn't quite in keeping with their historic reputation as "the smartest guys in the room." I have yet to hear a good explanation as to how giving out loans and mortgages which the lender can never hope to have paid back makes bankers richer and more evil. Seems more like a lose-lose from a straight-up dollars and cents perspective... which is exactly what it turned out to be.

One thing that is far less popular to discuss—but is very necessary to consider before buying a home—is the compassionately intentioned government legislation in the United States which mandated an across-the-board easing of mortgage lending requirements. This was done in the interest of helping lower-income families, particularly those living in predominantly minority neighborhoods, to buy their first home. On the flip-side, a little way to the north Canadian Prime Minister Stephen Harper vehemently opposed the implementation of similarly proposed legislation, as did the majority of lending institutions in Canada. As a result, the motions were rejected, and the housing market collapse did not directly impact Canada. The value of the Canadian dollar, which generally only averages around $0.75 of its American counterpart, actually surpassed the US dollar on September 20th, 2007. I know that a lot of people may not enjoy the realization, but America's equity-driven strategy of moving every eligible—or woefully ineligible—family into the ranks of homeownership seems to have played a huge role in tanking the global economy.

As with any global crisis, the exact cause is rarely as simple as the most common—i.e., "loudest"—talking points would have us believe, which is why Twitter is the stupidest and most worthless innovation in modern history. (It's not enough to just delete your account and remove the app: If you have Twitter, and if you can do so safely in accordance with any state-mandated campfire bans... *literally set your phone on fire!*)

The bottom line is that we have to figure out if even home-ownership is a necessity or a purple elephant we can live without. We have to carefully examine every option of our financial lives, and do a little "calculator and napkin" work for ourselves, rather than just signing on dotted lines and believing the soothing reassurances of whoever's pushing the pen into our hands.

Short version: Buying a house is great. But it may not be necessary or even beneficial for you.

Recently, many successful financial strategists, including the infamous billionaire investor and notably blunt-mannered *Shark Tank* star Kevin O'Leary, aka "Mr. Wonderful," have touted the advantages of remaining in a rental home for as long as possible, particularly for lower-to-middle income households. Before I was even aware of this being a legitimate long-term strategy, I knew for a fact that I had been able to save and invest far more money while I was renting. This realization caused me no shortage of frustration after I bought my first home, even though my rent and mortgage payments were almost identical.

If nothing else, renting can be a fantastic opportunity to kick-start our investments for a few years while we also put away money for the down payment on a mortgage. If we can get enough wealth growing in investments early on, it more than compensates us in the long run for getting a later start on our mortgage. And, by that, I mean that some people may choose to rent a home throughout their working years or longer, sometimes only buying a home when they are ready to retire, or even years after retirement. Some people have even rented homes for the entirety of their lives and still managed to have a very comfortable retirement. That's where smart early investing comes into play.

Again, the decision to buy or rent will often come down to our unique family circumstances. It is just prudent planning to be aware that we can live frugally and wisely with either a mortgaged home or in a rental property. I discuss money-saving strategies related to the home in much greater detail in my first book, *You Can't Have My Money!*, but I reiterate it here just to emphasize the point that a rental home may not be the sinister purple elephant that entire generations have told us it is. In many cases, it may be our best option with some truly shocking long-term benefits.

A mortgage is another purple elephant that can be restructured and reduced, creating a better financial foundation. There are three reasons why we might want to refinance: to lower monthly mortgage payments, to pay off a home sooner, or to use some of our home's equity. Since we are trying to reduce debt, refinancing mortgages to take out equity in the home is not really a topic for this book. Most people reading this book are probably more interested in lowering monthly payments to be able to pay off other bills and loans that have a higher interest rate faster, or they are on a very tight budget and just need a little breathing room. However, learning how refinancing a mortgage can lower our monthly payments and pay the principle off sooner are topics for us to discuss. Either way, refinancing the mortgage is an option. There are several options for refinancing that will help us lower our payments.

We may be in our forever home and know that we will never want to leave. If this is the case, refinancing for a longer length of time may be the best option. This means that our loan will have more payments over more years, but the payments will be lower, especially if the interest rate is lower than our current mortgage.

Another way to lower our mortgage payments is to refinance from the traditional mortgage to an ARM mortgage. An ARM mortgage gives us a lower interest rate for a specified length of time, and then the interest rate will increase to a specific rate. For someone who is hoping to move within the next few years, this may be the best mortgage option.

If we don't like the idea of paying for a longer time or having the interest rate change, and we can pay a little more on the mortgage at this time, we may want to consider refinancing our mortgage for a shorter loan period.

The most common change is refinancing from a 30-year mortgage to a 15-year mortgage at a lower interest rate. When choosing this option, we will pay off our mortgage sooner while having paid less in interest.

However, if we can't find a 15-year mortgage with a better interest rate than we already have, there is another way to D.I.Y. by paying off our loan early. Some banks offer this program, but doing it on our own is pretty easy. This option takes some commitment but works just as fast without all the paperwork and hassle of refinancing, and we keep our current interest rate. There are two ways to do this. Both work—one way just works in half the time of the other.

The first way is to pay half of our monthly mortgage payment every two weeks. We will still be making a full mortgage payment every month, and, in fact, we will make one extra full mortgage payment a year. Paying on our mortgage every other week means we will make 26 payments, adding up to 13 months' worth of mortgage payments every year. In 12 years, we will have paid for 13 full years of mortgage and also saved an entire year's worth of interest. Using the biweekly payment method is not the fastest way to pay off our mortgage, but it is faster than just paying monthly, and should still be able to shave years and thousands of dollars off our payments.

The second option is to make full mortgage payments every other week. With this option, we will be making 26 full mortgage payments every year. This more than doubles our regular annual payments, which will hypothetically pay off our mortgage in less than half of its regular amortization period. However, the obvious drawback to this is that many people can't afford to make more than double their regular payments, especially if they have as many purple elephants as the average American. On the other hand, that is where this book can come in handy: A lot of Americans could afford this expedited pathway to full home-ownership if they could only purge a few Tyrians and Amethysts from their credit card statements. As we have shown, in many cases hunting purple elephants can easily free up hundreds or even thousands of dollars a month.

Alternatively, a mixture of the two methods can also work. Making at least half of a mortgage payment every two weeks, but increasing the amount whenever we can, can merge these options and give us breathing room as well.

As a bonus, some mortgages will offer one day of the year, generally the home's closing date, wherein a certain percentage of our mortgage principal can be paid down without interest. For example, if we signed off on our mortgage on December 14th, then every subsequent December 14th we would have the opportunity to make a payment of up to 25% of the balance owing on our mortgage principal, interest-free. It is *definitely* worth our time to run the numbers on that early on. We can carefully save up for that annual lump payment, which can also save us thousands of dollars and years of payments. Even if we can't save up the full 25%,—which, honestly, the majority of Americans would find very difficult —we should still try to save up as much money as we can for that one special day. And, the more we can pay toward the principal balance in the early years of our mortgage, the sooner we can pay off our home, as that interest-free 25% will be reduced to a smaller eligible amount with each passing year as our mortgage is paid down. If we can do it, let's try to make that additional payment in the first five years and see how much of a difference that can make.

Knowing if, how, and when to refinance is half the battle, so we need to talk with our banks and a variety of mortgage companies. We need to know what they can offer us before we decide if refinancing is our best option, or if we can restructure the debt on our own.

### *Educational Loans*

Many people in today's society have an extreme problem with student loans. These loans are easy to become ensnared in, because they are generally low-interest with long amortization periods, and we all want the education necessary to procure our dream jobs. However, in the process, we may end up making payments to two, three, or five different loan companies to pay off educational debt. The good news is that there are ways to consolidate loans even between spouses so only one payment is made, and it is usually lower than all the payments we are currently making.

We must be aware that there are many scammers out there, and even legitimate companies that say they will help us lower our payments for an ongoing fee. Avoid anyone that charges repeatedly. Those fees are purple elephants, and precisely what we are trying to remove from our life.

Reputable student consolidation loans and refinance loans do not charge a fee and typically have a comparable interest rate to your current loans. We should reach out to several companies that offer student refinancing and see which one works best for us. We may be able to consolidate all the loans in such a way that we are paying less over a shorter period. Do a little research, and we can get rid of the student debt purple elephant.

### *Consolidation Loans*

Consolidation loans can be a great help, but they can also be a great destroyer. Many times, these loans have very high-interest rates, with zero wiggle room. For example, as opposed to an unsecured "safe risk" personal loan which we may be able to negotiate with the bank if we have sufficient income and a strong credit rating, others may require the loan to be secured to collateral such as our mortgage. Then, if we ever decide to sell the collateral item, the entire balance owing on the loan must be paid to the creditor first, which can take huge chunks out of our anticipated sale proceeds.

As a personal example, a very ambitious change in opportunity once compelled me to sell a home while another loan was still attached to it. It was the best move for my family and one which we have never regretted. However, while it was nice to have one less purple elephant to feed every month, losing several thousand dollars from a lump payout will always be very annoying, especially when you've already been getting the sneaking suspicion that your buyer is intentionally "nickel and dime-ing" you. (Note to skinflint home-buyers: After weeks of blatant undervaluation—It had a furnished two-bedroom rental suite in the basement with full kitchen and laundry, for Pete's sake!—those few bucks in mortgage payments that you managed to save every month on a FREAKIN' INCOME PROP-ERTY are thousands of "right now" dollars out of the seller's plans. Don't be that guy.)

I digress.

Some consolidation loans only deal with credit card debt, but others allow us to include all bills. These all-encompassing consolidation loans allow us to add credit cards, medical bills, student expenses, and other lines of credit so that we can make just one easy monthly payment that initially seems to be less. Just be sure that it is.

Before we decide on a debt consolidation loan, we need to research what is required and what we are willing to accept. Any loan that has an interest rate of 20% or higher is ridiculous and should be avoided.

There are plenty of consolidation loans with low-interest rates, but don't sign anything until we are sure of what they are, and exactly what security is required. We have to be smart enough to not rush into debt consolidation, especially if we can competently strategize our own methods, as we will discuss next.

### Debt Snowball Method

Now let's discuss the Debt Snowball Method. This is a strategy to pay off all our debt, starting with the smallest amounts and ending with the largest amounts.

How does this work? It's not complicated. The first thing we need to do is list out all of our debt and bills, then organize them in order of how much we owe to each one, from least to most. Let's say we have a gifted store credit card that is only carrying a balance of $200. This credit card would be the first item on our list. We may still owe over $14,000 on a vehicle, and it is our most significant source of debt. The car payment would be listed last.

For the sake of a simple example, we will say that we only have the four following purple elephants which we need to snowball, with the interest rates of each one already factored into the repayment plans so the amounts are not subject to change:

1. A gifted store credit card with $200 owing, and a minimum monthly payment of $40. Making minimum payments, it will be paid off in five months.
2. A home renovation loan with $1,200 owing, and a minimum monthly payment of $100. It will be paid off in twelve months.
3. A home furniture set purchased on a payment plan with $2,400 owing, and a minimum monthly payment of $150. It will be paid off in sixteen months.
4. A new SUV with $14,000 owing, and a minimum monthly payment of $500. It will be paid off in twenty-eight months. At this time, we will be debt-free.

Please note: In reality outside of this simplified example, our snowball expense list will be dynamic, and, as we pay off debts and incur new ones, we will need to update it. Updating at least quarterly will be required to keep us on track, paying off everything as expediently as possible. But, for now, we will just look at the basic procedure to see how it works.

Do not stop making the minimum payments on any of our listed debts, ever. This method is entirely dependent on knowing and consistently making all minimum payments, and being able to maintain that payment rate for a long period... which is what we had miserably resigned ourselves to doing anyway, particularly if we've missed payments in the past, which increases our interest and lengthens our payment period.

Let's snowball these suckers.

Within three months of creating this list, we paid off the smallest item, the $200 credit card debt with minimum payments of $40 a month. This could be technically be done by making only the minimum payments for five months, but the fastest solution is throwing extra payments on that smallest debt whenever possible. In our case, we could afford a small $30 overpayment, so we paid $70 every month to pay it off completely in a little less than three months, and we'll round that up to three. At the same time, we were only making the minimum payments on everything else on our list. When the small credit card is paid off, we immediately cancel it and remove it from our list.

Now we're in the fourth month. We change focus to the second-smallest bill to be paid off, the $1,200 home renovation loan with monthly minimum payments of $100, which we have been dutifully paying for the past three months, so there is now only $900 left owing. We continue to pay the $100 minimum. However, we will now add to that payment the same amount we were paying for the credit card: $40 minimum payment with a $30 over-payment. Please note that we are still only paying the same amount that we've already been spending for the past three months, but suddenly our home reno is being paid at a rate of $170 every month instead of $100. Instead of twelve months, the loan is paid off in about 8.3 months. We'll say eight for simplicity.

We're not done yet.

It's month nine, and we're moving on to our second-largest bill, the $2,400 furniture set with $150 monthly payments. Having been faithful in our payments for the past eight months, there is now only $1,200 owing. But now, while still only paying the same amount that we've paid from the beginning, we can add the $170 we paid for the reno to our furniture payment plan, so we're paying $320 a month instead of $150. And, instead of sixteen months, the furniture is paid off in 11.75 months—Call it a year for simplicity.

It has now been a year of making minimum payments on the SUV, so the $14,000 balance owing is down to $8,000. We snowball the $500 minimum payment with the three other combined payments and the original overpayment, so we can now pay our vehicle off at a rate of $820 a month. 9.75 months later,—let's call it ten—our SUV is fully paid off.

We are now debt-free. It happened in twenty-two months, six months ahead of schedule, and all we had to do was pay the exact same amount every month, in this case about $820. And what would happen if, since we're already in the groove of it, we just kept making that same payment into a long-term investment fund for the next six months?

At the end of twenty-eight months in either scenario, snowball or no snowball, we're debt-free, having paid a total of $17,800. But with the Debt Snowball, we're debt-free six months earlier, and we have an extra $4,920, conservatively earning 6%-8% a year if we've got a good financial manager or life agent.

The whole idea behind a Debt Snowball is that it gets us accustomed to regularly paying a set amount, but that amount becomes more and more beneficial the longer we can continue doing it. For example, what if we also had a home mortgage, making biweekly minimum payments of $500 for an annual total of $13,000, but hadn't included that in our original snowball, which was reasonable at the time because we wanted to start with something simple and not complicate things too much. However, after twenty-two months, all of our other debts have been eliminated, and we are now excited by how manageable the entire process was. We decide to continue, now adding that same monthly payment of $820 we had been using in the snowball to pay down our mortgage faster. While still only paying the same amount which we have grown accustomed to paying monthly for almost two years now, we are suddenly paying down our mortgage at a rate of $22,840 a year: An annual payment increase of $9,840.

To make matters even better, our mortgage provider offers us a bonus in the form of an optional, interest-free payment directly against our principal balance, which can be made once a year on our closing date, December 14th. So now, instead of paying an additional $820 to our mortgage every month, we save even more money—and snowball our mortgage even faster—by paying the $82o into a High-Interest Savings Account, or HISA, every month. We set up an automated payment plan which will pay the total balance of the account, plus any accrued interest, to the principle of our mortgage every December 14th. Even if the HISA interest rate is only 1.2%, which is fairly decent for most banks, that still means that— instead of $9,840 being paid to both the principal and interest—we are now paying an extra $9,904.20 directly to our principal every year. This dramatically reduces both our amortization period and the amount of interest we will pay.

And it all started with budgeting in a single overpayment of $30.

People have asked if the Snowball Debt Method could be reversed, i.e., focusing all efforts on paying off our largest, and naturally most frustrating, debt first. The answer is yes, but it is far less efficient, both in cost and time. To pay off our largest debt at a considerably faster rate, we would need to have the available resources to make a considerable overpayment on it every month. Otherwise, most of our smaller debts would already be paid off at their minimum rate by the time our largest debt was even slightly reduced. It is true that once our largest debt is gone, we would have a very large amount of carryover to completely pay off the rest of our debts in a very short time. However, the amount needed to rapidly pay down our primary debt is more than most people can maintain over any amount of time.

Again, it cannot be overstated that in our previous example, the entire Debt Snowball sequence—which considerably shortened the amortization period of every single debt on our list—was triggered simply by making an additional overpayment of $30 a month. In fact, it could have been accomplished in a slightly longer amount of time with no initial over-payment at all, so long as each minimum payment was subsequently diverted to the next smallest debt after they were paid off.

So the Debt Snowball truly is a feasible plan and can be accomplished with nothing more than discipline, a list, and a slight initial overpayment if you want to utilize the fastest variation. If the Chowders were the family in our example, they could budget an extra $30 by diverting away less than 9% of their monthly coffee budget. Skip the maple flakes and whip.

We can see how this technique could be extrapolated to include every single debt we are currently stag-gering under, including the single-largest debt for most people, our home mortgage. If we were already able to consistently make our minimum payments right from the beginning, this technique simply maintains that for a longer time, ideally for as long as we're able. As our debt dwindles, our remaining payments are ramped up, and, once all of our debts are fully gone, we carry on into the wonderful world of surplus cash purchases and investable savings.

Technically, the Debt Snowball works because we just never stop paying the previously paid bills, in the sense that we are using what would have been allocated to them to pay off what's left of our current debt faster. The process gains momentum the longer we continue to use it. The more smaller debts we wipe out, the faster the largest debt is paid off, like gleefully rolling a snowball down a hill to build the base of a snowman.

You're picturing a bunch of adorable, chubby-cheeked elephants having a snowball fight right now. Stop it! They're psychotic! Ever heard of the Lindbergh baby? That was *them*.

And, just because I'm a red-blooded, flag-waving, Commie-smearing Capitalist bastard down to my putrid core, I will briefly mention that there is a *very* interesting variation of the Debt Snowball Method which I developed years ago. It is not so much for dealing with multiple debts, but rather related to matters of our home mortgage/rental and long-term investing. We can discuss it in much greater detail in my first book, *You Can't Have My Money!* Once you've read all of the calculations and done the math for yourself, I'm confident that you'll agree the twenty-ish bucks you spend to buy the book will in no way make me your latest purple elephant.

### Debt Avalanche Method

The Debt Avalanche Method is a slightly revised version of the Debt Snowball: We list our debts as before, only this time we focus on paying off the debt with the highest annual interest rate first. If our most significant interest percentage is a credit card with a balance of only $2,000 owing, but at a 19% APR, this will be the first debt on our list, and the one that gets overpaid every month until it is eliminated. If our lowest percentage amount is a student loan with a whopping $57,000 still owing, but at a much more manageable 2.8% APR, this is the last debt on which to focus our attention.

Note that this is NOT a purely reversed version of the Debt Snowball, as some people have mistakenly believed. We are not necessarily paying the largest debt first, only the debt with the highest APR. This might be our smallest debt, but it is the one that will spiral out of control fastest if not paid off. Our list might not have our total debt amounts in ascending or descending sequence at all. Only the APRs are listed in sequence, from highest to lowest, while the individual debt amounts might be completely random.

If our highest APR and largest debt happen to be one and the same, this can benefit us as well. In the example I gave in the section on consolidation loan strategies, I had to pay off a debt that had been secured to my mortgage when I sold my house. My consolation prize after closing the sale was that the eliminated secured debt had been my second-largest debt—behind only my mortgage—and my second-largest monthly payment, but it had also plagued me with the highest APR. That was my spoonful of sugar that helped the medicine go down and allowed me to successfully carry on with my own Debt Avalanche. As the highest APR was also attached to the largest debt, it created what I will call a "Super Debt Avalanche," and enabled me to pay off my remaining obligations very quickly without spending any further proceeds from the house sale.

As with the Debt Snowball, we continually pay the minimum payment on every bill while focusing a little extra money on the first debt on our list. Unlike the Debt Snowball method, however, paying off other debts can become confused.

For example, some people say to use balance transfers and put the new credit card on the list. However, if the card has an introductory offer of 0% interest for six months, this debt would go at the end of the list, i.e., paid last. After the teaser rate expires, then the card's prioritization will have to be adjusted to fit into our sliding debt scale. In the end, we would still be paying interest on it.

So which method is better? Again, that depends on our circumstances, but a simple rule of thumb is to use the Debt Snowball when our various interest rates are similar and lower,—perhaps only ranging from 2-9%—while the Debt Avalanche works best if our debts have a wider range of interest rates or are generally higher—maybe ranging more dangerously from 9-25%.

**FYI:** Compounding loan interest is the most overlooked and sinister purple elephant of all, particularly on credit cards, which is why it is essential to prioritize repayment of our high-interest debts.

**Real-Life Consolidation and Restructure Example**

Clem and Tottie reviewed all their bills at the end of their 45 days of journaling and realized that they were spending almost $300 in credit card payments a month. They had four school loans with a combined cost of $2,700 a month, plus a mortgage with a 7% interest rate. On top of that, they had some medical bills they had been paying on for the last few months.

They knew mortgage interest rates had dropped and were currently at 3%. They hadn't refinanced their home since they moved in 10 years ago, so Clem started researching refinancing the house and consolidating their student loans. In the meantime, Tottie created a list of all their bills, starting with the lowest balance to the highest.

They immediately implemented a Debt Snowball to pay off their medical and credit card bills. They also found an outstanding new mortgage and needed to refinance their house. Finally, Clem found an accredited and reputable company to consolidate their student loans.

The first month, they paid off two of the medical bills and went through the refinance and consolidation process. By the second month, they paid off the last medical bill and were ready to start using the money previously paid toward the medical bills to pay down their lowest-balance credit card.

They consolidated their school loans and were now paying only $1,200 a month. They decided to drop the difference—$1,500—onto their newly refinanced mortgage the following month. They decided to make one full mortgage payment a month and a $1,500 payment between full payments. This would help them pay off the mortgage faster and help them spend less money overall.

Please note: Additional payments to a mortgage may need to be negotiated with the provider in advance to avoid penalties. Be sure to discuss overpayment options with any provider before signing the contract.

Why did the Chowders put extra money from the school loans toward the mortgage instead of the credit cards or consolidated school loans? The answer is simple. In this case, they also incorporated the Debt Avalanche. The consolidated school loan had the lowest interest rate. They were already putting the extra money from the medical bills to the credit cards. Therefore, taking the extra money from the previous student loan payment and applying it toward the higher-interest mortgage made perfect sense.

When they finished paying off the credit cards, they diverted that payment toward the consolidated student loan to start paying it down faster.

In less than a year, they had only two major bills: Their mortgage and consolidated student loan, with the student loan being paid off at a greatly accelerated rate.

My first book, *You Can't Have My Money!*, dealt primarily with savings and investments, often concerning a variety of insurance products, so I would be remiss not to mention the importance of reevaluating our insurance needs when hunting purple elephants. Even if we want to keep our existing coverage for home, auto, etc...,—which is normally the wisest decision—there are excellent resources, including websites such as Gabi.com, which can replace our current level of coverage, but with the benefit of a considerably lower price. Changing insurance providers can save our family hundreds or even thousands of dollars a year, a little-noted fact that will often shock even smart investors.

Restructuring and consolidation have many forms, and none of them are overnight fixes, but they can still save us huge amounts of cash and time. When we review our purple elephants, consider which ones fall into these categories and reallocate them to achieve the most efficient payoff.

# 5

## SELL SOMETHING OR SELL EVERYTHING: WRING THE CASH OUT OF YOUR EXCESS POSSESSIONS

**Step 5: Sell things.**

Material possessions are important to everyone. So much so that the self-storage industry is showing a growth that is similar to when they were a new industry in American society.

What does this mean? It means that most people keep too many material belongings for a variety of reasons. However, if the item is not being used, is it worth keeping?

We are all guilty of saying things like, "I have to keep Great-Grandma's quilt," or "I can't get rid of Dad's tools." We are a society that attributes sentimental value to material items. This sentimentality leads to a booming self-storage industry because we need more room to store these "special" items.

This is not a push to do away with self-storage facilities, but it is here to remind us that they can be purple elephants. These facilities have a purpose, especially when used during a move but should not be considered as a long-term storage option.

If you have had a storage unit for more than a year, consider selling the items in it.

When we are getting rid of purple elephants, that means not only doing away with a storage unit but also doing away with unwanted, unneeded, and unused items in our lives, even if they have some sentimental value. Unless they are serving a useful purpose, they can be sold for money to put toward paying off and destroying our purple elephants.

This chapter will discuss several things to sell and ways to sell items that aren't being used, aren't needed for our daily lives, or are so expensive to keep that it becomes a more financially viable option to let them go.

## Yard Sales

We have all gone driving on a weekend and seen signs for yard sales and garage sales. In the last decade or so, there are even community yard sales advertising with signs, newspapers, and online social media. The yard sale is a mainstay and is a great way to make some cash over a weekend.

Many of us have had yard sales and loved the money we made from them. However, many of us also love to go to yard sales and buy stuff. While sometimes we find items we needed at a great price or items that we plan to refurbish and resell, most of the time somebody else's yard sale is a well-hidden purple elephant.

We can probably go through our house and storage unit if we have one, and find hundreds of items that have served their purpose and are no longer needed. These items could include clothes, toys, memorabilia,—more on this in a moment—furniture, and much more. One of these items could even be Great-Grandma's quilt for the right price. She's dead. She won't mind as much as we think she will.

Yard sales are only conducive to warm months because no one wants to sit outside in the cold, and people are less likely to stop and walk around our yard or garage in the cold. That is why "spring cleaning" is an ideal time to plan our yard sale.

Plan accordingly. If you are reading this book during the warmer months, you can pull together a yard sale with the greatest sales potential in a few days or weeks. It may not include everything that it should because of time constraints, but it would be a good start.

In colder months, we can slowly go through things and create a yard sale section in our house, garage, or storage unit. Then in the summer, plan to have two or three yard sales to sell most if not all of the items in our yard sale pile.

In some cases, there are online yard sales through social media platforms. These types of yard sales allow us to list items continuously throughout the year and are a great resource when we need a bit of cash.

As a personal example, I once sold some unused items on a Facebook buy-and-sell page. Most of them sold quickly, but it was my old Nintendo 64 console with twelve games that started an insane online bidding war. The barrage of offers was ratcheted up to three times my initial asking price within an hour. Apparently, the farming-based game *Harvest Moon* had become a coveted collector's item since 1998, and nobody had told me. Somehow, it had become even more in-demand than *GoldenEye* and *Mario Kart*. (I don't care about modern graphic resolution, frame rates, and celebrity mo-cap technology: Nintendo 64 remains the single greatest console in gaming history. Fight me.)

Having an in-person yard sale and participating in online yard sale groups will help us sell everything quickly and efficiently. All we have to do is plan. Deciding which items to put in online groups and which only to put in the in-person yard sale is always best. Do some research and see what are the bestsellers online.

Also, consider if our items are of general interest to the public or if they are more of a niche. Niche items, including extremely valuable collectibles, may need a broader, or even international, audience to find the best price. A professionally graded limited-edition comic book might fetch hundreds of dollars on eBay, but we might not even get an offer on a local Facebook buy-and-sell page or in a yard sale. The other thing to consider is listing fees. There is a small fee attached to eBay listings, but it is generally nominal and far-outweighed by the international exposure our items can receive.

However, if we do list items on eBay, or on any site that may result in long-distance shipping, be sure to account for the cost of shipping, and include that price—usually as a reasonably-averaged flat rate—in our listing, as well as any other limitations on shipping. For example, many Americans will only ship items to destinations within North America. Sending a collectible *Star Wars* action figure to Mexico or Canada is normally fine, but sending it across extremely large bodies of water can incur additional costs and risks.

Finally, be aware of our buyers. Be certain that we have been paid before shipping any item, and be very clear with the buyer in advance about any shipping insurances or return policies.

No matter what sale option we pick—front yard, online, or both—do it! Have the yard sale to part with any physical purple elephants that are taking up space.

**Sell Collectibles**

As previously mentioned, collectibles and memorabilia probably should not be sold at a yard sale, or even in an online yard sale group. While my example did end up being profitable, I could have gotten a lot better bang for my buck had I not been lazy with my research and offered my Nintendo 64 up for auction on eBay rather than on a community Facebook page. To get the most significant profit from rare items, we should only list them on specific websites, such as reputable online auctions or eBay.

No matter where we list, we have to strategize. Research the item and see how much other people are selling the item for, and also what condition their items are in because this information will help us to price our items appropriately: We may need to undercut the average to make a quick sale. We also need to decide when the best time to list the item is. Depending on the type of collectible or memorabilia, anniversaries can be a great time to make a nice profit.

This is kind of brutal, but the death of an artist can make the value of their memorabilia skyrocket. The *In Memorandum* segment is about the only part of the

Oscars that's still worth watching, and, even then, only for research purposes.

I have a couple of personal experiences I want to share to show you just how well selling these items at specific times works.

One of my favorite movies has always been *Jurassic Park*, and I loved dinosaurs long before its release in 1993. I collected the original Kenner Series 1 action figures, including all human and dinosaur figurines. Knowing something about the history of *Star Wars* action figures, I kept all of them in their original packaging, with additional storage precautions to avoid light exposure, pet dander, or other long-term damage. I listed the near-mint-in-box—NMIB— items in 2018, in celebration of the film's 25th Anniversary. Despite only having the human and dinosaur figures,—none of the vehicles or larger playsets—I easily sold the collection for $2,000. The largest *Tyrannosaurus Rex* figure was originally the most expensive back in 1993, and even then it only cost around $50. Its value has easily increased 3 to 10-fold, depending on the condition.

My next example is probably a little more obscure, but I mention it because that is exactly what eBay and auction sites are best for. On August 10th, 2010,

I first saw eight-year-old opera singer Jackie Evancho performing on an episode of *America's Got Talent*. She would eventually win 2nd place, and she has been one of my favorite singers ever since. On August 16th, 2010, I randomly looked her up on Amazon and saw that she had an independently-released debut album entitled *Prelude to a Dream*, which I immediately purchased for about $20. I didn't realize until several years later that Jackie's parents had pulled the CD from distribution in its only online listings—Amazon and CDBaby—just a few days after I purchased it, and it, too, had become a coveted collector's item. Only 4,000 copies of the album had been sold, and it was eventually determined that almost all of those sales had been in the form of digital downloads. As such, it was suspected that there were probably only a few hundred of the physical CDs in existence. Although the album had become one of my favorite writing ambiances and was thus well-used, I was still able to list it in "Used-Good" condition on eBay and quickly sold it for $400. In the years since I have seen mint auto-graphed copies sell for as much as $4,000. Pretty impressive for an artist who many people still only know as "Miss Kitty" from Season 3 of *The Masked Singer*.

One thing I quickly learned about collectibles is that fake items are rampant. It is important to know enough about our items to identify real from counterfeit, and also to be able to sell our genuine articles with confidence. Know the specifics of the original packaging, release dates, artist autographs, and production runs of limited editions, because savvy buyers will want to be able to verify that they are getting the real deal. They will absolutely grill us before they are willing to hand over hundreds or thousands of dollars, as well they should.

If we have successfully sold rare items before, we should show full transparency, and encourage prospective buyers to contact our previous buyers for verification that our items are authentic. eBay is also excellent for this, as our past sales and customer reviews can be easily confirmed, and previous buyers can be messaged for verification. In the case of my collectible CD, I was fortunate to have purchased it from my regular Amazon account with an archive of every past year's purchases, so I could provide my buyer with an online purchase receipt predating the album's known date of removal from sale listings. In addition, I provided evidence such as the professionally silk-screened disc label and laser-etched serial numbers, production dates, and barcodes on the underside of the disc, as opposed to the cheaply-burned discs with sticker labels which many scammers will try to pass off as originals.

It is also important to remember that we may not always come out with a profit compared to our original purchase, especially if we knew the value of the item when we bought it. When we bought that rare, 1st Edition *Spider-Man* comic from the 1970s for $1,000 back in 1995, we planned to keep it forever or sell it way down the road for twice that price. However, then 2007 rolled around and everyone in the world learned what a Subprime Mortgage was. Suddenly, our gleaming mantelpiece becomes a choice between selling an old comic book or missing that month's mortgage payment. We list it online and get an offer for $800. At that point, we must be pragmatic and think of our family. We can no longer think of our item as an appreciating investment, or even a treasure to hand down to our children. We have to think of it as an eight hundred dollar bill that's been sitting on the shelf while it could have been saving our home.

Owning collectibles and memorabilia is truly an enviable aspect of the American dream, but when we are trying to rid ourselves of purple elephants, the sacrifice of selling these items and paying off our debts to help our family is worth it. And, even when it's painful, it truly reminds us that "things are just things."

## Sell at Local Farmers' Markets

Do we love to bake and make homemade crafts and items? Maybe our side hustle is woodworking, but we're not sure how to get our items to customers. Then why not try our hand at selling our items at a local farmers' market?

From spring and well into the fall, these markets are a staple in most rural communities, although they are even found in major metropolitan centers including, quite famously, downtown Los Angeles. Depending on our county or parish, the markets may be in different areas on different days, usually starting Thursdays and ending on Sundays. Smaller communities may only host them one day a week.

Farmer's markets are a great second source of income, especially if we make items at home. Researching the farmers' markets in our areas will tell us exactly what types of products are allowed and what is not allowed.

Most of the time, the products have to be homemade or homegrown. During the week, we will be making the products. On the weekends, we're going to be selling them. Farmers' markets also have a fee associated with participating. However, the fee is usually nominal and will easily be covered with the first week of sales.

When we are just starting, using the farmers' market to get regular customers is a prime example of a purple elephant working for us. We pay the fee to be there, but the profits we make more than just exceed the cost. Once our name gets out to the community and people start buying our items regularly, we can open up a website to continue to sell the items over the colder months. We will also have some money for advertising. Again, advertising is a purple elephant, but when done properly and within reasonable limits, it will have a return on the marketing investment that is worth it.

**Sell a Vehicle**

Most families have two vehicles. Do you need that? That's all I have to say.

## RV Living

RV living was initially associated with seniors who had retired and wanted to travel the country. However, in today's world, more and more adults of all ages and in differing states of family obligations live the RV life.

What is RV living? It is selling our home, purchasing an RV that is comfortable for the family and living in it. This is not something we would do on a whim, but if we don't want the hassle of owning a house, condo, apartment, or such, an RV may be the best option for you. Maybe it is even just a temporary solution when we realize that our home is our biggest and most wasteful purple elephant when it could be the solution to almost all of our financial problems with the simple posting of a realtor sign.

If we work for ourselves or in a remote position, RV living is optimal because not only can we continue working but we can travel as much or as little as we like. We aren't stuck in one location. We can move around with the seasons.

While many people dream of driving across the country in a motorhome, many RV-living families prefer a pickup truck with a towed RV on a fifth-wheel hitch. This allows them to travel and live where they please, but also means they do not need a second vehicle when someone needs to go to work while the rest of the family is working from "home." Home and vehicle can be linked or separate depending on the circumstance since nobody wants to angle-park a motorhome in front of the bank.

However, before we put our house on the market or give up our lease, research RV living. Make a plan and find out about insurance needs. Have the yard sales and sell our items online to downsize enough to move into an RV. Don't just put our stuff in storage: Remember that a storage unit is just another purple elephant. Communicate with our family unit. If we have a partner and children, make them part of the decision-making process, since this type of change will affect them, too.

Maybe we all decide it is not the right time to do it now but maybe it will be a better option in a few years. Keep the idea open and stay on top of the trends. RV living isn't for everyone, but it is always an option.

No matter what we decide, we won't buy our RV until we have sold our house. Paying on a house and RV is like having two giant purple elephants, each with different extra expenses. Just as if we were hunting for a new home, put the current house on the market and don't buy the next one—the RV— until we close the sale on the current one.

Let's keep those purple elephants at bay and pick the lifestyle we want that best serves our family.

**Monetize Cancel Culture**

Here's a fun new addition to our purple elephant hunt: Cancel culture! What is cancel culture? To put it as bemusedly as I can, it is whatever the blue-haired people are screaming about today on Twitter. (I prefer the term "blue-haired people" to refer to any individual form or coalition of progressive activists, because their primary tact is the weaponization of language, and I don't feel like memorizing that many brand new words and acronyms. Normally, I would end this jocular, bracketed segment with the playful challenge to "Fight me," but, in this instance, most of the people who would take me up on it are incredibly low-T and I would feel bad.) So, basically, to bring some joy into cancel culture, we are going to consider it hunting blue-and-purple elephants. The only difference is that we want these to exist because they are often only hurting themselves in the end, as has been repeatedly demonstrated in recent years.

Cancel culture can affect almost any aspect of public life: free speech, celebrity careers, toys, books, movies and TV shows, regular people who made a joke 20 years ago, and so much more. If blue-and-purple elephants are offended or don't like the concept, item, or person, they push to ostracize and ban them from society.

Why? The short answer is "Commies." The long answer would require me caring enough about resolving the issue to write a third book. Either way, the best and most hilarious way to deal with it is to wave an American flag and make a buttload of money from it.

If any readers find this segment offensive, I'm not too worried. They probably aren't the kind of people who are going to shoulder enough personal responsibility to follow all of the steps in this book anyway. But thanks for the royalties!

Fun brain-detonating fact: You don't have the right to NOT be offended.

Now, while it is possible to successfully rally a Twitter mob against something or somebody that gave somebody else "the sads," it often has a glorious side-effect: The non-blue-haired people immediately recognize the mob's bullying, harassment, discrimination, virtue-signaling, violence incitement, blatant racism, and lack of meaningful employment for what it is, and then they rally to the support of whatever or whoever is being canceled. Suddenly, the "cancel-ee" sees a sharp boost in their market value.

Let's say that a Twitter mob demands the cancellation of a popular "problematic" character from a television series, whether that be live-action or cartoon, or demands the firing of the actor portraying the character. Does that series have associated merchandise relating to the character? Action figures, video games, canonical novelizations, posters, or even Lego sets? The brakes are about to be stomped on the production of all of those. The cogs of Hollywood and merchandising corporations are regularly operated by blue-haired, yellow-spined people, so their knee-jerk reaction is to immediately cave to the mob, rather than just laughing hysterically at them while counting the stacks of money which the protested property has raked in for the company.

The Black Box "Slave Princess Leia" action figure from *Star Wars: Return of the Jedi* was pulled from shelves almost immediately, and this was more than 30 years before the term cancel culture was coined. Why? The enslaving chain around her neck offended someone. Never mind the fact that, in the movie, the chain was deliberately used as a symbol of Leia's table-turning liberation from her evil captor: Our favorite butt-kicking space princess used it to strangle Jabba the Hutt to death, in the process freeing the citizens of Tatooine from a reign of terror going back 50+ years according to the time-line established by the prequel trilogy. (Did I just find a way to validate the existence of that entire stupid pod-racing sequence from *The Phantom Menace*?) That so-called enslaving chain deserves to be on prominent display in The Museum of Free-dom, right beside George Washington's powdered wig, Abraham Lincoln's stovepipe hat, and a Blu-ray copy of that movie where Sam Elliott kills Adolf Hitler and a Sasquatch.

Either way, the action figure is now worth around $300 if you can even find it.

In the case of Princess Leia wearing the most famous bikini of the 1980s—If you bought the poster for your son and then wondered why his bedroom door was always closed, don't operate heavy machinery—the figure was canceled for supposedly demeaning the character. However, more recent action figures have been canceled on account of the actors who originally portrayed the character.

Without a doubt, the most infamous example of this is another beloved character in the *Star Wars* universe: The even more butt-kicking Rebel shock trooper Cara Dune from the hit Disney+ series, *The Mandalorian.* Since her introduction, the character quickly became a huge fan-favorite amongst both male and female viewers, a widely-praised example of a strong female role model, and has even been called the show's second breakout character, right up there with Grogu/Baby Yoda.

Then the actress playing her—former Brazilian JiuJitsu and MMA champion turned action star who I would not want to mess with, Gina Carano—was fired from the show for statements she made on social media. All advertising and merchandise featuring the Cara Dune character were immediately canceled, including a production halt on all Hasbro action figures.

The fan backlash was overwhelming and almost wholly in support of Gina Carano, who was perceived as being targeted solely for her political viewpoints. (Shortly thereafter, equally larger-than-life action star Arnold Schwarzenegger made the televised statement, "Screw your freedoms," but apparently we're all good there.) Disney+ lost countless subscribers in the following months, the official Disney social media accounts saw a severe ratio of dislikes on every new post they made, and the company's historical reputation was brought sharply into question. The ongoing furor has been called a dramatic paradigm shift in public perceptions of Hollywood.

Starting bids on both of my NMIB Cara Dune action figures will begin shortly at $300 each.

And Gina Carano is making movies with the legendary "destroy with facts and logic" Ben Shapiro. Good luck canceling her now.

Even cartoons aren't safe. The blue-haired people screamed that *Looney Tunes'* most hilariously amorous skunk, Pepe Le Pew, was a symbol of toxic masculinity and rape culture, and also that Mexican mouse Speedy Gonzalez was a racial stereotype or an example of mice appropriating Latino culture or some other such bull-crap: Both of their individual compilation DVDs are now only available from private sellers on eBay, and will put you at least $100 in the hole. (In a hypocritical pattern that becomes increasingly noticeable the more we study it, Pepe Le Pew was removed from the 2021 film *Space Jam: A New Legacy*, because he might have been unthinkably smitten by a black cat who had an unfortunate run-in with wet paint. However, a few more questionable Warner Bros properties *were* included in the film as background characters, such as the child-killing Pennywise the Dancing Clown from Stephen King's *It,* and the gang-raping droogs from *A Clockwork Orange*. But we're all good there.)

And let's not forget Dr. Seuss! The most famous children's book series in history now has six titles which gave the blue-haired people soy-infused lachrymose secretions, because a guy in a wok hat was using chopsticks or something. These include: *And to Think That I Saw It on Mulberry Street* (1937), *McElligot's Pool* (1947), *If I Ran the Zoo* (1950), *Scrambled Eggs Super!* (1953), *On Beyond Zebra!* (1955), and *The Cat's Quizzer* (1976). Sell 'em if you got 'em because they're going like hotcakes!

Fun fact: If you feel oppressed by a kids' book that was written more than 84 years before the writing of this book, your society probably isn't as oppressive as you think.

Let's be clear about something. The bestselling book titles on Amazon are not like a Twitter mob, which generally consists of an ear-piercingly vocal minority with a fear of red meat. The Amazon bestseller list is an international compilation of the bestselling books on the planet.

Within days of Dr. Seuss being canceled, his books accounted for more than 30 of the top-50 bestselling titles on Amazon.

---

*"And there was much rejoicing!"*

— MONTY PYTHON AND THE HOLY GRAIL

---

If you are short on cash, and you own something which the blue-haired people have decided is their "outrage *du jour*," be of good cheer: You're about to make some money.

If I may be half-serious for a moment, we need to develop a predictive algorithm to more fully monetize cancel culture. They have algorithms that can track the extrapolating pattern of online arguments initiated by trolls on Twitter, at least if we're to assume that the entire Season 20 of *South Park* wasn't lying to us. We need a new, computer-aided "big short" to figure out who's going to provoke the next bellowing, blue-crested stampede, utilizing determinative factors which go far beyond the baseline triggers of "voted for Trump" or "named Chris Pratt." I accurately predicted that both the 2021 Oscars and the 2021 Olympics would have an all-time, record-low viewership, so now it's time to channel my eerie prescience into the realm of zeros and ones for the benefit of Capitalist bastards everywhere.

**Sell Your Pet**

The last item we should consider selling is also the most heartbreaking: A pet.

I only mention it here because you need me to say it. Sometimes the sale of a pet is a necessity when all else has failed and we are falling behind in essential payments. It can easily cost over $1,000 a year for one healthy cat or small dog, and this estimate doesn't even include the additional cost of bowls, toys, leashes, carriers, veterinary visits, vacation kennelling, or other needed equipment and supplies. That is just factoring in dog food and maybe some kitty litter.

I have not mentioned this idea lightly, and I genuinely believe it should only be considered as a last resort: When the needs of our family must come before the luxury of an animal that feels like family. In some cases of people living alone, pets are the closest thing to a family that they have. I would suggest using our pets as a scale to measure our other purple elephants against: Ask ourselves what expenses and subscriptions we are willing to give up to keep our beloved family pet. When it comes down to a choice between keeping the chocolate lab that we raised since he was a pup or some lingering purple elephant, suddenly that Netflix subscription doesn't seem so important.

No matter what our final decision is, try to include everyone involved before we act on it. Again, let's make sure there are no other areas that can be cut or items that can be sold before we even consider this one. I may make fun of the blue-haired people, but I wasn't chiseled out of a rock.

It's make or break time. If the items we love are no longer serving a purpose in our lives, sell them. Sit down with the family and decide what to sell, what to keep, and what to do with the sale proceeds.

## Real-Life Paring Down Example

Rosemary and Herb are in school, and the Chowder parents aren't able to work from home, so they are not going to be able to sell their home and live in an RV at this time. However, Clem and Tottie have been intrigued by the possibility, and are making this a goal for retirement.

Until then, and while the kids are still in the house, they have decided they need to pare down on their material possessions. This is hard for everyone, but they agree as a family that they need to do it. The Chowder parents tell the children that 50% of the money they raise will go toward their next vacation. This motivates Rosemary and Herb, and they all start purging their areas for the yard sale.

Rosemary goes through her room and the garage attic. She decides that she will sell her large collection of Barbie dolls, except for the first one she got when she was four years old, which she wants to give to her own daughter one day. She is keeping most of her books, but many of her other childhood playthings and adolescent crush memorabilia— which now make her cringe—are going in the sell pile.

Herb decides to keep his board games, larger Lego sets, and three of his video games, as he realizes that he plays those three games 90% of the time. All of his many other video games, and a variety of stuffed toys from when he was younger go into the sell pile. He gives the video game collection to his father to sell online because some are in near-mint condition and known to be in demand. The ones that will garner less money will be taken to a local video game shop and sold for store credit toward his next game purchase.

Clem and Tottie go through old baby items they have kept for sentimental reasons: Cribs, playpens, mobiles, baby clothes, toys, and baby bottles. In the end, they only keep Rosemary's first baby bottle with Herb's first pair of baby socks inside it as a mantel-piece memento... and just to ensure that the old wives' tale about getting pregnant again the minute you sell your last baby item doesn't come true.

Tottie has some jewelry inherited from her grand-mother that she decides to appraise and sell. She also has a fur coat she has never worn, as well as some paintings and other odd and ends that are just packed away at this point.

Clem doesn't have much to go into the yard sale, as he has always been more interested in hunting rare collectibles, so he has a vintage baseball card collection and an original set of 1977 Star Wars figurines. He decides to research these items and sell them online for the best profits.

They all have clothes to contribute to the yard sale, as well as some older pieces of furniture and an old TV which they had replaced long ago and just stored in the garage. Also in the garage, they find boxes of old VHS tapes, audio cassettes, and vinyl records from before the children were born. Although they are long outdated forms of home entertainment, these items will still sell quickly at most garage sales: Never underestimate how many people still have a VCR or record player in their homes. In fact, prices on VHS tapes and vinyl records can go up if the title is rare enough: For example, a lot of movies that were released on VHS were never transitioned to DVD or Blu-ray, with the same certainly going for old "long-haired, bell-bottomed" records from our youth that never made the crossover to CDs or music streaming services.

On the day of the yard sale, they all help out. It was decided that, since 50% of the money was going toward their family vacation, the yard sale was a family affair. Tottie and Rosemary took the first shift since Rosemary worked her part-time job later that afternoon. Clem and Herb had the second shift.

At the end of the yard sale, they still had quite a few unsold items. They counted the money and realized they had made just over $700 in that one day. They decided to add more to what was leftover and have another yard sale in a few weeks.

Before the week was out, Clem's baseball cards and action figures had been auctioned off online for an additional $480. It was about 30% less than he had hoped for, knowing the appreciated value of similar items in recent years, and also because he had first purchased several of the items for a high price many years ago, with no intention of ever selling them. However, he accepted the hit for the sake of his family, as the auction brought their one-week household purge up to a total of $1,180.

Of the sale proceeds, $590 was added to the tail-end of their ongoing Debt Snowball, which fully paid off their smallest debt and a good portion of the next-smallest. The other $590 was budgeted toward their hotel reservation, a guided castle tour, and one special dinner at a prestigious restaurant for their upcoming trip to Ireland.

Be under no illusion: Budgeting each day of a vacation is just as important as budgeting our weekly routines, or we risk it turning into a nonstop, two-week splurge-fest.

When we have collectibles and items we no longer use, it is time to let others enjoy them. Don't just throw everything into a yard sale. Some items have more value or a value that may only be appreciated by a niche community online. Research items and decide if we'll be selling them in a yard sale, to a broker, for store credit, or online so that we always get the best returns possible.

# 6

# DECLARE WAR ON SCREEN-TIME: IT'S MOST LIKELY NOT MAKING YOU MONEY, AND IT'S DEFINITELY COSTING YOU MONEY.

**Step 6: Cancel streaming services, expensive phone plans, and other superfluous subscriptions.**

Do we know how much time we sit in front of a screen? This is not referring to work time if we work in front of a computer or some type of screen. We're talking about the TV screen—watching TV shows and movies or playing video games. We're talking about computer, tablet, and phone screens; watching YouTube, surfing social media, or doing a host of other largely useless activities.

In December of 2020, a study revealed that most Americans spend approximately 17 hours a day looking at screens (Lee, 2020). It averaged out to four hours and 30 minutes watching TV or movies, four hours and 33 minutes on a smartphone, over three hours on a gaming device, and nearly five hours on a laptop.

Now, let's take out those five hours on the laptop and two hours on the smartphone that we can associate with work, and we have a whopping 10 hours—more than we work or sleep—in front of screens.

While this is not true for all people or families, this is still a scary statistic. As we're completing our time journals, start adding up how much of our time and our family's time is spent in front of screens. Is the time useful or wasted?

If we have just started a side hustle or part-time job, that number is going to drop dramatically since we are working on our other money-making endeavors instead of wasting time looking at a screen. Of course, if our side hustle or part-time job has us parked in front of a screen, we get it: We'll still have lots of hours in front of a screen, but these arent wasted hours. They are useful and help us defeat our purple elephants.

I want to mention that this doesn't mean we can't ever play a video game or watch a movie or TV. It means we have to budget our time. We may have created one day a week as a family day. Use time on that day to watch a movie as a family or to play a video game.

What we are trying to accomplish in this chapter is removing the screen as much as possible and creating more time to work toward slaughtering our purple elephants. Unless we are actively making money online, then it is time to step away from the screens.

**Cancel Subscription and Streaming Services**

One of the easiest steps to get the whole family away from screens is to cancel all the streaming services. There are hundreds of streaming services out there, and people are signing up for new ones all the time.

As a way to get away from cable, people have started signing up for Hulu, Peacock, Sling, and other TV channels. Even YouTube has a TV subscription plan. Initially, having one of these streaming services was cheaper than cable or satellite and offered the same shows and service.

However, the prices are now soaring, and more subscription-based services are starting up. Initially, subscription services gave us access to networks like NBC, ABC, and CBS or movie channels like HBO and Starz. Those networks were separate, but they soon found that moving to the streaming services was a better option, so they never truly went away.

In the most recent years, special networks, such as Disney and Discovery, have created their own subscription service. Disney+ and Discovery+ are now gaining more subscribers because they are changing what is available on streaming services like Hulu and Sling. We have to subscribe to them to have access to everything. Discovery even has a subscription for Discovery Archives, which gives access to older shows that we can't find on the normal streaming services or Discovery+.

The new network subscriptions don't even take into account the movie channels, like HBO, Starz, and others. This also doesn't consider Amazon Prime or Netflix.

However, streaming services are more than TV shows and movies. Radio programs, podcasts, music streaming, online news outlets behind a paywall, and more are also included under this heading of subscription services. It covers any service we pay for monthly.

Look at our finance journal and see how many of these subscription and streaming services we currently have. How many of these services make us money instead of costing us money? That is what we need to ask.

Each subscription seems to be such a small price. Most are between $5 and $15 per month. However, if we have 6 to 10 or more of these services, we are probably paying around $1,000 a year. Some may be part of our side hustle, but not all of them. We need to consider reducing the number of subscriptions.

Here is an example. How many radio and podcast subscription services do we have? How many do we need? Chances are we have at least one, such as Pandora, Apple Music, or Spotify. Do we have SiriusXM in our car? Do we pay extra for the subscription so everyone has their own login? If we have a partner and children, we probably do. Upgrading "for just a dollar a month!" to any form of unnecessary family plan can sink us even further.

We need to ask ourselves these types of hard questions and figure out how much our family can let go of without feeling like we are sacrificing our life. We don't necessarily have to cancel all of them, but we must trim it down to the bare essentials.

**Change Your Phone and Phone Plan**

Many people today live by their phones. Their contacts, their calendar, their tasks—everything is on their phone, but that is not all.

If a person has a smartphone, they have all those smart apps to keep them on track—a fitness tracker, pedometer, food diary, calendar with reminders, book tracker, and so on. However, most people also have Facebook, Instagram, LinkedIn, YouTube, Twitter, and a host of free phone games with in-app purchases.

The problem isn't all the smart apps unless they are associated with a subscription. Many of the fitness apps are subscription-based, but not all of them. Find a free one or one that has a free option and use it. There are plenty out there. The calendar, contacts, and other smart apps are always free and useful in our busy lives.

The problem arises when we decide to spend a minute just checking Facebook or Instagram. Maybe we have a few minutes, and we choose to watch a quick video on YouTube. Sometimes we just sit back and play a game on our phones, calling it self-care and a needed minute away from work or stress. These are the time and money-eaters that we call purple elephants.

Think about how many times we had to write in our journal that we spent over an hour on Facebook or such when we initially were only going to spend a minute or two. Time gets away from us. We become engaged with the screen, and, when we feel ashamed of our time-wasting, we will certainly be tempted to downplay that time in our time journals. Just remember that we only hurt ourselves if we can't even be honest with ourselves about our screen-time problem.

We play those free games on our phones. But have we ever purchased extra energy/weapons/coins for $1.99? How many times in the past month or three months? Take a minute to look back and find out how much we have actually spent while playing this "free" game.

One of the best ways to get rid of the smartphone purple elephants is to get rid of the smartphone. Instead, get a dinosaur of a cell phone that doesn't have Internet access, such as a flip phone. When we have a flip phone, we don't need any data on our plan so we can downgrade to a talk-and-text plan. Fair warning: You will face mockery. All the way back in 2011, a dear friend of mine wrote and produced a stage musical in Hollywood, wherein a hilariously elitist character mocked the small-town heroine's phone with the memorable line, "Oh! And it flips. That is so adorably 2006."

When I was searching for my purple elephants and realized how much time I spent on my phone, I downgraded immediately, and not because I run in those circles that believe 5G is an Illuminati-crafted transmitter of testicular cancer and is making the frogs gay. I bought the Alcatel One Touch, which cost me $70.00, and downgraded my phone plan to a simplified talk-and-text plan. Again, even a lack of apps can open us up to mockery. My standard response is, "Yeah, it has this great 'Does Nothing' feature that I love." Nine times out of ten, the person who was laughing will stop and admit, "Yeah, I kinda wish mine had that."

This is a fast and easy way to save money and time without sacrificing too much. A simple change of phone or plan can save us hundreds of dollars a year.

### "Ma'am, Step Away From the Video Games!"

This is a constant reminder of how old I'm getting, but anyone who was born in the 1970s or later probably grew up with a love for video games. Starting with the classic simplicity of *Pong* and floppy disks drives, and then exploding in the 1980s with the innovation of the first Coleco, Atari, Sega, and Nintendo systems,—to say nothing of the surge in quarter-fed arcade games in every movie theater, shopping mall, and laundromat—video games were a purple elephant of enraptured time-consumption, but little did we know just how big this purple elephant would become.

Moving from simple blocks and stick figures to life-like celebrity motion capture technology within a few decades has been another huge innovation, and the thrill of entering an entire virtual world of fantasy has never been more of a draw for both children and adults. Be under no illusion: The kids from the 1980s who fell in love with video games are not going to grow out of that particular hobby, even in their 40s and 50s. This is no longer a waning childhood pastime like the Easy-Bake Oven.

Consoles cost around $500, and these come out every few years. The worst part is that the new games can't be played on the old consoles, so we have to buy the new ones. Plus, the old games can't be played on the latest consoles, so we have to keep the old ones and pray they don't break. Then a retro collection of our favorite NES or old Playstation games comes out as a way for new consoles to milk some nostalgia dollars because we all miss those classic 2D side-scrollers. So we buy for a second time the same games we already spent too much on 25 years ago. Because *Earthworm Jim* was just that good.

When the systems originally came out, we played by ourselves or with others at our house, and the Nintendo 64's 4-controller, 4-way split-screen was considered mind-blowing. Nowadays, we buy passes for a specific time frame, usually three months to a year, that lets us talk to people from around the world and play games with them online. These passes cost about $20 for three months or $60+ for a year, and of course, we have to keep buying them.

In addition, the games themselves often start at $40 with a basic version. However, if we want all the bells and whistles, we'll pay an extra $20+ for downloadable content, which gives us extra weapons, maps, quests, and more. If we don't want the basic version, we can get the deluxe or collectible versions. These come with extras such as a soundtrack, posters, plushies, and more, but we still have to purchase downloadable content most of the time. These deluxe and collectible versions usually start around $120 but will range all the way up to $400.

This means that not only do video games waste about four hours a day—that's 28 hours a week if played daily—the one basic game with downloadable content and season pass can be $120 easily. While we only pay for the season pass once a year, that is still $60 per game if the basic version is $40.

Let's not forget the hungry, hungry arcade hall, which is less prevalent than it was a decade ago as more people turn to home consoles played on big-screen TVs, but they are still a mainstay in most movie theaters or shopping malls. Feeding endless quarters from a styrofoam cup into a Pac-Man machine was the downfall of many an allowance back in the day, and the cost of inflation has not skipped over this: Most games today cost $1-2 at minimum, which needs to be replenished every 5-10 minutes depending on how many mutant spiders you get swarmed by, and, of course, the hall employees are more than willing to sell us recharge-able cards for $30 or $100.

And don't even get me started on 4D virtual-reality experiences that let us put on a visor and pick up a plastic blaster/proton pack to fight Darth Vader or Slimer for 10 to 15 gloriously-nostalgic minutes... usually for $70 or more.

Moving away from video games is a way to save time and money. There are several ways to do this, and depending on the children's ages, some options are better than others. Particularly when some of the children are creeping up on 50 and have children of their own.

### *Cancel the Game Passes and Switch to Board Games*

If our children have begged us for the online pass that allows them to play with others online and we purchased it already, no problem. Just don't renew the pass, as they only last for a specific amount of time. The longer we buy the pass for, the less it will cost—but it will still cost.

Not renewing a pass for younger teens will be much easier than for older ones in most cases. How can we move this purple elephant from our wallet to theirs?

For the younger teens, if they have an allowance—or do jobs for neighbors and such—they can pay us for the pass. The same goes for the older teens that have part-time jobs or side hustles. They can get a reloadable credit card, put their own money on it, and pay for the pass themselves.

If they want games, have them save up and get the game. Also, if we get the game for them for a holiday or birthday, only get the basic version. If they want the deluxe or collectible version, that should be on them—not our problem.

Our youngest children will not be using passes since there is no filter or parental control on them. This means that, as they get older, we just refuse to pay for the access. As before, when they are teenagers and making their own money, they can pay us for the video game passes or buy the passes themselves.

However, no matter their age, we should use this type of expense and their wanting of it as a teaching moment. Make them create a budget that includes saving for this expense. Have them decide which purple elephants they are willing to pay for themselves and which ones will be going away. They make the decisions about what they can live with and without.

If our kids are young enough, then instead of buying a video game console, buy board games and play them as a family. Having a family day each week to spend time together is a perfect time to play board games instead of spending time in front of screens.

Switching to board games may be a little harder for older children, but it is not impossible. Make the picking of the game to play a family decision and make it fun rather than overly competitive. Just remember that Cribbage is the worst thing ever invented, rivaling even TikTok, and no one under the age of 70 should be playing it.

When the family starts having fun playing board games, then the switch is much easier for everyone. They're a low-cost, one-time investment, and they last for decades in many households.

### *Making Money on Video Games*

We can't leave this topic until we acknowledge that many people make money playing video games as a job. Some make enough to call it a career.

If anyone in our family is making money streaming their video game playing, do not get rid of new games or passes. The income from video streaming should more than cover these businesses expenses.

Instead, make it a business and treat it as a business. Make money and use the expenses of the passes, the new consoles, the new games, and anything else needed as write-offs for the business if allowable. Talk with an accountant first, but just know that video gaming streaming is a viable income if the person already has followers. It is not a good side hustle when starting because it can take a lot of money to be on top of the newest games and will take a lot of time in front of the screen to gain followers. But sometimes all it takes is an energetic person with a magnetic personality and a knack for the game to draw a considerable crowd.

If the followers are already there, consider monetizing our video game passion and turning it into a side hustle.

**Cancel Your Internet**

This tip is probably the hardest one to acknowledge or accept because I know people who would sell the family cow for dubiously magical beans before they would ever "go off the grid." But the truth is that if we don't have the Internet at home, our bills and spending will decrease, often drastically.

Think of it this way. If we cancel our home Internet, we will be canceling all our streaming and subscription services. (Just don't forget to actually go online and cancel all the subscriptions first, because they will gladly continue to gouge our credit cards every month for the rest of our lives whether we have an Internet connection or not.) In fact, we will be doing away with most television shows and movies altogether because most TVs require the Internet unless we have a media player.

When we disconnect the Internet, we will be disconnecting from online retailers, including Amazon, Wayfair, Target, and so many other ones. We will have to go to the store to purchase what we need. If we are following the tips in the third chapter, we'll only be shopping with a list anyway.

Having to get dressed, pack people into the car who don't necessarily want to go shopping, and then drive to the store to walk around looking for items is not what most people enjoy. We have become acclimated to sitting in front of our computer or tablet and shopping by typing in the item we want and being taken directly to it, particularly in the wake of COVID-19 lockdown measures: We just got used to it, and the top online sellers have flourished as a direct result. The convenience makes spending money so easy, and that is why we need to stop shopping online.

In fairness, shopping online is a time-saver and the best way to purchase in bulk. However, we spend a lot of our money without even thinking about it when we shop this way because we have limitless shiny, pretty things to hook our wallets like fish. It's basically the real-life version of that classic *Family Guy* episode where Peter and Brian trap James Woods in a crate using a trail of M&Ms.

"Ooo! Piece o' candy... Ooo! Piece o' candy... Ooo! Piece o' candy…"

One more important thing to remember if we do continue to shop online, as this may legitimately be the best financial option for many people: It's not just about discipline, it's also about exact numbers. Maybe those woodworking tools Clem needs for his Texas business aren't available on amazon.com, but they are available on the British and Canadian sites, amazon.co.uk and amazon.ca, and international shipping can be quite reasonably priced. His receipt for the tools will likely be in British pounds/pound sterling (GBP) or Canadian dollars (CAD), so Clem must accurately calculate and record what the purchase cost him. At the time of this writing, for example, 1 USD is the equivalent of £0.73 GBP, but also $1.27 CAD. That's quite a variance that must be accounted for, even across first-world nations with many economic similarities.

Fortunately, almost any search engine such as Google or Bing has free online calculators. Just search "currency calculator" and we can easily determine the values of almost any international currency. Simply choose our currency from the drop-down menu on one side, and the foreign currency on the other, and then enter the total cost of the foreign purchase in its column. For example, if Clem spent £38.45, the actual cost to him would be $66.79. If he just assumed the currencies were more or less equivalent, he would throw his budget off-course and come up short by about $28.34.

However, it's not just shopping that slurps us into an online vortex. The Internet has another purple elephant that consumes hours of our time every day.

Social media!

Yes! Social media, that glorious fantasyland wherein people with blue hair scream at you because words are violence. A place where US presidents get censored while self-proclaimed terrorist groups do not, and a place where, once upon a distant time, friends used to block friends because they were getting too many damn *FarmVille* requests. (*Cafe World* was better. Fight me.)

Americans spend almost five hours a day on social media. This could be Facebook, Instagram, TikTok, Twitter, Twitch, Discord, Snapchat, YouTube, Parler, Rumble, Odysee, Gab, Tinder, Match, other online dating sites, independent blogs, and even LinkedIn. Yes, LinkedIn is social media, and unless we are using it to network or find a job, it is wasting our time. I'm not immune. I still miss *Lemmings*.

More and more people are starting to pull back from all forms of social media, but it is still one of the biggest time wasters we have. However, if we do away with our smartphones and do away with our home Internet, the amount of time we spend on social media will drastically decrease. Unless we are somewhere like the library where we can use their computers, access to social media is limited to almost never.

The Internet is a primary source of our screen-time usage and the main source of impulse spending, so canceling it only makes sense in most cases.

### *When to Keep the Internet*

There are some cases when keeping the Internet and being on social media are appropriate and necessary.

If we work from home or use our computer for our side hustle, accounting, paying bills, banking, and so forth, then we need the Internet daily. Turning it off completely would be detrimental to us finding and getting rid of our purple elephants. In this case, the Internet is working for us. Our income should cover a portion of the Internet service fee, and we should include that portion in our monthly business expenses and even our tax returns.

Another time to keep the Internet is if we are making money on social media. Believe it or not, top influencers are making careers of being on social media. A person that has a certain amount of subscribed followers, generally 10,000 or so, is eligible to monetize their account, run ads, and generate ad revenue. Influencers on Instagram charge people to have their products endorsed. Even Facebook has a marketplace where people sell their products on their business pages.

Just like video game streaming for income, the use of social media to make money is not impossible. If we run our business through a social media outlet or use ads on these platforms to bring in business, then we will want to keep our Internet. As long as the Internet is contributing to hunting our purple elephants and killing them, then use it as a tool to help in the fight.

Just remember that "Tub Twitch" is basically the gateway drug to OnlyFans, and you have failed as a parent if your daughter ever ends up there.

**Real-Life Scenario of Cutting Screen-Time**

Clem and Tottie both work in corporate offices, regularly using computers every day. They also watch their phones for messages from work, friends, the children, and each other. When they got home, they weren't much better. Clem looked up instructions for DIY projects, sports, news, recipes to try on the grill, and such, and also listened to audiobooks and podcasts. Tottie liked to read ebooks on her tablet or play her free game apps.

Rosemary and Herb used computers for homework and games. Herb played video games every evening. Rosemary had her phone in her hand and her face staring at the screen even when she was watching TV with Herb at night.

When the family reviewed their screen-time, they all cringed. They realized that they were exactly the average American family. The parents spent at least 17 hours a day staring at a screen while the children were closer to eight or nine hours a day.

The family sat down and looked at how they spent their time.

They all agreed that they didn't need all the different streaming services. They settled on two services: One for TV and movies and one for anime that Rosemary and Herb loved. They also agreed that they would only watch TV two to three times a week and for less than two hours.

This TV time didn't include Herb's video game time, but he did agree that he shouldn't play as often. He decided to use playing video games as a reward for grades and finishing school projects and chores. He gave everything minute ratings, and however many minutes he earned that week was how long he was able to play his video games—not to exceed two hours a week. There was no need to cancel his video game pass because they had already paid for the year of online access but would reevaluate it next year or have Herb pay for it himself through chores or money from odd jobs in the neighborhood.

Tottie could not reduce her screen time as much, but she reallocated it to be for her freelance marketing side hustle. However, thanks to her marketing know-how, she was able to launch her freelancing business quickly and had clients in a relatively short time. Clem also still used the computer to find new ideas for his woodworking side hustle, but he scheduled two hours each week specifically for this research task. During this time, he searched for design inspirations or used his software to design his ideas. He also used this time to research places to sell his items and knew that once he had an inventory built up, he may need to schedule more time on the computer or hire Rosemary and Herb to enter his items for sale.

Rosemary took this the hardest. Being a teenager whose friends all had phones and were on social media constantly, she decided to give herself an hour each night to be on social media with her friends. She would still check her phone for messages but used the evenings for studying or reading.

Sundays are family days, and instead of the family sitting in front of the TV or going to the movies, they have family adventures—weather permitting. They research different state and national parks, hiking trails, and fishing locations. They have also found new museums and historical sites nearby to visit for the day when it is rainy or cold.

On Sunday evenings, they cook dinner together and prepare food for the upcoming week. Tottie usually pulls up the recipe on her tablet, but it is on an app and saved for the week. She only pulls up what she needs. After dinner, they all sit around the family room coffee table and play a board game or work on the puzzle that lives there during the week.

Sundays in the Chowder household are screen-free days for the most part. It was a little hard for everyone when they first implemented this rule, but the family is closer than ever, and they all love having this day just to themselves.

Now that we realize screen-time is a significant time and money waster in many cases, think about the number of screens we have in our homes. Look at our journals at the end of the 30 to 45 days and see how much time each person has spent in front of a screen.

When we analyze this information, ask the family if the Internet is helping or hurting our financial situation. If there is hesitation, make it a discussion, but get to the bottom line and answer the question. If it is not helping us purge purple elephants, it's time to start purging screen-time.

Refocusing our time away from screens can be challenging, but the time we gain to learn something new, work at a part-time job or side hustle, or spend time with our family is worth giving up the screens for.

Also, blue-screen eye fatigue is real and taking a collective toll on our REM sleep as a society. Go get some sunshine.

# 7

# YOU COME FIRST: YOUR MENTAL AND SPIRITUAL WELL-BEING IS THE HIGHEST-CALIBER ELEPHANT GUN IN YOUR ARSENAL.

**Step 7: Heal your psyche, and your money will follow suit.**

E very generation has seen its share of tragedies and suffering, whether personal, by group, or as a collective nation. Wars, diseases, and financial crises have been as much of a mainstay throughout history as death and taxes, and, in many ways, the advent of 20th-century technology seems to have exacerbated them: It was a heck of a lot harder for a global pandemic to be declared back in the 1870s when Wyatt Earp was cleaning up Tombstone because he couldn't just catch a flight to Paris on a whim whenever he needed a little Me-Time while also being unknowingly asymptomatic.

At the time of this writing in 2021, COVID-19, an ongoing economic crisis, and increasingly rampant civil unrest have brought fear into many lives across the globe. Despite their comparative prosperity, Americans have been hard-pressed to feel good about themselves or their fellow countrymen, no matter what decision they make in the face of hardship. The unexpected shortages that we have seen, such as gas, flour, and even plywood are materials we use in our everyday lives that are rising in cost and are helping to throw our economy out of whack. (Remember the Great 2020 Toilet Paper Wars? Pepperidge Farms remembers.)

Even a crippling blow to the global economy is not something new. It has happened frequently throughout history, but it is still something that all of us have a very hard time preparing for. I'm no exception. I was working an excellent job when COVID-19 restrictions were put in place, which required my company to implement a comprehensive downsizing strategy across multiple worksites, and I was laid off. I found myself doing smaller jobs, and even picking up random day jobs, with considerably less pay for several months, and I'm not going to say that was a fun time. I'm also not trying to boast, but I had been following the strategies in my books, and that planning was what helped me and my family get through.

However, even I didn't escape unscathed. I had to cancel some things I really didn't want to cancel, sell some things I really didn't want to sell, and restructure some debts that I really did not want to take on in the first place. However, despite the personal setbacks, I still count myself among the highly blessed in our world. I was able to get back to work at my old job, and I was even able to pay off some lingering debts amid the chaos. It took some very careful planning and a tough decision or two, but the chaos was survivable.

Sadly, many others were hit much harder, which is what further inspired me to write this follow-up to *You Can't Have My Money!* Countless people lost their jobs, were forced to shutter small family-owned businesses or saw substantial reductions in their available work hours. Personal debts spiraled out of control. Depression, suicide, and violent crime all reached record highs. Money can't protect us against all of that, but we would be fooling ourselves if we said that there is no connection between suffering and poverty.

Even worse, there is a strong connection between suffering and foolish spending. We received stimulus checks, and instead of using them to survive, we bought giant TVs or items that we thought would make us feel better. Did these extravagant purchases make us happy? After the dust settled, we were still overwhelmed and despaired because we couldn't afford to buy necessities. We were still in debt.

Even many of those who worked during the pandemic have more debt than before because with everyone home and doing all of our shopping online, we spent more and impulse-purchased more often because we had no other outlet. Sometimes, there's a simple catharsis in just knowing that we have a new package en route from Amazon.

I mention all this because our mental and physical health are affected by our purple elephants. Many of the changes we have discussed in this book so far will help us have stronger physical and financial health. However, in this chapter, mental health is the focus, and there is nothing that will help us get our financial life back on track faster than maintaining strong and determined mental health.

We need to stop listening to our purple elephants. We need to evaluate and accept the moment, and figure out how to move from feeling overwhelmed to feeling financially stable.

This book has given tips and ideas to help us destroy the purple elephants and their incessant need to keep us in the spending mode of financial insecurity. Now, let's consider how to move us back to a stronger state of mental health as well.

**Despair Spending**

When we feel overwhelmed, Amethyst and Tyrian love it. When depression is our primary mindset, our purple elephants rally together and whisper in our ears from every side. If we listen to their foul, peanut-scented mockery, we become defeatists who believe that we deserve whatever suffering we're trying to deal with.

That is not you. That's your purple elephants talking. Why would they say this to you? They want you to spend more because purple elephants are almost synonymous with instant gratification. And because they're a bunch of evil Baal worshippers.

Our society equates happiness with spending. Remember how many times we have seen someone on TV or in a movie go shopping because they are sad?—And remember how well that worked out in both *Zoolander* and *Anchorman?*— We are told to buy ourselves a present to make ourselves feel better, and we do feel better, at least initially. Then, we look at our bank account or credit card balance and regret the purchase.

Another way we spend through depression is by eating or shopping for food. This is probably the most common form of despair spending.

What is our comfort food when we have a bad day? When we're feeling down, maybe we decide it's pizza night. If we had a stressful day at work and can't even think of cooking, we order takeout. On a personal note, this is probably my biggest vice, having struggled with my weight for most of my life. Convenience stores have these heavenly steam trays full of things I call "roller food," and saying no to that particular midnight impulse is an ongoing battle. The temptation of taquitos and hot dogs is my own personal *Call of Cthulhu.*

Unfortunately, when we start this cycle, it is hard to stop it. The more we spend on food, clothes, games, books, or whatever our vice, we end up feeling inadequate or worse because we spent the money so frivolously and now have nothing substantial to show for it.

Just because an item is solid and physically substantial—like video games, books, or DVDs—doesn't mean they are significant. They are luxuries or extras. Not necessities.

Have you ever bought something while saying to yourself, "I've had the worst day ever, and I deserve (insert product placement catharsis of choice here)?" We all have. Let me share a couple of my worst moments of despair spending.

I mentioned struggling with obesity. With that comes depression, almost without exception. In years past, I would take entire luxury vacations to Los Angeles or Las Vegas based on little more than an overwhelming sense of despair. Please take note that I didn't just do this once. There are two very different and equally expensive locations noted there.

I paid for the trips, beginning to end, on credit. I was well-paid in my job, and I worked a huge amount of hours, so I couldn't even bring myself to care if I accumulated more debt by putting the entire trip on a credit card. I even used my earnings and time worked as justification to spend far more than I should have. I was depressed and lonely. I was in despair.

This wasn't my only form of despair spending, but it was by far the most extravagant. I realized that if I stayed on that path, I would destroy more than just my finances.

Whether we are taking extravagant trips, buying luxury big-screen TVs with stimulus checks, or buying takeout every night because we just don't have the energy to cook, we need to stop. If we continue down this path, we will not just destroy our finances and credit, but we will destroy our already-fractured spirit. And I'm not preaching from a pulpit when I say that. I was in the same trenches that so many of us have been in, and may still be in. If you bought this book, we've probably been in the same trench together at some point and never even known it.

Like me, you know you need to stop. You know you need a change. Reach out to family and friends and take those first baby steps toward meaningful change.

We can reach out to our local church or trusted religious leaders. Seek the aid of a counselor, crisis helpline, or begin therapy if that is what's needed for our spiritual healing and beginning to regain a healthy mental state. Listen to motivational speakers and read self-help books to motivate ourselves out of this rut. Consider alternative methods of meditation, medicine, and healing. Considering the number of conspiracy theories that were proven correct over the past few decades, the one thing we surely should have learned by now is to investigate everything and to be dismissive of nothing.

We all have to do something to stop listening to our despair and depression. Quiet our purple elephants. Create a better mindset, find a focused plan that works for us, and start on a path toward the healing of our souls and the destruction of our debts.

Because if there is one thing I know with 100% certainty that I don't have to convince you of, it is that debt has been your unshakeable burden. It has been filling your mind day and night. It distracts you while you're driving. It keeps you awake when you need to sleep. And it destroys more families and marriages across America than we can imagine.

**How to Overcome Your Overwhelm**

Yes, we are feeling overwhelmed, but once we reach out to others and start coming out of this pit, we are ready to start taking action.

This is not a fast change. It will take time and commitment from us. We must want to feel better or it will not work at all. We can't fight against ourselves. If we try to feel better and all we do is negative self-talk, then we are defeating the purpose.

I can't promise rainbows and gumdrops, but I can promise that taking the steps to create a better mindset—and taking steps to create a more stable financial foundation for our family—will help the process of feeling mentally and physically better.

### Self-Care Is Free

Self-care isn't just spending money. Self-care is about healing. Use our self-care time to de-stress, recharge, and regroup from hard days, weeks, months, and years, as well as challenging situations and circumstances. We have to take care of ourselves before we can take care of others, which means taking care physically, financially, and mentally.

If we are constantly stressed, we will lash out at those who love us most of the time. Why? They are the people to who we feel safe releasing those emotions. Would we do that to a co-worker or supervisor? Not if we wanted to keep our job... and the exceptions to the rule are the primary cause of toxic work environments around the world.

Our families will always take the brunt of our frustrations, but remember, this is a two-way street. We will bear the brunt of their frustrations, too. Partners, spouses, parents, and children all lash out at one another because they feel they have no one else, and because they feel we are the ones who should already have the deepest understanding of how they are feeling. In that way, even the most emotional of outbursts are based on trust. While there is never an excuse for emotion to escalate into abusive behavior, it does help us to understand where the emotions are coming from, and why we are the ones who get to see it up close.

Self-care is not just for the parents. Kids have these same emotions and can pick up on the emotions of their parents, particularly when something like debt is driving a wedge between loved ones. This means that it is even more important to take time for ourselves and teach them to take time for themselves.

When the term self-care is used, most people think of something like a bubble bath with candles. Yes, that is a form of self-care, but it is only one form.

Self-care is more than that. It's not about a feeling in a moment. It's about purpose.

Taking a hike in the woods with the family is a form of self-care. We are away from everything that is stressing us out. We move ourselves to the outdoors, get sunshine and fresh air, and spend time with those we love. We might feel a twinge of regret when we return home and the realities of life start to resurface, but even that regret is bittersweet, and I can promise you that the healing and renewal of the hike are what we will remember for the longest time. Ask yourself this: Have you ever come back from a hike with your family or friends feeling mad or stressed, even when you're exhausted, sweaty, and windburned? I doubt it. (Unless your kids are spoiled, whiny brats who hate any form of physical exertion and shrivel like a vampire in direct sunlight, in which case your biggest household problem is probably less related to a surplus of purple elephants and more related to a deficit of butt-whuppings with a birch switch. And I haven't written a book for that yet.)

Other forms of self-care are socializing with friends and peers. Have lunch with co-workers. Go to company events and gatherings. Get to know the people around us. Not so that we can vent, but rather so we can smile, say hello, and not feel so isolated. Have friends over for dinner, or go to their house. Socialize and remove ourselves from our sources of stress. Again, it won't resolve problems, but it will give us a clearer mind so that solutions begin to come organically. I cannot count how many times a friend has come to me saying, "I can't fix this!" and I tell them, "Then, for this moment, stop trying." A stressed mind will only ever come up with the most irrational or extreme form of quick-fix. Never once will it produce a real solution.

Exercise, better sleep routines, eating well, and even getting a haircut are also ways to provide self-care. If we are healthy, sleep well, and exercise, our stress levels will begin to calm like a placid sea. Many people use exercise and the gym to burn off the frustration and stress of the day, and it's a very wise decision. Instead of taking frustrations out on the family, take it out on a bench press or the kick-boxing bag. Grab an ax and chop some wood. Mow the lawn. Even 10 minutes of moderate-to-light physical activity can put things into perspective far more than hours of sulking in a beanbag chair ever will. When I'm at work and just can't seem to get a focus on anything, I take one minute out of the day, drop to the floor, and do 30 push-ups. My armpits might be a little damp and my breathing a little heavy when I crawl back into my chair, but my brain is ready for the next challenge.

Understanding that self-care is more than just essential oils, baths, candles, and endorphins,—or, in my backwoods case, going out in a cow pasture and popping gophers with a .22 Remington for a few hours—will help us find ways to create a self-care routine that works. Sure, the bathtub is always an option, but it shouldn't be the only thing we use for self-care. Let's be creative and find ways to take our minds off the stress and frustration and onto the things that truly make us happy. And here's the best part: We will realize that most of those things involve our family in some way, and we will realize that's where we want to devote our time. Our psyches will thank us. Our families will thank us. Even the gophers will take a moment to extend their silent gratitude... the evil, flea-bitten, ankle-rollin' little buggers.

Once we have our routine, and our family has theirs, then we can start to repair the family unit even more. And we will find those routines intersect more often than not.

*Repair Your Family*

The next step is to repair our family. Monetary problems will attack a family first and foremost. Studies have shown that couples who fight about money at least once a week are 30% more likely to divorce than couples who don't ("Divorce statistics and facts | What affects divorce rates in the U.S.?", 2018). Worse yet, if our partner believes we are spending money foolishly, or despair spending, then the likelihood of divorce rises another 45%.

We can add these two percentages together to say that if both these situations are in our life, then we are 75% more likely to get a divorce. We can glean from this that if we, our partner, or both are despair spending, and fighting about it at least once a week, then we are very likely heading toward the one end we never foresaw when we first walked down the aisle.

We can fix this. Us, our partners, and our kids can get through this tough time. Remember, our despair and depression are based on the things happening around us in our immediate circle. Nothing wrings more despair out of us than a loss of control, whether real or psychological.

There is always a way out. We just have to find it. As a family, we need to work together to find the solutions that work for all of us. Repairing our family unit has no quick fix, and it takes work, but if we want to save our marriage and family, then we are fighting to save a treasure that no one can put a value on.

Let's consider some ways that we can stop despair spending and, if needed, repair our relationships with partners and children.

***Use Your Journals***

In the first two chapters of this book, we discussed two different journals which everyone in the family is expected to use diligently for 30 to 45 days. The first of these journals tracked expenses for the month, including all monthly bills and their totals—all the everyday expenses, including jelly beans, paid subscriptions, pizza delivery, new earbuds, and everything in between. Everyone in the family was to keep this type of journal but especially the parents and adults in the home. Any time we spent money for any reason, what we purchased and how much we spent were to be entered into the journal.

The second of these journals tracked our time. We didn't need to track every task at work or school because that would be one entry, i.e., Work: 8 a.m.–5 p.m. However, we were expected to write down everything else. If we need a refresher, see the example in the second chapter of this book. Again, everyone in the household should be keeping a time tracker journal within reason.

With the two journals complete, it is time to start searching for those purple elephants in both areas.

In the finance journals, look for the following items:

- Shopping habits - Chapter 3
- Subscriptions and streaming services - Chapter 5
- Credit cards and loans - Chapter 4

If our shopping habits are out of control and we are spending much more than needed, take those chapters' advice on how to curb the debt. Make shopping lists and go to the store to do our shopping. Buy only what is on our list. This can be done for grocery shopping, household/furniture shopping, and clothes shopping. Write down what we need to buy and only buy those items.

Cancel streaming and subscription services that are duplicating one another. For example, Hulu has many Discovery+ and Disney+ shows and has an option for current live TV for under $100. This option will also have many specialty shows but not all of them. It's worth our time to examine our interests and exactly which service most closely aligns with them before we purchase, or before we decide which to cull. There are similar overlaps in such services as Amazon Video, Netflix, Disney+, CraveTV, HBO Max, and Paramount+, i.e., the extremely popular Marvel Cinematic Universe or DC Extended Universe movies. (*Batman v Superman* is a good movie, particularly the Director's Cut, and Warner Bros should have let Zack Snyder play out the rest of the franchise. Fight me.)

My lifelong love of movies is admittedly another blind spot in my life, although my greatest weakness is in buying them on physical media such as DVD and Blu-ray, rather than paying for streaming services where my favorite titles might be there one day and gone the next. With forced purple elephant hunting, I have pared down my spending on those purchases a LOT over the years and even sold online or in yard sales many of the titles which I no longer watched. However, I freely confess that the receipts for my entire film collection would likely burst a blood vessel behind my left eye if I ever took the time to backtrack them over the past couple of decades.

If our children or teens love anime—which, along with manga, is exploding in popularity and profitability in western markets, in the tragic wake of more and more blue-haired people continuing to plumb Hollywood, television, and the entire comic book industry down the toilet—and you are willing to keep that subscription, VRV is one of the best family options at only $10. It carries the majority of the anime streaming services, and it can give western kids a new cultural perspective on the world of entertainment.

Again, I am not recommending one service over any of the others, as that is up to the personal preferences of you and your family. These are just things to consider in regards to what we can keep, and what needs to go. Know what's in our services. Know how long the titles we like most will even be there. Know what's coming up next. We might even want to consider the purchase of a VPN, not only for wisely protecting our online information, but also to enable access to specific TV shows and movies that would not otherwise be available in our region. No, Express VPN is not sponsoring me, so don't try entering promo code "Finnegan," as it won't do you any good. I'm just saying that when we have three subscriptions and don't use them, we might be better off just paying for one service plus a VPN to get the shows and movies which we absolutely cannot live without.

Another subscription to cancel is music. Pick one subscription for our music service. We don't need a combination of Pandora, Spotify, and SiriusXM. We can have one and access it on our phones, computers, and vehicles. There is no need for more than one service.

Fun money-saving fact: Type the name of literally any song or piece of music into regular old YouTube. It's there. Everyone in the family makes a personalized playlist. Suddenly, there is no need for any music streaming service.

If we have credit cards and loans, start researching, consolidating, and restructuring them to save money and lower our monthly payments. This will help with paying off our debt and feeling better about life.

If we need more money coming in, start our side hustle or get a part-time job. If we are not willing to pay for a subscription our teenager wants, have them get a job to pay for it. We are not responsible for everything, and part of a parent's job is to teach their children financial responsibility. A financial journal and deciding on what things to keep and which to cancel can be a great teaching moment.

In our time management journals, look at our:

- Phone screen-time - Chapter 6
- Computer screen-time - Chapter 6
- Video game screen-time - Chapter 6
- TV screen-time - Chapter 6

We are all guilty of excessive screen-time. If we are trying to become more financially stable and teach our children the same, we need to show them how working extra and budgeting time and money go hand in hand with a strong financial foundation.

Do not judge or shame one another, but learn from this activity to be more productive as a family.

### *What Are Options for Savings?*

There are several options to help with creating savings for our family.

One is selling items that are no longer being used or collectibles that may have aged like fine wine. We can all make a little extra money selling things we no longer want through yard sales, garage sales, online marketplaces, and websites.

The best idea is for you to learn more about other sources of investments and savings, to maximize the benefits of our increase in household income. Debt reduction lays a firm foundation for a strong future, but the walls and really nice window treatments come from learning what to do with the hundreds or thousands of extra dollars we've saved or earned every month.

Shameless self-promotion time! (It's for your own good, I promise.)

My first book, *You Can't Have My Money! A 6-Step Guide to Grow Tax-Free Wealth and Retirement Income by Smart Investing in After-Tax Accounts, Active-Managed Funds, and Cash-Value Life Insurance,*—Hey, you get the full title this time!—gives some great information on different types of retirement saving options while legally frustrating the omnipresent tax man. And don't forget your gift link from the beginning of this book, *The Law-Abiding Pirate*, if you want to know more about how we can boost the value of our money by thwarting the whims of inflation.

And I don't mention my titles again *only* because I'm the aforementioned greedy Capitalistic bastard who haunts the dreams of Bernie Sanders. *Hunting Purple Elephants* really is a companion guide to the first book, and I sincerely believe that using the strategies of the two books in tandem, with a few extra tidbits from our website and private Facebook group,—also titled *You Can't Have My Money!*—can help you create the stable and prosperous financial future you've always dreamed of.

Learn and read about investments, savings, and even how to grow your side hustle if that is something you're interested in doing. Making extra money to help you in the future is never a bad thing.

Remember, unless we teach our children about these types of financial options, they usually do not learn until later in life, when it may be too late. Teaching them about investments now can help them be more financially secure faster, and we all want to make sure our children are safe and happy. They may think it is boring now, but they will appreciate it when they are older with their own families.

### Each Person's Contribution

Even though the need to find and remove purple elephants is a family affair, this is not a one-size-fits-all type of formula. The fact is that every household will be different. Some people reading this book are fresh out of school, single, and live alone but want to start now and build a solid financial foundation for their future. Others may have young children and have just bought their first house. Maybe some people will be divorced and/or single parents trying to rebuild their lives. Others may be only years from retirement but have so much debt they fear they will never be able to survive without work. There is no one-stop-shop to building a solid foundation for any of these people, but utilizing the strategies that work for you, your situation, and your household type is what will help you destroy your purple elephants. And this book has plenty of sound options for you to try.

We know that no two households will be working in the same way, so we also have to consider that every person in our specific household will be contributing in their own way.

Some of us are in single-parent households. Some are in a household where only one person works. Still, others have both parents working with children of all ages. Just as each family is different, so is the dynamic within the household.

This means when we are reviewing the journals of our household, they need to be looked at as individuals and not compared to each other. We have to be able to analyze them for what they can contribute based on their age, ability, and understanding. A six-year-old can do more chores but can't contribute financially. However, a 20-year-old going to college but living at home can help pay some of their bills, such as portions of the streaming and subscription services, phone bills, car insurance, food, and more.

Consider each person individually, and then start to figure out how we all will team up and get rid of our household purple elephants.

## The Chowder Family's Purple Elephant Hunt Summary

Let's take one more look at the Chowder's and how they destroyed their purple elephants or at least reduced them to a more manageable level. The first thing they did was look at their finances. When they added up everything, they were spending around $11,185 a month. It is no wonder they couldn't get ahead and often felt they were falling behind.

Their monthly expenses before they did the activities in this book were as follows:

Morning coffee and more: $336
Kids lunches/school: $106
Parents' workplace lunches: $480
Takeout and restaurants: $880
Groceries and shopping: $2000
Student loan (one in default): $2,700
Mortgage: $2,700
Credit cards (minimum payments): $300
Car payments: $650
Car insurance: $500
Cell phone: $140
Internet/phone/TV: $200
Video game console subscription: $60
Amazon Prime: $10
HBO/Starz/etc. (3 average): $45
Netflix: $18
Other miscellaneous streaming (Verve, Crunchyroll, YouTube): $75
Music subscription (SiriusXM): $22

Other music subscriptions (Spotify/Pandora):
$16
**Total:** $11,185

They realized that they hadn't included some minor outstanding medical bills but knew now why they had to pick and choose which bills to pay every month. Clem and Tottie both earned good money,— roughly $4,083 a month each—but it didn't cover their spending. They also noticed some of these items that were paid during their journaling time were annual subscriptions. Therefore, the Amazon Prime and video game subscriptions could be taken off when they created their budget. However, that only accounts for $70 every month. They knew they needed to reduce their purple elephants even more.

To do this, Clem started to research refinancing options for the mortgage and student loan consolidation options to put all the student loans into one. He was able to refinance the home at a lower interest rate and lower payment of $2,000. It saved them money at the moment but not necessarily in the long term.

It's also noteworthy that, since selling a lot of excess items, the family is considering selling their home and buying a smaller one, which could cut their monthly mortgage payments by as much as 50%, while providing additional money for eliminating other debts such as their student loans.

When Clem was able to consolidate all the student loans into one loan, the payment dropped to $1,200 a month. They decided to use the saved $1,500 from the student loans to make extra payments every month to the mortgage. While they ended up with a 30-year mortgage, and are actually paying more per month toward it, this allows them to pay it off early and save money.

Tottie, on the other hand, researched consolidation loans for their credit cards and medical bills. She decided that the consolidation loan interest rate of 22% was not worth it and chose to use the debt snowball method to pay off these bills. They were able to use the $700 in savings from the mortgage to snowball their credit cards and quickly started paying off these purple elephants.

Clem realized he only needed a basic cell phone for the majority of his work and side hustle, so he got a simplified version. The family also reduced their family phone plan to a more basic form to save additional money.

The subscriptions, streaming services, and other excess bills were next. Since they had already paid for the Amazon Prime and video game subscriptions for the year, they left these alone and decided to reevaluate them in a year.

They decided to keep only one TV/movie streaming service and agreed that because Herb was doing more chores, they would keep his anime streaming service. They also kept one music streaming service. After realizing that their landline telephone service was being used no more than 4-6 times in a month, they canceled it as well. The multiple landlines and cordless phones throughout the home were added to the sell pile of yard sale items.

Clem and Tottie gave up their morning coffees and ate a homemade lunch every day. They also began making sack lunches for the kids or had the kids make their own. As the family had also begun grocery shopping more responsibly, they found that this eliminated the cost of the school lunches with no additional impact to their monthly grocery bill, and, in fact, the total grocery budget had also been reduced by $500. Clem and Tottie did budget for one lunch out a week for each of them, but they didn't always use it. When they didn't use it, the money went straight into investments... probably the best compensation strategy of all. They also decided as a family that they could eat out once a week at most. Again, they didn't always do this, so the unused budgeted money was put into a family vacation fund.

The car payments and car insurance were still high, so Tottie started researching refinancing for the cars and getting quotes for car insurance, as many of these options can halve current insurance costs. This led to combined insurance savings of $200 a month for the family's two vehicles.

They knew that they still were not done. Both parents started working side hustles: Clem did woodworking and leatherwork, and Tottie started a freelance marketing business and did all the marketing for Clem's business. They conservatively estimate that Clem is now earning an additional $1,300 a month, and Tottie, who found faster growth than anticipated in her marketing, is bringing in an additional $1,500 a month.

They got the kids in on the action as well. Rosemary babysat for neighbors, and took part-time jobs as both a fast-food worker and a lifeguard, earning an average of about $1,000 a month across the year, factoring in variations such as working a lot more hours during the summer months when school was out. Herb was too young to be employed in a workplace, but he offered to do more chores around the house, as well as beginning to do landscaping and yard work for neighbors. He earns an average of $300 in a month, again working and earning a lot more in the summer months.

The additional free time, side hustles, and part-time work brought in an additional $4,100 a month for the household, increasing their annual income by $49,200, for a total household income of $147,200 a year. This is particularly exciting, as both Clem and Tottie expect their still-new side hustles to see a growth of 30-50% over the next 1-2 years as they take on more clients and projects. With the rapid success that Tottie is seeing, she is considering eventually leaving her day job to work on her marketing business full-time, as she believes that it could easily replace her current income.

This was just the beginning, but the Chowders knew they were now on the right track. Clem and Tottie finally started saving for retirement, and the kids were learning what it took to have a strong financial foundation. They all also realized that this was not a one-time deal, but rather one which needed to be re-evaluated at least once a year to ensure they were all still on track, with quarterly assessments being even better.

One unexpected benefit of the activity was that each family member has found that they are actively challenging themselves to find the next purple elephant to cull, and, more importantly, that they don't miss Tyrian or Amethyst nearly as much as they thought they would. It turns out that some of those old board games Grandma was always nagging them to play with her are kind of fun.

Except for Cribbage. That one is still the worst.

Their new monthly budget is as follows:

Parents' work lunches: $96
Takeout and restaurants: $400
Groceries and shopping: $1500
Student loan: $1,200
Mortgage (minimum payments + overpayment from consolidated student loans): $3,500
Credit cards (minimum payments + overpayment from refinanced mortgage): $1,000
Car payments: $650

Car insurance: $300

Cell phone: $100

Internet/phone/TV: $120

Video game console subscription: $0 (Annual fee already paid)

Amazon Prime: $0 (Annual fee already paid)

Other miscellaneous streaming (Verve, Crunchyroll, YouTube): $22

Music subscriptions (Spotify/Pandora): $16

**Total:** $8,904

**Total Savings:** $2,281 a month. $27,372 a year.

It's very important to note that the family made the conscious decision to keep some of their monthly payments high—or even increased them consider ably—when this was not required, such as in the cases of their mortgage and credit cards. They could have had a more satisfying bottom line of $6,704—for a whopping total savings of $4,481 a month or $53,772 a year—had they not opted for those overpayments, but they knew that debt reduction is not necessarily about paying less. It is about paying smarter. By boosting their payments in these cases, they were eliminating years of payments and thousands of dollars in interest, while still freeing up well over $27,000 a year to put into vacation funds, family events, and long-term investments.

Bottom line: When looking at their combined savings ($27,372) and increased income ($49,200), the family has an extra $76,572 a year. That alone is more than $20,000 over the national median household income.

Take that, purple elephants.

And this aggressive plan is not etched in stone. In a few years, the family's annual reevaluation may determine that they have sufficiently offset their ongoing payments and resolved enough debt. They may then eliminate or reduce the overpayments as they have become unnecessary, or they may be able to work fewer hours since they have found their solid financial footing: They may earn less money, but they will still have more free cash available to invest or use to enjoy some of the finer things of life more responsibly.

To quote the villainous but eerily-pragmatic Wilson Fisk from *Marvel's Daredevil*, "Because I play the long game, Mr. Castle. You see, when I'm finally let out of this cage, it won't be to wage war. It will be to win one." (Vincent D'Onofrio was a dang *gift* to the MCU's rogue gallery.)

Even when we look at our expenses and time, it can be hard to decide what to get rid of and what we want to keep. We probably want to keep it all because that is what we are used to, but the truth is that purple elephants don't create happiness, and they usually are not in any way essential to living a good life.

Trimming down, selling things, canceling subscriptions that take us away from living, and seeing beyond the screen or out from under all our material items can be scary. However, it is worth it. Many people have a hard time stopping once they start. They move from extremely materialistic to extremely minimalist. Once you find the things in life that matter most and realize that your spouse, Rosemary, and Herb are what you are fighting for, all the "things" just kind of fade into the mist.

This may work for some people, but again, this process is individualized by the persons within each household. The example of the Chowder family is purely hypothetical, and their previous earnings, potential earnings, and projected savings may not be anything close to what you will experience. But almost all of the same strategies can be used by anyone, regardless of how much we earn or how much debt we have.

You and your family have to analyze your life. You have to decide what is worth keeping and what you can do without. When you reevaluate in a year, you may be at a point financially where you can add back in a purple elephant or two, and by that time you will know which ones you have missed the most. Just don't let it become the norm, and put any new additions right back into the budget.

Being debt-free may seem almost impossible in today's world, but being as debt-free as possible should be our goal. Sacrifice a little now, so we have something to live comfortably on later. Plus, for most of us, that sacrifice will bring the family closer together and let us have new experiences that we would have missed out on if we hadn't done away with unneeded subscriptions, streaming, and screen time.

# CONCLUSION

Well, are we ready to go hunting or are we still not sure? If we have come this far, then we know it is time. We know this is what we want to do. What is holding us back?

For many of us, the fear of giving up something we love or enjoy makes us stop short of actually hunting our purple elephants. We love our TV time or our video games. We love tapping a couple of buttons on a phone and then a pizza magically shows up. We don't want to do anything that messes with those areas of our lives, because mammoths no longer require us to chip a spearhead from a flint rock. So why should we?

We all feel that way about something. Nowhere have I said, "You have to give it ALL up." In fact, in most instances, we can agree that it has been about deciding as a family what areas can be sacrificed and what areas can't. Again, the fascinating outcome of this culling process is finding out not only what we love most, but how we can increase our income and reduce debt from that. Suddenly, we're making money doing what we want to do, and there's a good chance that we were not doing that while still drowning in debt.

Don't just look at what to get rid of forever. Look at what makes sense for our household to remove at this time. This process may take several sessions of sitting down as a family to come to a final decision. Maybe we want to get rid of the Internet at home, but the kids need it for school. Therefore, the Internet is not an item that can be canceled. However, screen time can be limited.

Look for compromises when needed, and especially look for reciprocal and compensatory practices when it comes to buying those special treats. Don't think of anything as an all-or-nothing type of situation. We'll build our hunting strategy for our family's needs and then go hunting.

This will not be an easy hunt, but if we find our purple elephants and get them under control, then our hunt will be a success, and we will be on our way to creating a solid financial foundation that will carry us into a brighter, more appreciative future.

In a way, it is like when men used to hunt mammoths. They were probably crapping their leopard skins on their first hunt. But, with every subsequent hunt, they acquired the skills, courage, and mindset needed to take down their quarry until it became second nature.

Now, let's ask that question again. Are you ready to go hunting? I think you are. I think all you need to do is get your expedition participants together, and your journals, and the hunt will begin.

Make it easy on yourself and your family. Start on the first of the month and go until the last day of the month—September 1st through September 30th. You can even push it out until the 14th of the next month, such as September 1st through October 14th.

Then, as a family, sit down and start analyzing the journals one at a time. Start with your finance journal. You may want to include the children in this so they know the truth, or you may want to have two sessions for finances: One for the family and one for you and your partner. The following household session will review screen time. Once the family has had these two sessions, they can decide which elephant to hunt first, Tyrian or Amethyst. Or they can decide to just start cleaving both of them into weird, purple stew-meat at the same time.

And that's about it. Get out there and make your life better. If you found the content of this book useful or enjoyable, the best way you can express that is through a detailed review on Amazon, Audible, or any other bookseller from which you may have purchased. I read as many as I can to glean new ideas and improve my content. Your feedback is always greatly appreciated, and I have enough humility to recognize that my next big idea might come from an innocuous comment from a reviewer.

One final fun fact that I intentionally withheld from you until now, just because it will make your upcoming journey a lot easier: I am 100% confident that by the time you sit down with the family for the journal analysis, you will already be in a far better situation than you were when you started journaling. The change in your life is already well under-way, and you didnt even realize it.

Because it only takes a few days of glancing at receipts and doing a few internal calculations to say, "FOUR THOUSAND THIRTY-TWO BUCKS A YEAR ON FREAKIN' COFFEE?!"

Suddenly, even the maple flakes can't justify it.

(I think purple elephant stew would be delicious. Fight me.)

# REFERENCES

*Amazon.com help: The amazon prime membership fee.* (2021). Amazon.com. https://www.amazon.com/gp/help/customer/display.html?nodeId=G34EUPKVMYFW8N2U#: ~:text=Amazon%20Prime%20membership%20fees%20are

Bergen, A. (2021, July 2). *The true cost of eating out (and how to save).* Moneyunder30.com. https://www.moneyunder30.com/the-true-cost-of-eating-in-restaurants-and-how-to-save

*Black box slave leia collectible.* (n.d.). Www.google.com. Retrieved July 23, 2021, from https://www.google.com/search?q=black+box+slave+leia+collectible&rlz=1C1CHBF_enUS838US838&sxsrf=ALeKk01T2QZZiDWOD1LIRyLLNGmbeNilyA:

1627068710814&source=lnms&tbm=shop&sa=X&
ved=2ahUKEwiCr6Gk9_nxAhXhEFkFHT-
YAx0Q_AUoAXoECAEQAw&biw=1920&bih=937

Boersma, M.P.H, P., Villarroel, Ph.D., M., & Vahrat-
ian, Ph.D, A. (2020, September 10). *Products - Data
Briefs - Number 374- August 2020*. Www.cdc.gov.
https://www.cdc.gov/nchs/products/
databriefs/db374.htm

Brenoff, A. (2018, April 27). *The Amount Of Money
You Spend On Drinking May Blow Your Mind*.
HuffPost.

https://www.huffpost.com/entry/money-spent-on-
drinking_n_5adf49d9e4b07be4d4c54401#:
~:text=%E2%80%9CIf%20you%20have%20three
%20drinks

Burke, E. (2018, April 10). *What's a reasonable amount
to spend on lunch every day?* Www.moneymanage-
ment.org. https://www.moneymanagement.org/
blog/whats-a-reasonable-amount-to-spend-on-
lunch-every-day

Chase. (n.d.). *Consolidate your credit card debt*.
Www.chase.com. Retrieved July 22, 2021, from
https://www.chase.com/personal/credit-cards/

education/basics/how-to-consolidate-your-
credit-card-debt

Chase. (2021, July 22). *Refinance your mortgage | refinance.* Www.chase.com. https://www.chase.com/
personal/mortgage/mortgage-refinance

Consumersadvocate. (2021, July 22). *10 best student
loan refinance of 2021.* Consumeradvocate.com.
https://www.consumersadvocate.org/student-loan-
refinance/a/best-student-loan-refinance?pd=true&
keyword=student%20loan%20refinance&
gca_campaignid=413265422&gca_adgroupid=
18980165222&gca_matchtype=e&gca_network=g&
gca_device=c&gca_adposition=&
gca_loc_interest_ms=&gca_loc_physical_ms=
9008020&
gclid=Cj0KCQjw0emHBhC1ARIsAL1QGNebkCh1
W5tg68NSTihJPoKq4DBGggOi9XG69YG_Ree_EU
MHAYs2LWMaAhliEALw_wcB

Crawford, L. (2021, February 9). *Shop the grocery store
perimeter.* Recipe Idea Shop. https://recipeideashop.
com/grocery-store-perimeter/

CreditDonkey Staff. (2020, July 2). *Average cost of food
per month will scare you.* CreditDonkey; CreditDon-

key. https://www.creditdonkey.com/average-cost-food-per-month.html

*Divorce statistics and facts | What affects divorce rates in the U.S.?* (2018). Wilkinson & Finkbeiner, LLP. https://www.wf-lawyers.com/divorce-statistics-and-facts/

*Famous People Victims of the Cancel Culture.* (2021, May 13). Ethics Sage. https://www.ethicssage.com/2021/05/famous-people-victims-of-the-cancel-culture-now-that-i-have-created-a-series-of-blogs-on-the-cancel-culture-and-its-effects.html

FreshBooks. (n.d.). *What is expense tracking and how can it help your business?* FreshBooks. https://www.freshbooks.com/hub/accounting/expense-tracking

Gaille, B. (2019, January 22). *34 convenience store industry statistics and trends.* BrandonGaille.com. https://brandongaille.com/34-convenience-store-industry-statistics-and-trends/

Garner, C., & Young Entrepreneur Council. (n.d.). *Council Post: Four Predictions About The Self-Storage Industry.* Forbes. https://www.forbes.com/sites/theyec/2019/11/25/four-predictions-about-the-self-storage-industry/?sh=2d1fb7ed7814

*Get the package that fits your groove.* (n.d.). SiriusXM. Retrieved July 7, 2021, from https://www.siriusxm.com/plans

Green, D. (2018, September 18). *Bi-Weekly mortgage program: Are they even worth it?* Mortgage Rates, Mortgage News and Strategy : The Mortgage Reports. https://themortgagereports.com/11183/bi-weekly-mortgage-payments-will-you-pay-your-mortgage-faster

Hamm, T. (2019, September 17). *Here's When Buying in Bulk is Really Worth It.* US News & World Report; U.S. News & World Report. https://money.usnews.com/money/blogs/my-money/articles/when-buying-in-bulk-is-really-worth-it

*How to Make Money by Mowing Lawns.* (2021, May 6). WikiHow. https://www.wikihow.com/Make-Money-by-Mowing-Lawns

Jefferson Center. (2020, July 24). *Self-care: It's not always bubble baths (but it can be!).* Jefferson Center - Mental Health and Substance Use Services. https://www.jcmh.org/self-care-its-not-always-bubble-baths-but-it-can-be/

Lee, C. (2020, December 26). *Screen zombies: Average person will spend 44 YEARS looking at digital devices -*

*and that's before COVID!* Study Finds. https://www.studyfinds.org/screen-zombies-average-person-spends-44-years-looking-at-devices/

Levy, A. (2021, June 22). *Netflix could raise prices again soon.* The Motley Fool. https://www.fool.com/investing/2021/06/22/netflix-could-raise-prices-again-soon/

Linton, A. (2021, June 10). *How much money you will save when you quit smoking.* Verywell Mind. https://www.verywellmind.com/how-much-money-does-smoking-cost-you-4143324

Maryalene LaPonsie. (2021, May 13). *10 best expense tracker apps.* US News & World Report; U.S. News & World Report. https://money.usnews.com/money/personal-finance/saving-and-budgeting/articles/best-expense-tracker-apps

Mayo Clinic Health System. (2018, March 23). *Shopping the grocery perimeter.* Www.mayoclinichealthsystem.org. https://www.mayoclinichealthsystem.org/hometown-health/speaking-of-health/grocery-store-tour-shopping-the-perimeter

Meyers, S. (n.d.). *Council Post: A Look At Self-Storage Growth Trends Now And Post-Pandemic.* Forbes. https://www.forbes.com/sites/

forbesrealestatecouncil/2020/12/01/a-look-at-self-storage-growth-trends-now-and-post-pandemic/?sh=7a8fcc1c2165

Morin, A. (2021, March 8). *How to make a profit with your lemonade stand*. The Balance. https://www.thebalance.com/lemonade-stand-math-2086842

Netflix. (2021). *Netflix streaming plans*. Help Center. https://help.netflix.com/en/node/24926

Palomino, C. (2021, May 6). *How to get a babysitting license*. WikiHow. https://www.wikihow.com/Get-a-Babysitting-License

Petersen, L. (2011, January 28). *Difference between a grocery store and convenience store*. Chron.com. https://smallbusiness.chron.com/difference-between-grocery-store-convenience-store-19023.html

Price, S. (2015, July 17). *Average household budget.* ValuePenguin; ValuePenguin. https://www.valuepenguin.com/average-household-budget

Ramsey Solutions. (2021, April 22). *How the Debt Snowball Method Works*. Ramsey Solutions. https://www.ramseysolutions.com/debt/how-the-debt-snowball-method-works

S.H. Block Tax Services. (2015, September 29). *Why is it important to keep receipts? -*. Mdtaxattorney.com. https://www.mdtaxattorney.com/resources/why-is-it-important-to-keep-receipts/

Saeed. (2016, November 16). *81 legit ways to make money online (for beginners & without paying anything!)*. Money Pantry. https://moneypantry.com/ways-to-make-money-online

*School Meal Trends & Stats*. (2020). Schoolnutrition.org. https://schoolnutrition.org/aboutschoolmeals/schoolmealtrendsstats/

Spencer, S. (2021, February 16). *Gina carano "the mandalorian" toys scrapped by hasbro*. Newsweek. https://www.newsweek.com/mandalorian-gina-carano-cara-dune-toys-action-figures-1569495

Spotify. (2019). *Music for everyone.* Spotify.com. https://www.spotify.com/us/premium/

Stokes, J. (2018, July 18). *Beginner's guide to full-time RV living: 8 tips for life on the road*. Rollick Articles. https://gorollick.com/articles/consumer/beginners-guide-to-full-time-rv-living/

Stregowski, J. (2021, June 28). *How Much Does It Really Cost to Own a Dog?* The Spruce Pets. https://

www.thesprucepets.com/the-cost-of-dog-ownership-1117321

Vera, A. (2019, December 9). *Here are just some of the people who were canceled or threatened with cancellation in 2019.* CNN. https://www.cnn.com/2019/12/08/us/2019-canceled-stories-trnd/index.html

Wells, L. (2021, July 23). *Best debt consolidation loans for July 2021.* Bankrate. https://www.bankrate.com/loans/personal-loans/debt-consolidation-loans/

Whitney, A. (2018, February 7). *17 ways to save money on groceries.* Bon Appétit. https://www.bonappetit.com/story/save-money-on-groceries

*Work harder, earn more: 2013 incomes by hours worked.* (2014, October 13). DQYDJ–Don't Quit Your Day Job... https://dqydj.com/work-harder-earn-more-2013-incomes-by-hours-worked/

www.ingramcontent.com/pod-product-compliance
Lightning Source LLC
Chambersburg PA
CBHW030449210326
41597CB00013B/599